Pino Arlacchi

Mafia Business

The Mafia Ethic
and the Spirit of Capitalism

Translated by
Martin Ryle

VERSO

The Imprint of New Left Books

British Library
Cataloguing in Publication Data

Arlacchi, Pino
    Mafia business: the Mafia ethic and the
    spirit of capitalism.
    1. Mafia——Italy——History
    1. Title   11. La Mafia imprenditrice.
    English
    364.1'06'0458   HV6453.18

First published as *La Mafia Imprenditrice*
by Società editrice il Mulino, Bologna
© 1983

Verso Edition first published 1986
© Verso 1986

Verso
15 Greek Street, London WIV 5LF

Typeset in Imprint by
Cover to Cover, Cambridge

Printed and bound in Great Britain by
Biddles Ltd, Guildford and King's Lynn

ISBN 0-86091-135-7

Contents

IV Afterword to the English Edition

For
Giovanni Arrighi

Introduction

In this book I offer a synthesis of the research work on the mafia in southern Italy which I began in 1977–78. I have put forward a theoretical framework, within which I have analysed the forces that have moulded the modern mafia, and I have also tried to illustrate some of the latter's leading characteristics.

Since scholars do not pluck their subject-matter from the clouds, it may be helpful if I give an idea of the reasons which led me to carry out this work. Two circumstances stimulated my interest. First of all, the rise in mafia activity, and its widely publicized consequences, began to arouse increasing concern in the regions of Calabria and Sicily from the mid-seventies on. Living as I do in Calabria, and working in a Department of Sociology, I found it difficult to avoid becoming to some extent professionally concerned with what was an urgent public problem. The second factor was scholarly and academic in nature, and lay in my strong conviction that the interpretations of the mafia then current were altogether unsatisfactory.

I had held this conviction for some time, having formed it in the course of my investigations into the traditional social and economic systems of the *Mezzogiorno* [Southern Italy], whose results were published in my book *Mafia, contadini e latifondo nella Calabria tradizionale* (which appeared in English under the title *Mafia, peasants and great estates. Society in traditional Calabria*).[1] I had devoted a chapter of that volume to outlining

[1] Pino Arlacchi, *Mafia, Peasants and Great Estates*, Cambridge 1983.

some of the economic and cultural 'preconditions' underlying the mafia phenomenon in the period from 1860 to the end of the 1940s. As I compared the information about the traditional mafia which was emerging in the course of my research with the evidence coming to light, during this same period, about the contemporary situation, I grew more and more certain that existing theories were inadequate to deal with the most recent developments of the problem.

It was for these reasons that I decided to undertake fresh research in order to construct a schema for the understanding of today's mafia—a schema which would complement Hess's account of the traditional mafia.[2] Hess's work can be regarded as the classic account of its subject, drawing together a series of studies running from the late nineteenth century up to the 1960s. The present study's tripartite division—Part I deals with the traditional mafia, Part II with the post-war transformation, and Part III with the contemporary situation—strongly reflects this 'bent' of my initial researches.

Between the autumn of 1977 and the first months of 1978, I carried out a series of pilot research projects in various parts of Calabria, whose results gave rise to the hypothesis that became central to my work throughout the following years—the hypothesis of the entrepreneurial mafia. In the summer of 1978, I wrote an essay entitled *Mafia e tipi di società*.* This was a preliminary attempt to give an overall interpretation of how the mafia had changed and developed over the last thirty years.

I had the good fortune to receive a research grant from the Ford Foundation, enabling me to spend almost the whole of 1979 in the USA, in New York. Here, I was able to gain a close acquaintance with the state of the mafia art on the other side of the Atlantic. My research continued to follow its original lines, but I found myself taking on a rapidly broadening spectrum of problems. In 1981, I began to concern myself with the questions raised by the Sicilian mafia's intervention in the world heroin market, and in December of that year I went back to the USA to gather valuable documentary evidence from a trial then taking place in Brooklyn, and also to hold a series of conversations with police officials and experts on drug-trafficking.

Meanwhile, the problem of the mafia had become a matter of

[2] H. Hess, *Mafia*, Bari 1973.
* *La Rassegna Italiana di Sociologia*, 1980.

the most urgent public alarm, no longer just in Sicily and Calabria, but at national level. In little over two years, the mafia had killed several leading Sicilian political and judicial authorities, including the President of the Regional Government himself. All these people had been murdered in Palermo, in broad daylight and right in the city centre, in front of dozens of witnesses. Each murder led to an outcry in the press, and to solemn promises from government officials that justice would be done and that the struggle against the mafia would be waged in earnest. And yet none of these murders led the central authorities to enact even the smallest legislative measures or to undertake even the slightest anti-mafia action.

At the beginning of 1982, several proposed anti-mafia laws awaited the consideration of the Italian Parliament. One of these had been put forward by the communist parliamentary group, its first signatory being Pio La Torre, MP. La Torre had taken part in the anti-mafia campaigns of the Sicilian Left ever since the years immediately after the second world war, and had been one of the most active members of the Parliamentary Commission of Inquiry into the mafia.

The proposed La Torre law incorporated the analysis of the contemporary mafia that I had made in my 1978 essay, turning some of its categories directly into legislative provisions. The projected legislation was aimed at the mafia enterprise, which enjoyed lethal competitive advantages vis-à-vis 'normal' firms; its provisions as a whole were designed to strike a blow against the mafia's accumulation of capital.

On the morning of 25 April—the anniversary of Italy's liberation from Fascism, and a former national holiday—Pio La Torre was murdered, with his chauffeur, as he drove along a Palermo street. There was an outcry in the press, government officials made solemn promises that justice would be done and that the struggle against the mafia would be waged in earnest. This time, the government acted, at once dispatching to Sicily General Carlo Alberto Dalla Chiesa, whom they described as the 'cutting edge of the anti-terrorist struggle in Italy'. Dalla Chiesa was appointed Prefect, and a solemn promise was made that extraordinary powers would immediately be conferred upon him to enable him to combat the mafia.

Four months later, on the evening of 3 September 1982, General Della Chiesa—who still had no extraordinary powers, and was unaccompanied by any escort—was killed, together with his wife, in a Palermo street. A week later, the Italian Parliament approved anti-mafia legislation very similar to that put forward by Pio La Torre.

A Note on Method

The first part of the present book is devoted to a fresh examination of the chief characteristics of the mafia as it existed in the traditional *Mezzogiorno*. It covers the period from the unification of Italy to the immediate aftermath of World War II. Since the aim of this account is to establish certain basic analytic points of reference, these early chapters contain none of the usual references to the mafia's historical origins. The traditional situation is outlined in terms of ideal types.[3] Accordingly, it is in no sense a historical reconstruction of the mafia; nor does it pretend to describe all its most obvious aspects within any given part of the *Mezzogiorno* during any given space of time. The image of the traditional mafia and the traditional *mafioso* presented in my first two chapters has been created by a process of 'one-sided' emphasis upon one or more points of view, in which connections are established between phenomena drawn from a variety of social, geographical and temporal contexts. The resulting framework is coherent, but provisional—to be used as a compass or guide by which to plot later stages of the analysis.

The account of the 'typical-ideal' structure of the traditional mafia in the first part of the book comprises two successive surveys, each corresponding to a different aspect of that structure. First, I describe the workings of a social phenomenon that plays a key role in any understanding of the relations between the mafia and the environment that has given rise to it: *mafia behaviour*, and the closely-linked phenomenon of the *competition for honour* which has held sway in certain parts of southern Calabria and western Sicily.

Studies of the traditional mafia have almost entirely neglected this honorific-competitive basis of its vitality. They have for the most part stressed the elements of fixity and stratification in

---

[3] This methodology closely follows classical Weberian precepts. See Max Weber, *Il metodo delle scienze storico-sociali*, Torino 1974, pp. 107 and ff.

Sicilian society. Most scholars discuss the nature of property relations and relations of production in traditional Sicilian mafia areas in terms of 'feudalism', 'the fief', 'feudal survivals', and—above all—the *latifondo* or great landed estate. Concepts of this kind evoke a world in which there is but slight vertical social mobility, and in which honour and power are allocated to the members of the local community along pre-established lines.

My own approach, by contrast, highlights horizontal conflict between individuals and groups, and emphasises the degree of social instability and vertical mobility as well as the modern nature of the economic structure. These are the characteristic features of the mafia areas. Here I relied upon my own earlier research, which identified a particular socio-economic system—the 'society of permanent transition', found in its most heightened form in western Sicily and southern Calabria, in which there was a marked asymmetry between the mercantile-capitalist economic structure and the traditionalism of the cultural structure—as the womb of the classical mafia and its manifestations.

The survey that follows illustrates the second component of the mafia phenomenon: *mafia power*, and the functions it fulfils at local and national levels. The debt I owe to the work of H. Hess, A. Blok and the Schneiders is too evident to require further emphasis: my second chapter draws on this both for its conceptual organization and for the examples it provides. Understanding of the mafia has made fundamental advances thanks to their contributions—Hess's identification of the category of *mediation* as the special and cardinal activity of the *uomo di rispetto*, the Schneiders' analysis of the social and familial composition of mafia groups, and Blok's exploration of the relation between the notion of the territorial monopoly of violence and the genesis of mafia power.

The second part of the book is devoted to a rapid description of the effects that the great post-war transformation of society, in Italy and in the *Mezzogiorno*, had upon the traditional forms of mafia behaviour and mafia power. The story of the mafia during the 1950s and 1960s cannot be understood (literary and scholarly treatments to the contrary notwithstanding) in terms of a gradual development, running parallel to simultaneous changes in the economic system. My reading of the voluminous documentation amassed by the Anti-mafia Commission, together with evidence from a range of other sources confirmed the opposite conclusion: during the two decades following the war, the mafia underwent not a development but a crisis, and a deep crisis at that. The sociologists, anthropologists and historians who studied the question between the mid-'fifties and mid-'sixties are in agreement as to the ways in which mafia power and mafia behaviour were declining both in Sicily and in Calabria.[4]

As the State took back the powers over public order which it had delegated to the *mafiosi*, as emigrants left southern Italy for the North and for the rest of Europe, and as mafia areas became caught up in the 'cultural revolution' of the post-war years, so the authority of the mafia eventually lost its general legitimation. In the course of the 1950s and the 1960s, the *mafiosi* found themselves ousted from the centre of the social system, and squeezed to its margins. The role of the man of honour grew uncomfortably like that of a common criminal. Thus the spectacular upsurge in the mafia's entrepreneurial activity, which has been taking place from the 1970s up to the present, is the result of the interplay between the mafia's changed economic position and the *institutional disintegration* of Italian society that marked the 1970s.

The third part of the book is devoted to an account of the ideal type of the mafia, and the *mafioso*, as they exist in our own time. In the absence of previous studies, I have had to carry out a series of ad hoc investigations into many of the most important aspects of the question. These investigations have led me to conclude that the mafia's present features derive from the culmination of three processes that have been at work over the last ten or fifteen years: a) the birth of the entrepreneurial mafia; b) the attainment by Sicilian mafia firms/families of pre-eminent positions in the world drugs system and in the illegal sector of the international economy; c) the development, on the part of the mafia, of very considerable *political autonomy*. At times, these three processes have followed parallel courses; at times, they have overlapped; and at times, they have fused together as in a chemical reaction—giving rise to some of the most disturbing episodes in recent Italian history.

The fact that the mafia and the *mafiosi* have ceased to play the role of *mediators*, and have devoted themselves to *capital ac-*

---

[4] E. J. Hobsbawm, *Primitive Rebels*, Manchester 1959; A. Blok, *The Mafia of a Sicilian Village 1860–1960*, New York 1974; D. De Masi, *Sopraluogo nella Sicilia della mafia*, Nord e Sud no. 46, 1963.

cumulation, is crucial to any understanding of the qualitative differences between the traditional mafia and the mafia of today. Only by turning to the concepts of the *enterprise* and of *entrepreneurial activity* (or 'entrepreneuriality'), as used by Schumpeter, rather than to more strictly sociological or criminological categories, was I able to make progress in my research. The great advantage of these categories lies in their ability to bring together three strongly contradictory aspects of the object of investigation: a) the aspect of innovation, of rupture with the most recent past, constituted by the entry of *mafiosi* into economic competition; b) the element of rationality and of capitalist calculation present in the economic behaviour of the mafia entrepreneur, and in the way he selectively resuscitates some facets of traditional values and traditional culture; c) the irrational, aggressive aspect of mafia activity itself, which finds expression in the 'animal spirits' involved in the accumulation of wealth.

As regards the first dimension of the mafia's entrepreneurial activity, its innovative quality as compared to ordinary economic operations, I am anxious to emphasize that here, the application of this schema is in no way forced. The *mafioso*-entrepreneur is indeed an innovator, introducing 'new productive combinations' that give him competitive advantages over other entrepreneurs. It follows that the difference between Schumpeter's innovator-entrepreneur and the mafia entrepreneur is to be found, not in the intrinsic character of his activity, but in the different effects that his presence has upon economic development. The introduction of mafia methods does not give the productive system in which the *mafioso* is operating any sharp 'push forward': but in Schumpeter's theory, economic development is seen as the product of the innovative activity of the entrepreneur, who helps achieve social goals of development even as he pursues his own individual goals. (This theory of course rules out any consideration of the conflict which may, and often does arise between the behaviour of the entrepreneur on the one hand, and the overall development of the economic system on the other. For this reason, it has the same well-known limitations as Adam Smith's notion of the 'invisible hand' that supposedly transforms private vices into public virtues.)

The case of the *mafioso*-entrepreneur clearly demonstrates that there is no automatic correspondence between entrepreneurial activity and the collective good, and that the question of what *institutional rules* govern that activity is one of the crucial problems for any theory of entrepeneurship.

If the *mafioso*'s entrepreneurial activity is marked at once by an economic-rational dimension and by an aspect that is irrational and extra-economic, he is not alone in this. Several of the best-known theories of accumulation and of capitalism have recourse to categories from outside the economy when they seek to explain the so-called 'reasons' for accumulation. Keynes sees the long-term rate of growth as a function of a rather ill-defined 'animal spirit' in the entrepreneur's breast; and in Kaldor's model, this is conceived, precisely, as an extra-economic factor influencing economic activity.[5] Max Weber wrote of the 'protestant ethic' and its affinity with the 'spirit of capitalism'. Marx, moreover, had already turned to concepts of a religious type, expressed in the idea of 'fetishism', of an 'inhuman power' governing the actions of the capitalist entrepreneur and forcing him to accumulate for accumulation's sake: 'Accumulate, accumulate! That is Moses and the prophets!'

In order to differentiate between the capitalist entrepreneur and the mafia entrepreneur, we must consider the relations between the two contrasting spheres of their activity. In the case of the mafia capitalist, his pursuit of rational goals interacts very differently with the extra-economic and irrational sphere of his entrepreneurial activity. Far from progressively enlarging the sway of values and conduct of a rational-capitalist type, the entrepreneurial practices of the *mafiosi* extend the domain governed by archaic and predatory attitudes.

Mafia capital accumulation is encouraging the recrudescence of a whole range of primitive behaviour patterns. One sees this in the growing tendency for economic conflicts to become inter-family wars, and for market competition to be transformed into vendettas and bloody personal struggles. The entrepreneurial activity of the mafia is poisoning large stretches of territory, and entire sectors of production, with heavier and heavier doses of destructive anarchy and barbarism, and is proving one of the gravest threats to democracy and development.

[5] N. Kaldor, *Essays on Economic Stability and Growth*, London 1960, cited in Giovanni Arrighi, *Sviluppo economico e sovrastrutture in Africa*, Turin 1967, p. 651.

In a final chapter, I discuss the growth of international, large-scale crime; its effects on world consumption of narcotics and the role of drug profits in the financial system.

Research into a phenomenon such as the mafia presents certain special features, making it different from the usual investigations of social scientists into more 'peaceful', and more readily observable, objects of inquiry. Members of mafia groups do not willingly talk about their activities; and when they do, they are seeking to defend and justify themselves. This strongly influences the quantity, and above all the quality, of whatever information they divulge. The organizations that systematically collect data on organized crime (consisting of three official bodies of the Italian police) collate this data in order to identify and prosecute professional criminals, and not in order to provide information for students of the social sciences.

Moreover, renewed public attention has of late been focused, in Italy, on the relations between the world of the mafia and of organized crime on one hand, and the legitimate political and economic world on the other. This has meant that obtaining reliable data and information about the nature of mafia activity has been a major difficulty for any researcher. If to all this we add that a) there is a time-lag between changes taking place in the mafia and criminal world (changes themselves accompanied by the emergence of new social groupings and phenomena), and the reactions of the State and the academic community, which are always several years behind the actual, changing social objects of inquiry; b) there is, consequently, no existing body of research, and no organized collection of data; and c) official Italian judicial and criminal statistics are in a parlous state—then some idea can be had of the difficulties that confronted me when I began my inquiry.

But scientific research is rather like the voyages undertaken by the explorers of the past: rational and scientific method play their part, but so do luck and fortune, good and bad. In the case of my own research, fortune smiled on me in that, as I began work, an extensive series of judicial inquiries into the mafia was getting under way, both in Calabria and in Sicily; and their proceedings were published in time to be of great use in verifying the hypotheses I was framing. These inquiries—they included Judge Cordova's investigations into the sixty mafia bosses of Tyrrhenian

Calabria, and Judge Falcone's investigation of the biggest heroin-trafficking operation from Europe to the USA ever set up by a Sicilian mafia group—were carried out with great professionalism and intelligence. The several hundred volumes in which their proceedings were collected spared me some years of uncertain (and risky) fieldwork, and allowed my investigative barque to return, despite some difficult passages, safely to its home port.

Acknowledgements

In the course of my research, I have contracted a large debt of gratitude to a number of people. I must give particular thanks to a group of brave Calabrian and Sicilian magistrates, whose valuable collaboration I have enjoyed at every stage of my inquiries. Enzo and Carlo Macrí, Augusto Di Marco and Saverio Mannino in Calabria, and Rocco Chinnici, Peppino Di Lello and Giovanni Falcone in Sicily, helped me to get a 'feel' for the unusual object of my research, and to keep my bearings in the labyrinthine maze of overlapping jurisdictions that is the criminal justice system in Italy, without ever failing in the secrecy and discretion to which their office binds them.

Giuseppe Viola, the President of the Reggio Calabria court, and Giovanni Montera, President of the same court's preventive measures department, allowed me to consult the court's archives, while Giuseppe Tuccio, the Public Prosecutor at Palmi, helped me in my investigations of the composition of mafia families.

Several journalists, from a variety of regional and national publications, followed the development of my work with close interest, and contributed to it by offering much good counsel, many suggestions and a great deal of information. I would like in particular to thank Daniele Billitteri, Alfonso Maddeo, Luigi Malafarina, Gianfranco Manfredi, Franco Martelli, Antonio Padalino, Pantaleone Sergi and Marcello Sorgi.

Among the political representatives of the Left who have supported and encouraged me in my research, and have helped to make it into a weapon of anti-mafia struggle, I must give especial thanks to Pio La Torre, Ugo Pecchioli, Francesco Martorelli and Nadia Alecci, of the Italian Communist Party; and to Aldo Rizzo, MP, of the independent Left.

In my fieldwork, in my interviews with eyewitnesses, and in

collating the statistical data, I was helped at various times by Vito
Barresi, Rino Bernasconi, Pino Canale, Rita Neve, Anna Reda
and James Walston. I am particularly grateful to Antonio Tucci
for his help in preparing the statistical material.

The first stage of my research was funded by the Calabrian
regional authority. I must express my thanks to Pino Del Grande,
an official in the Department of Public Education, for the sympathetic interest he showed in my research project.

Giovanni Bechelloni, Arnaldo Bagnasco, Alessandro Cavalli,
Giuseppe Colasanti and Jonathan Steinberg read and commented
on my manuscript. Their criticisms and suggestions were most
useful.

I regret, finally, that I am unable to give thanks individually to
all those police officers and judicial officials, Italian and American, who gave me information that proved extremely useful in
understanding the most inward workings of the power of the
mafia.

Pino Arlacchi
Arcacavata

I

The Mafia
and *Mafiosi*
in Traditional Calabria
and Sicily

And, as a rule, it has been neither dare-devil and unscrupulous speculators, economic adventurers such as we meet at all periods of economic history, nor simply great financiers who have carried through this change, outwardly so inconspicuous, but nevertheless so decisive for the penetration of economic life with the new spirit. On the contrary, they were men who had grown up in the hard school of life, calculating and daring at the same time, above all temperate and reliable, shrewd and completely devoted to their business, with strictly bourgeois opinions and principles.

Max Weber, *The Protestant Ethic and the Spirit of Capitalism*,
London 1984, p. 19.

1.

The Behaviour of the *Mafioso*

Mafia, *'Ndrangheta* and *Omertà*

Social research into the question of the mafia has probably now reached the point where we can say that the mafia, as the term is *commonly* understood, does not exist:

> . . . Most people, and especially most people outside Italy, have a fairly clear image of the mafia as a centralized criminal association, with a strict code of honour and its own constitution and initiation rites. Information has been freely available to the public in the specialist literature, as well as in the daily press, in detective stories and horror comics, and in sensational TV series. But to try and find out more, to go back to the sources, is to get an altogether different picture . . . and conclude that Mini [*the accused in a mafia court case*] was speaking nothing but the truth when, asked whether he belonged to the mafia, he replied, 'I don't know what that means'. In fact, he knew that an individual was what we call a *mafioso*, not because that individual belonged to a secret society, but because he behaved in a certain way—behaved, that is, like a *mafioso*.[1]

What did it mean to *behave like a mafioso*?

It meant to *make oneself respected*. It meant to be a 'man of honour', *un'uomo d'onore*, strong enough to avenge himself for any insult to his person, or any extension of it, and to offer any such insult to his enemies. Such behaviour, whether defensive

[1] H. Hess, *Mafia*, Bari 1973, p. XI.

or aggressive in kind, may run counter to the state's prohibition of violence; but in the culture which the *mafioso* inhabited, it was not just accepted, but encouraged and idealized. Indeed, the fact that the comportment of the *mafioso* openly violated the rules and judicial institutions of officialdom was one important factor in the prestige that it conferred.

The mafia was a form of behaviour and a kind of power, not a formal organization. To behave as a *mafioso* was to behave honourably (*onorevole*). It was to conform, in other words, to certain rules of cunning, courage and ferocity, of robbery and fraud, that even as late as the 'forties of the present century continued to play a crucial role in the culture of many areas of western Sicily and southern Calabria. 'He was really a tough customer, nobody could stand up to him'; 'he wasn't violent as a rule, but when he had to be, then he amazed everyone, he stunned his enemies. This happened six or seven times, and people still talk about it like something from a legend'—this is how a village *mafioso* is described in a book that might be taken as a kind of popular manual on the traditional mafia. To members of the society depicted in *The True Story of the Outlaw Marlino Zappa*,[2] the word '*onorevole*' ('honourable') denotes, simply, the possession of superior strength and force. To be 'honourable' is to be 'exceptional', 'worth your salt'; it is to be 'overbearing'. An honourable act is, in the last analysis, not much more than a successful act of aggression (whether in response to some previous insult or on the aggressor's own initiative).

Until a few decades ago, most of the population of Reggio Calabria province used the Greek word '*ndrangheta* to indicate a high degree of heroism and virtue. This was embodied in a superior élite, the '*ndranghetisti*. '*Ndranghetista* means 'member of the honoured society', but more generally it referred—as in classical Greece—to any brave man who was proud of his valour, scorned danger, knew no scruples and was ready for anything.[3] The key to the '*ndranghetista's* system of ideas was *omertà*, which means *the ability to be a man* ('*uomo*). To keep to the rules of *omertà* was to follow a *double moral system*, with one set of norms applying among the members of a given group, and

[2] P. Familiari, *La vera Storia del brigante Marlino Zappa*, Vibo Valentia 1971.
[3] P. Martino, 'Storia della parole "'ndrangheta"', in *Quaderni Calabresi*, 44 (1978).

another, opposing set governing relations with those outside.[4] In relations with fellow-*'ndranghetisti*, 'tact and fine manners' were required, together with 'education, courtesy, kindness, and persuasion by argument and without compulsion'. But dealings with the common people and with one's enemies obeyed the opposite principle of *false omertà*, 'feigned *omertà*: 'false kindness, false condescension, false courtesy, which are snares concealing death to unsuspecting trouble-makers . . . and to the wicked and contemptible.'[5]

Despite the formal hostility of the official authorities, the *'ndranghetisti* enjoyed popular admiration and esteem. Traces of this attitude occasionally filter through into important judicial documents. In 1939, a local mafia chief, Paolo D'Agostino, was found killed near a shrine in the commune of Ardore, in Calabria. Sentence was passed on his murderers by a court at Locri, 12 of the 142 accused receiving life sentences and the remainder being acquitted. The judgement described the murdered man as 'a dangerous character, whose personal courage was matched by his daring spirit, his rare determination to have the upper hand, and his readiness to take advantage of others at the first opportunity. He had the courage needed to make these qualities count, and was able not just to defend himself against two or three antagonists, but to take the offensive and put his enemies to the slaughter.'[6]

Mafia and *'ndrangheta* are synonyms, as are *mafioso* and *'ndranghetista*. They are terms denoting the idea of honour and the man of honour in the eyes of the local population. In the traditional mafia areas of Sicily and Calabria, honour was the unit that measured the value of a person, a family or a thing. It was expressed in the respect and esteem in which certain people were held, and was strictly linked to the possession of particular qualities and the accomplishment of particular *gesta*—feats, deeds and actions.[7] The behaviour of the *mafioso* was part of a cultural system whose central theme was honour attained through

---

[4] M. Sahlins, 'La sociologia dello scambio primitivo', in *L'antropologia economica*, Turin 1972, pp. 113–116.

[5] L. Asprea, *Il previtocciolo*, Milan 1971, p. 174.

[6] S. Gambino, *Mafia, La lunga notte di Calabria*, Reggio Calabria 1976, p. 74.

[7] J. K. Campbell, *Honour, Family and Patronage*, Oxford 1964, pp. 268–297. G. Pitré, *Usi, costumi e pregiudizi del popolo siciliano*, vol. II, Bologna 1969, p. 292.

individual violence. These values are to some extent expressed in the well-known definition of the mafia, and of the *meaning* of the *mafioso*'s acts, which Pitré gave at the end of the nineteenth century:

> The mafia is neither a sect nor an association, and has neither rules nor statutes. The *mafioso* is not a robber or a brigand . . . The *mafioso* is simply a brave man, someone who will put up with no provocation; and in that sense, every man needs to be, indeed has to be, a *mafioso*. The mafia is a certain consciousness of one's own being, an exaggerated notion of individual force and strength as 'the one and only means of settling any conflict, any clash of interests or ideas'; which means that it is impossible to tolerate the superiority or (worse still) the dominance of others.[8]

Honour

The concept of honour referred, intrinsically, to two fundamental ideal attributes: virility in the case of men, virginity and sexual shame in the case of women. Apart from the very lowest class, every member of the local community was held to be *naturally* endowed with a certain degree of honour. But in the conditions of insecurity and competition typical of the society where the mafia flourished, it was easy to forfeit either virility (or—the term was synonymous—*diritezza*, 'uprightness': the capacity to 'stand up for oneself', acknowledging no superior) or virginity. 'To be a man—that's the hardest thing, in this lousy life we lead', exclaims one of the characters in the novel *Il selvaggio di Santa Venere*.[9]

In a mafia area, 'to be a man' meant to display one's pride and self-assurance, and to show oneself ready and able to respond quickly to the threats that life constantly posed to one's own honour and that of one's family. 'To live in these parts,' writes L. Asprea in his autobiography, 'you needed to be not so much a peasant or a worker as a wild beast. You had to be cautious, you had to show respect; but if anyone provoked a fight, you had to be ready to bite them.'[10]

Virtility and sexual shame were linked to a clear opposition

[8] G. Pitrè, *Usi, Costumi e pregiudizi del popolo Siciliano*, Vol. II, Bologna 1969, p. 292.
[9] S. Strai, *Il selvaggio di Santa Venere*, Milan 1977, p. 127.
[10] L. Asprea, op. cit., p. 23.

between the sexes that governed a large part of the *mafioso*'s cultural world. Except among relatives, the two sexes represented qualities in constant antagonism: the *uomo di rispetto* ('man worthy of respect') had the task of demonstrating his virility at every opportunity, even if this meant committing violence against women or seizing them by force.

In terms of the honour of any given family, however, virility and virginity-shame complemented one another. The virility of the men in the family protected the women's honour against threats and insults from outside. The women, for their part, had to preserve their virginity and their modesty if their menfolks' virility was not to be dishonoured.

Among the limited category of possessions crucial in determining the degree of honour of an individual or group, women represented something especially precious. Indeed, they were themselves the most precious of possessions, to be guarded with unflagging watchfulness.[11] Women who, through some particularly unfortunate chain of events, found themselves without menfolk to defend them were hard put to retain the respect or consideration of society. In most cases they fell to the lowest social stratum, and passed their own dishonour on to their descendants.

In mafia areas, feminine honour typically symbolized unbroken family honour. If an outside enemy destroyed it, he gained superiority over his victims, proving himself the more powerful by exploiting a potential weakness of his adversary. He showed that he could oblige a member of another group to violate the sacred bonds of loyalty in order to satisfy his own desire. Under such circumstances, blood-vendetta was the obligatory recourse: the father or brother must first kill his own daughter or sister, and then her violator or lover. A husband, in the same way, must kill first his unfaithful wife and then her lover. Not to pursue the vendetta was to forfeit beyond recovery any claim to social standing: individuals and groups who lost their honour in this way were very often excluded from the local community. In his autobiography, L. Asprea describes a Calabrian village of the 1930s where those in the category of the irretrievably dishonoured were segregated from the rest of the community even in the literal, territorial sense:

[11] Gambino, op. cit., pp. 57–58.

To the south of *il Calvario* was *il Piliere* . . . There, alongside the main sewer of the town, was a string of huts, battered by the east wind . . . They were unbelievably smoke-blackened. This was the refuge of the most wretched and feeble-hearted men: their women, wives and daughters, were at the mercy of any more powerful man.[12]

Social life had no place for individuals and groups who had lost their honour. For this reason, emigration was often the only alternative to civil death:

In one quarter of Taurianova, during the war, a peasant-woman whose husband was in the army became the love of an *'ndranghetista* who had managed—*per diritezza*, he said: because he knew how to stand up for himself—to avoid going to the front. When the husband got back, he realised at once, from the coldness of people's greetings, that something serious had befallen his own and his family's honour. When he had found out from his old father what had happened, he didn't have the courage to kill either his wife or the *'ndranghetista*. A few months later, he had to leave for America. Nobody held him in the slightest regard any longer. Even the children in the street had started to make fun of him.[13]

Heightened sensitivity in matters of feminine honour was one of the most frequent sources of conflict between *uomini di rispetto* in traditional Calabria. Of all the mafia-type murders committed between 1940 and 1950 in the Plain of Gioia Tauro, over 60 per cent stemmed from conflicts caused by acts of sexual violence, abductions of women, or broken engagements. In this last case, conflict arose, not from any direct physical attack on the woman's honour, but from the implicit suggestion that for some reason or another she was not worthy of becoming a wife. In these communities—in ordinary families, as well as among the mafia—marriage was entered into only after long discussions and searching enquiries. No-one, therefore, could say their decision was mistaken, and any attempt to go back on what had been settled was seen as a challenge to the family honour.

[12] Asprea, op. cit., pp. 14–15.
[13] Interview no. 6.

Challenges, Combats, Competitions

In cultural systems of the mafia type, the individual's personal
strength and force had a more immediate and obvious role than
elsewhere in determining the degree of honour accorded to competing individuals and family groups. Neither birth nor institutional factors were decisive in determining the distribution of
honour. Men of honour were made, not born, and the pursuit of
honour was a free competition, open to all. The élite of men of
honour was formed by a demanding process of selection, based on
competitive confrontation between individuals. The culture of
the mafia differed from other cultures in that such antagonistic
confrontation was a matter of course within it, and found expression in a whole range of events. Balls, festivals and pilgrimages
were among the classic opportunities for status and prestige to be
assessed. Hundreds and even thousands of people, drawn from a
wide area, came together for these annual festivities and collective
celebrations, making them an ideal arena for trials of honour and
for the spreading of mafia values.

One of the most important of these recurrent festivals was the
pilgrimage made each year to the shrine of the Madonna di Polsi,
in the heart of the Aspromonte region. Here, 'the young men have
to make an impression, they have to show the whole family what
they are made of (literally, that they are *mascoli di fegato* : "men
of liver")'.[14] It was during a festival that don Nino, the mafia chief
described by Strati, demonstrated before a crowd of two thousand people that he was precociously endowed with the qualities
of a man of honour:

> During a summer festival which was taking place outside a church in
> the open country, one silly fool tried to make himself look big by
> taking Nino's place at the head of the dance, which he had been
> leading. With a single back-handed slap, Nino sent his head spinning.
> The women cried out in fright, and everyone grew excited and
> uneasy. The two *carabinieri* on duty came running to restore order,
> but Nino was in such a rage that he lifted one of them bodily in the air
> and threw him against a wall. The whole crowd gathered round, to see
> what was going on and say what they thought of it.[15]

[14] Strati, op. cit., p. 97.
[15] Ibid., pp. 56–57.

In mafia areas, competitions, challenges and fights were also the fundamental means by which people were socialized. The distribution of power and prestige within the family was not preordained, as in families of the patriarchal type; rather, it was established through a series of very intense conflicts. The entire domestic world was dominated by *vertical* relations (parents-children; husband-wife; elder brother-younger brother, and so on). Family solidarity prevailed only in the case of conflict with another family group. Relations within the family obeyed the rule, not of *intimacy* or *solidarity*, but of *subordination*, which involved a mass of obligations and values emphasizing the prerogatives attached to each position within the reigning domestic hierarchy.

The father-son relationship, for instance, was not based on an established, stable hierarchy derived from the parent's greater age and experience, but on the latter's ability to emerge victorious—through physical strength and through cunning—in any competition for supremacy. What mattered was the establishment of a hierarchy based on the predominance of the strongest. The strongest member of the domestic group might also be the oldest, or he might simply be the most aggressive or the wiliest. Family roles were thus fluid and temporary, and subject to considerable tensions and reversals. In time, one of the sons might grow sufficiently bold to 'challenge' the father's superiority, struggle against it, and dethrone it.[16]

Success in competition was an end in itself, independent of the material advantages that victory brought within reach.

Mafia culture therefore offered numerous symbolic representations and simulated forms of competition for honour. These found their fullest expression in the game of *passatella*. A number of players, whose roles and hierarchical relations were fixed as required by the drawing of lots or by suitable sub-competitions, competed for the control and distribution of a resource, represented by wine, beer, fruit, or even water. The way in which this was to be distributed was decided in negotiations that could last for hours, and whose course depended on the changing relationships of alliance and antagonism between the players. As the game proceeded, its ruthless and dramatic character often transformed it into a *real* struggle for supremacy, with fights, wounding, and

[16] Ibid., pp. 8–10.

murder. A case in point is recounted in the biography of Gerolamo Piromalli, the most important Calabrian *mafioso* of the post-war period:

> Towards midnight on 27 August 1950, a seriously injured man was admitted to the General Hospital at Reggio Calabria. This was Francesco Ippolito—the late Francesco di Pellegrina di Bagnara. He was immediately operated on, and died without informing the authorities of the name of his attacker . . . The local *carabinieri* proceeded to investigate . . . The events leading up to Francesco Ippolito's death can be reconstructed as follows: on the afternoon of 27 August, Francesco Ippolito, his brother Carmelo, Girolamo Piromalli and Carmelo Marafioti met up near the Pellegrina Railmen's Club . . . They passed the time with a game of *padrone e sotto* (that is, *passatella*), adding interest to the game by using bottles of beer as stakes.
>
> It fell out that chance more than once favoured Francesco Ippolito, making him the *padrone* of the beer; and he, while offering drink to his other friends, each time left Piromalli *all'olmo* (without a drink). Piromalli took good note of this, and eventually—perhaps because Ippolito was giving himself airs on account of his good luck—he declared that Ippolito was nothing but a kid, and that he for his part had come along to have some fun and not to quarrel.
>
> Ippolito answered by saying that he was afraid of no-one, and that even if the other was Mommo Piromelli, he was not going to eat dirt. This exchange of insults inevitably created a tense atmosphere among the players. However, the game continued; and when chance made Piromalli *padrone* of the beer, he repaid Ippolito in kind, leaving him *all'olmo* in his turn.
>
> With the game going on in this way, the tension showed no sign of breaking. Indeed, it must have been clearly apparent, for when Vincenzo Oliviero arrived, he realised that 'something must have happened between Piromalli and Ippolito'. In fact, understanding the situation and what it might lead to, Oliviero suggested to the onlookers that the game should be brought to an end.
>
> . . . The game ended and, once they had paid for the beer they had drunk, everyone went out, stopping for a few moments outside the bar. Here . . . Ippolito went up to Piromalli, and the two of them moved a few paces away from the others. They exchanged a few words . . . Everyone felt certain that they had challenged one another, and had made an appointment to meet again. . . .[17]

[17] Reggio Calabria Court, *Procedimento contro Piromalli Gerolamo, Protocollo*, no. 298/50, 1950.

In communities where the mafia was present, this general tendency towards combativeness in its most extreme forms, regardless of the rules laid down as the basis for competition, sometimes made itself felt even in the most innocuous encounters, such as football matches or children's games.[18] The competition for honour was not precisely delimited and institutionalized, as it is in modern forms of sporting, scholastic and commercial competition, and in the struggle between classes and groups. As in war, rules were reduced to a minimum, and any means were justified. Struggle between people thus resembled the most primitive forms of social conflict: robbery, wanton destruction, the taking of prisoners, slaughter. Aggression was a socially sanctioned form of action.

Intermediate kinds of institutional regulation, such as the duel, never became established. Thus even where conflicts between *mafiosi* began by acknowledging the rules of chivalry, their outcome was determined by the unbounded use of fraud and deceit.

This is well illustrated by Familiari's account of the clash between the mafia chief, Criazzo, and his young challenger Gemina. Gemina, a goat-herd, accused Criazzo of having colluded with the judicial authorities and with the wealthy people of the district in order to 'get something out of it for himself'. The duel between the two ended in victory for the younger *mafioso*, and the mafia chief, seriously wounded, was taken to hospital. 'After two months and five days in bed, Criazzo returned home. The following night, he went round to see Vincenzo Gemina, who was sleeping in a hut. He called him outside and killed him in the doorway with two rifle-shots . . . The funeral was an impressive one. The whole town followed the brave goat-herd's coffin, and his murderer was in the first row.'[19]

In mafia areas, acts, people and events were habitually judged in terms of the honour acquired through victory in struggles and competitions. It follows that aggressiveness and violence were positively endorsed. In consequence, those who for biological and cultural reasons were least disposed to take part in conflict (such as women, children, and the elderly) found that their participation in the life of the community was severely limited—unless they adopted the manly and pugnacious bearing of those in the

---

[18] Asprea, op. cit., p. 13.
[19] P. Familiari, *La vera storia del brigante Marlino Zappa*.

superior categories. Asprea, describing his mother, emphasizes her strength, her courage, and her rather bloodthirsty temperament.[20] In the eyes of the inhabitants of Reggio Calabria province (and of the author of the novel *Emigranti*), the women of Bagnara owe their fascination to the fact that 'people said they wore razors in their hair, and used their knives with more daring than the men'.[21]

The society into which the *mafioso* was born was a tragic and brutal world, sparing neither the weak nor the defenceless. Although women and children, being excluded from the competition for honour, were rarely involved in woundings and killings, members of the marginal categories of the local community sometimes became the object of the most sadistic crimes. The mafia chief Michele Navarra, a doctor from Corleone, had no hesitation in killing a boy, the son of poor shepherds, with a cyanide injection simply because the child might *perhaps* have been present at the scene of a murder which Navarra had committed.[22] And at Oppido Mamertina, Peppinello, the son of a prostitute, was killed by a group of young men on Easter Monday afternoon. The youths had made the child their target in a shooting-competition.[23]

Honour and Justice

One important consequence of the war of each against all that prevailed in mafia areas was the fact that nothing, at bottom, could be really unjust. Honour was connected less with justice than with domination and physical strength. The local community remained largely indifferent to questions of 'right' and 'wrong', or 'justice' and 'injustice', when there was a conflict between two families, groups of relatives, or individuals. The preference tended to be given to whichever party proved victorious in the end, irrespective of the original causes of the conflict:

[20] Asprea, op. cit., p. 18.
[21] F. Ferri, *Emigranti*, Rome 1976, p. 198.
[22] D. De Masi, 'Sopraluogo nella Sicilia della mafia', in *Nord e Sud*, 46 (1963), p. 23.
[23] Asprea, op. cit., pp. 58–59.

The assassination of Andrea in Genuardo in 1919 and that of Cesare in the following year were carried out by Alessandro Cassini to get his territorial claims recognized. In the village of Genuardo, these claims were not disputed: Andrea's father accepted defeat, and even complied with the action of the Cassinis by charging innocent persons.[24]

In the carrying out of his day-to-day 'duties', the *mafioso* did not follow any abstract ideal of morality and justice. He sought honour and power, and in pursuit of his goals he was quite ready to flout *any* established rule of conduct. There does not exist, and there never has existed, any coherent system of 'just, unwritten laws', enforced by the power of the mafia as against the 'unjust written laws' imposed by the State.

As we shall see below, traditional *mafiosi* assumed public functions, safeguarding the socio-economic *status quo* against the threat posed by subversive forces. Such functions, however, were the product—recognized as such both by the local society, and by the State—of the mafia's possession of a territorial monopoly of physical violence, and not of its general 'allegiance' to any traditional order. If anything, this 'allegiance' is a later rationalization, temporally and logically consequent upon the gaining of the monopoly of violence.

The conviction that the law is an instrument of physical force has deep roots in mafia culture. When an enemy threatens him with recourse to the State's laws, the *mafioso* of *La famiglia Montalbano* replies that 'law is force, and can never be separated from force'.[25] Force and supremacy, here, create the law much more than they represent the efficacy of any law valid in itself. Of all historical and social worlds, none demonstrates more clearly than the world of the *mafioso* the extent to which physical force can be independent of any pre-established distributive justice. Individual *mafiosi* were perfectly aware of the ultimate foundation of their power, and on some occasions took care to emphasize how the concrete 'justice of force' prevailed over the ideal force of justice.[26]

When power was at stake, *mafiosi* had no hesitation in violating

[24] A. Blok, *The Mafia of a Sicilian Village, 1860–1960: A Study of Violent Peasant Entrepreneurs*, New York and Oxford 1974, p. 174.

[25] S. Montalto, *La famiglia di Montalbano*, Chiavalle Centrale 1973, p. 84.

[26] Familiari, op. cit., pp. 20–21; Strati, op. cit., pp. 17–18.

the most deep-rooted cultural and ethical norms. '*Mafiosi* used to stress relations of friendship in order to accomplish a killing effectively without raising the suspicion of either the victim, public opinion, or the law,' wrote Blok. Blok also recounts a struggle that took place in 1922 between two western Sicilian mafia groups. A serious disagreement had broken out between Bernardo Cassini, a member of the leading mafia cell (*cosca*) in Genuardo, and the *cosche* of Adernò, Corleone and Bisacquino. When his brother was killed and his animals were stolen, Bernardo realised that his own life was in danger, and that he would have to give in to his opponents, whose leader was the famous Vito Cascio Ferro.* Bernardo asked for a meeting to be organized, at which the whole affair could be discussed. It was decided that Bernardo must pay a money indemnity to each of his adversaries. He went to Corleone and paid up. He then took money to Bisacquino, to Cascio Ferro's house:

> Cascio Ferro himself and the other *mafiosi* involved reassured Bernardo, and told him that he could leave the house without incurring any danger. Thus appeased, Bernardo did not suspect that his 'friends' were preparing his elimination.
> Bernardo was shot twice by Don Pipineddu, one of Cascio Ferro's right-hand men.[27]

What determined the power of the *mafioso* was victory in the struggle for supremacy—victory by whatever means. Respect for traditional legal and cultural obligations was a subsequent, derivative phase in the dynamic of mafia power (which we shall, however, discuss later in this account). The fact that all hierarchical relations operating in mafia areas were governed by this strict link between right and might, law and physical force, gave them a distinctive formal character, which could recoil at any moment upon the heads of those currently in power. When the leader of a cell was physically eliminated or defeated in a fight, his followers accepted the new state of affairs quite calmly, and the

---

* *Vito Cascio Ferro* : Together with Calogero Vizzini and Genco Russo, Cascio Ferro was one of the most important traditional Sicilian *mafiosi*. Born in Bisacquino, in the province of Palermo, he emigrated to the USA for a time at the beginning of the century. He was arrested under the fascist regime and condemned to life imprisonment, dying in jail in 1943.

[27] Blok, op. cit., p. 173.

victor was quickly installed in his place: 'Guiseppe Damati . . . was only twenty-six years old when he killed and replaced the much older and established Bernardo Cassini in November 1922.'[28]

It was just this formal quality of mafia power, linked to its honorific-competitive origins, that explained the apparently curious phenomenon of the 'transfer' of authority from one man to his opponents.

His understanding of these 'Hobbesian' roots of mafia power brought the *prefetto* (Prefect) Cesare Mori much early success in the anti-mafia campaign that he began in Sicily in 1924. 'If Sicilians are scared of the mafia,' Mori told his colleagues, 'I shall convince them that I am the most powerful *mafioso* of the lot.'[29] The linchpin of his whole strategy was the setting up of a competition for honour with the *mafiosi* of Sicily, a competition that would take place partly on their own terrain but which also relied upon the State's military and organizational superiority.

His language and his methods were thus steeped in the spirit of the mafia. When the elite of Palermo gathered in the Teatro Massimo to celebrate his victory over the mafia brigands of le Madonie, Mori declared that it was 'no good trusting in the inadequacy or incompleteness of the law. The law will be re-written, completed, and put right. And in any case, wherever it is lacking, we shall step in, with arguments of unquestionable force.'[30] His struggle against the *mafiosi* of le Madonie clearly shows how he tried to bring about a transfer of collective authority from outlaws to State officials by demonstrating his superiority in political, military and—above all—honorific terms.

After surrounding the town of Gangi, where the *mafiosi-banditi* had taken refuge, and occupying it with a military force for some ten days, Mori gave the bandits twelve hours to leave their hiding places and surrender:

> It was my firm intention to deny them the honour of armed combat. I did not want the prestige of crime to benefit once again from the glory . . . of a battle with the forces of law and order. I proposed not just to win—that is, to bring the bandits to justice—but to give the people concrete proof of the cowardice of crime.[31]

[28] Ibid., p. 173.
[29] A. Petacco, *Il prefetto di ferro*, Milan 1975, p. 105.
[30] Ibid., p. 105.
[31] C. Mori, *Con la mafia ai ferri corti*, Verona 1932, p. 296.

However, the police campaign achieved no notable success until Mori put into practice his plan of showing himself to be 'the biggest *mafioso* of all':

His first trick was to have rumours spread that the Gangi hostages were suffering all kinds of maltreatment in prison, and in particular that 'the cops are screwing the bandits' women'. The ruse was only partially successful . . . Many of the bandits came into the open and gave themselves up to the authorities . . . But from the chiefs, there was not the slightest movement . . .

. . . 'If these characters care nothing for the virtue of their women-folk,' Mori commented ironically, 'let's see how they react when their interests are attacked.'

There and then, he published a decree confiscating all the bandits' goods. The confiscation was carried out in broad daylight, and so publicized that no-one could avoid noticing it . . . Mori then had the fattest calves from the confiscated herds slaughtered in the *piazza*, ordering the meat to be distributed free to the public. The people, hungry after the long seige, all came rushing to collect the unexpected gift. The giving out of the meat became in some ways like a town festival. The policemen-butchers made the most of the public mood, pouring scorn on the timidity of the bandits.

. . . Cesare Mori continued with his psychological warfare, author-izing his immediate colleagues to issue personal challenges to the most celebrated brigands. He himself challenged Gaetano Ferrarello: 'Let it be known to the so-called King of le Madonie,' he proclaimed, 'that I am ready to meet him single-handed and carrying my musket. I shall be waiting for him this evening at six, in the *fondo Sant'Andrea*. If he is a man, he will be there.'

Similar challenges were then issued by Francesco Spanò to Carmelo Andaloro and by the police-chief, Crimi, to Salvatore Ferrarello. These pieces of bragadoccio may at first sight seem transparent, and it is clear enough that the bandits never had the slightest intention of accepting the challenges. But Mori's aim was in fact to make an impression on the imagination of the people, who were accustomed to respect only those who behaved like *mafiosi*.

It was at this point that Mori decided to issue his ultimatum to the bandits in hiding . . . But it proved unnecessary to wait for the full period to elapse . . . Gaetano Ferrarello emerged from his hiding-place, which was actually in the attic of the building that housed the police-station.

'My heart is pounding,' he said in an agitated voice. 'For the first time in my life, I am face to face with justice.'[32]

---

[32] Petacco, op. cit., pp. 91–93.

Honour and Murder

In a system whose basis was the struggle for supremacy, the most unequivocal way of asserting one's own pre-eminence was to take another man's life. When Bernardo Cassini was murdered, as Anton Blok describes, his killer gained not just land and power, but the honorific title *don*. In the mafia scale of values, where conflicts of honour played such a central role, it was in the highest degree honourable to take life and to kill a fearsome adversary. 'So-and-so is an exceptional man; he has "got" five murders'. 'He is *un'uomo di rispetto* : people say that he's "rubbed out" four people'—phrases of this kind recur in mafia conversation. The more fearsome and powerful the victim, the greater the 'worth and merit' of the killer. Vito Cascio Ferro boasted of how he had killed with his own hands his long-standing adversary Joe Petrosino, the New York police lieutenant, enemy number one of the American mafia, who had visited Palermo secretly in 1909: 'In my whole life I have only killed one person, and I did that *disinterestedly* . . . Petrosino was a brave adversary, and deserved better than a shameful death at the hands of some hired cut-throat.'[33]

Any man of honour had to commit at least one act of murderous violence. Without killing someone, nobody could hope to inspire fear or to gain the recognition and respect due to a *mafioso*.

> It often happens that the *campiere* (estate guard—often an agent and representative of the mafia) gets the name of having pegged out one or two scalps to dry—that is, of having committed one or two murders. And then, because of the aura this gives him, he is made. Everyone's afraid of him. He becomes someone who causes an impression, makes an impression. People can't do without him and for that reason his services are better paid.[34]

Murder was the root of the *mafioso*'s prestige, transforming an anonymous shepherd or farm labourer into a man who must be reckoned with. Among the mafia of Sicily and Calabria, the act of murder—especially if committed in the course of a struggle for supremacy, of whatever kind—was a mark of courage and manly force, and automatically enhanced the killer's credit. This was an

[33] A. Petacco, *Joe Petrosino*, Milan 1978, p. 182.
[34] A. Cutrera, *La mafia e i mafiosi*, Palermo 1960, p. 95.

important form of *conversion* between illegal action and mafia action: to break the law of the State was honourable, because it showed contempt and defiance of powerful persons and institutions. Many *mafiosi* began their careers (and still do so) in the ranks of common criminals:

> It is by a series of well-defined steps that the *mafioso* enters the world of crime. These steps are always the same. They are monotonously familiar in judicial life-histories. At a very early age—as young as fifteen or sixteen—there will be a charge of illegal carriage of fire-arms. Next comes a charge or conviction for causing actual bodily harm. This accusation of wounding is a sign that the young man of honour has distinguished himself by his arrogance and boastfulness at some brawl or in some vendetta, though as yet the affair is only a minor one. At this stage, he is not yet certain to become involved with the mafia . . . Then the young man's desire for dominance, his wish to be a cut above the rest, and his friendship with undesirable characters push him a step further. He finds himself convicted of robbery or extortion. The more serious the offence, the better for his reputation in the underworld. And so he attempts a murder, and then commits a murder, or carries out a massacre—by which he gains, so to speak, his battle honours, and is entitled to 'claim his place' alongside other men of honour.[35]

Anyone who studies the careers of the most important *mafiosi* will indeed be struck, not only by the number and gravity of the conflicts from which they have emerged victorious (especially during the early part of their apprenticeship), but by the fact that there does exist a progression of illegal acts tending always to pass through the same stages. Thus the *curricula* drawn up by the judicial authorities for the lives of Gerolamo Piromalli (the mafia chief of the Tyrrhenian part of the Reggio district) and of Antonio Macrí (the Ionian mafia leader) are almost identical in their earlier phases (see Table 1 over).

This honorific dimension of murder, with homicide seen as an expression of the killer's predominance and of his ability to avenge himself, casts a haze of glory over every murderous act and over its agents and accessories. To get an idea of the impact which a murder makes on the population of a mafia area even today, one need only flick through the best-selling Reggio

---

[35] Interview no. 4.

Table 1

Judicial curricula for the lives of
Antonio Macrí and Gerolamo Piromalli

Year	Antonio Macrí Charges and Convictions	Gerolamo Piromalli Charges and Convictions	Year
1929	illegal carriage of firearms	illegal carriage of firearms	1939
1932	grievous bodily harm	grievous bodily harm	1940
1945	robbery with violence	robbery with violence	1944
1947	attempted murder		
1958	murder (with aggravating circumstances)	murder	1950

Calabria newspaper the day after the murder happens: page after page is crowded with photographs, including close-ups, together with the most minute particulars of the victim, all giving the event a touch of symbolic grandeur. The reports usually emphasize the execution's cruellest and most violent phases; they tell how the blood spilled out, how the dead body was mutilated, how the victim spent his last hours, and how his disconsolate relatives are coping with their grief.

To carry and use firearms was a mark of honour in mafia areas. In Reggio Calabria province in 1950, several thousand licences to carry arms were issued; there was a still larger number of statutory declaractions in respect of the domestic keeping of rifles, pistols, knives and bullets; and a yet larger number of cases of unlawful carriage and possession of arms.

2.

The Power of the *Mafioso*

The Power of the *Mafioso* and its Functioning

So far, we have been considering the traditional mafia in its aspect of individual violence, as seen in the anomic competition between those who vie for the supremacy that is the source of public esteem and consideration. However, the mafia also appeared in another guise, as important as the first and of a fundamentally opposite kind. We can define this in terms of a process of *institutionalization* : honour is institutionalized and transformed into a *power* acknowledged as legitimate.

What happened, in point of fact, when the competition for dominance was resolved by the victory of a particularly powerful aspirant, who attained to the highest degree of honour? The latter sought to bring the local area and its people under his patronage, establishing a monopoly of physical violence that allowed him to maintain his own position as long as possible. He tried to 'freeze' the existing distribution of honour, and to soften—by regulating and controlling it—the war of each against all that underpinned the system.

In pursuing these goals, he couldn't any longer rely simply on the archaic virtues of courage, ruthlessness and strength that helped him in his rise. The *mafioso* who wanted to die in his bed, honoured and revered as a gentleman, had to know the arts of government. He must imitate the action not just of the lion, but of the fox. If his power was to be accepted and acknowledged by the population, he must have demonstrated his prudence, his level-headedness, his cunning. In him, people would have to see not just a victorious he-man, with the strength and the ability to wipe out any rival, but also a figure of authority—the father and friend of all, the protector and mediator, the counsellor and judge. In the areas where the mafia flourished, moreover, some principle by which to regulate social conflicts was keenly sought. The socio-economic system faced a constant and real threat of disintegration, and there was thus an urgent need for some supra-individual and public power, capable of creating even a semblance of public order.[1]

Long-drawn out feuds (*faide*) and conflicts of honour, leading to many deaths and the destruction of much wealth, left a deep mark in local consciousness, both as historical memory and as everyday actuality. Large families and groups of relatives were often reduced to penury by the endlessly recurring savage vendettas and devastation typical of mafia areas. These results, clearly visible as they were, stimulated a particularly pressing demand for some principle by which the use of physical violence could be governed.

This need for some self-regulation of the system met with the need felt by the *uomini di rispetto* to maintain their honour, and as a result the latter came to be entrusted with a series of important public functions, protecting traditional laws and criminal judges, arbitrators and executioners, exercising in their own persons many sensitive powers that were normally the prerogative of the State.

Honour was thus transformed into legitimate power, into authority. The latter then appeared in its turn as a means by which honour was itself confirmed and extended. If the authority of the mafia was generally accepted, this was not on the whole due to any esteem or spontaneous admiration felt by the crowd for the deeds performed by the man of honour during the time when he was establishing himself. Honour acquired by such exceptional acts set too great a gulf between the *mafioso* and the common people for it to form the basis of any lasting identification. The mechanism of 'representation' in mafia areas owed something to this elitist dimension, but was based on the propagation of an anti-heroic and anti-charismatic ideal. 'The real *mafioso*, the

---

[1] See P. Arlacchi, *Mafia, Peasants and Great Estates. Society in Traditional Calabria*, Cambridge 1983 (trans. Jonathan Steinberg), pp. 113-120.

authentic *mafioso*, almost always behaves modestly, speaking and listening with an air of humility.'[2] Unlike the gangster or the bandit, the *mafioso* had no taste for the conspicuous consumption of power. He liked to veil his own potency. When the journalist Montanelli asked Calogero Vizzini's* permission to take a photograph of him, Vizzini replied:

> Me, in a photograph!
> I'm nobody, I'm just an ordinary citizen. . . . How strange it is! . . . People think that I say little out of caution. But if I say little, it's because I know little. I live in a small village, I seldom come to Palermo, I know few people . . .[3]

Once the *uomo di rispetto* established his position, he did not try to legitimate this by presenting himself as someone gifted with extraordinary qualities, unattainable by others; on the contrary, he presented himself as an ordinary man, one of the common people, particularly well endowed with the basic attributes of personality—a sort of model valid for everyone. The 'exaggerated notion of individual force and strength, as the one and only means of settling any conflict' must henceforth be understood in the context of a strongly marked institutionalization and self-limitation, which circumstribed the *mafioso*'s range of action.

In this second aspect, the action of the mafia was characterized by its notable *conformity* with reigning cultural norms, and not by any tendency to subvert them. The typical *mafioso* was a simple man, who nonetheless unquestionably spoke for everyone. A man who kept faith with his friends, knew how to repay a favour, held honour and gratitude in high esteem, and was *ready to use violence* to ensure that these values were respected—such a man was an honoured citizen of his town. No longer could anyone think of calling him a criminal, an outsider, a rebel:

> Every year, Momo Grasso of Misilmeri played the part of Jesus in the festival of the Passion. . . .[4]

---

* *Calogero Vizzini:* Celebrated Sicilian capomafia, he was born and lived in Villalba, in Agrigento province. He died in 1954.
[2] A. Vaccaro, 'La mafia', in *Rivisto d'Italia*, anno II, vol. III, p. 688, Rome 1899.
[3] I. Montanelli, *Pantheon minore*, Milan 1958, pp. 280, 282.
[4] H. Hess, *Mafia*, Bari 1973, p. 100.

The *mafioso* recoils with shocked surprise from any suggestion that he is a criminal: by talk of that kind, journalists and *carabinieri* are simply setting out to ruin honest family men. His actions, in his own eyes, are by no means criminal, they are ordinary 'social behaviour'; and to behave like this is quite simply a necessity in Sicilian society. It is in a spirit of altruistic self-sacrifice that he undertakes the burdensome responsibility of arranging things and protecting people . . . after all, someone has to take it on if life is to run smoothly.[5]

The power of the mafia was understood, by those who wielded it, in terms of a disinterested service of communal order and the general good. This was how Giuseppe Genco Russo* reflected on himself and his functions:

I was born like this. I don't have any ulterior motives. If someone asks me a favour, I'm inclined to do it, because that's how nature made me . . .

Suppose someone comes along and says, 'I'm having a bit of trouble with Tizio, see if you can put things to rights.' I get the person in question to come along, or maybe I go to see him, depending how things stand between us: and I put matters to rights between the two of them. But I don't want anyone to get the idea that I am telling you these things to make myself look big. No, I absolutely don't want it to seem as though I were saying all this to make myself look big—I'm saying it out of politeness, because you have come all this way to see me. I'm not vain, or ambitious. If people ask me how they should vote, that's because they feel it's their duty to ask advice, as a way of showing their gratitude and appreciation, and also because they feel that they themselves are in the dark, and want to follow the example of those who have done them good.

Tomorrow, for instance, I've got to leave the threshing, I've got to leave the animals and everything, so that I can go to Agrigento and mention someone's name to the examiners—recommend him, to be sure they pass him.[6]

Genco Russo's understanding of his own role does of course represent a self-serving distortion of reality. But this must not

---

* *Genco Russo:* Calogero Vizzini's nephew, active as a *mafioso* in the area of Mussomelli, he was interrogated by the Anti-mafia Commission in the 1960s.

[5] Hess, op. cit., pp. 100–101.

[6] D. Dolci, *Spreco*, Turin 1960, pp. 68–69 (see D. Dolci, *Sicilian Lives*, trans. J. Vitiello with M. Polidoro, London 1981: but here and elsewhere, we have translated afresh from the original Italian—*trans.*)

disguise the fact that behind the rationalizations he uses, there
exists a serious problem of cohesion and social stability. The
mafioso's actions were often a blend: outward fidelity to the
traditional order mixed with the man of honour's quest for profit
and personal power. At times, the *mafioso* may truly have behaved like a 'knight at the service of the weak'. As any true man
must, he disinterestedly defended those who find themselves in
difficulty:

> Any citizen, even a stranger or a foreigner, is best advised, should he
> need a favour, to go to one of the so-called mafia chiefs. He can be
> sure his request will be granted, and willingly too. In fact, the *mafioso*
> will go to great lengths to serve his new friend, disinterestedly and
> without expecting any reward.[7]

In reality, the *mafioso*'s disinterestedness at this initial stage
was a small long-term investment, for 'he knows that his labour is
never without its profit, since, apart from the growth in his
reputation, he has also added to the number of people who look
up to him.'[8] The more people there were who believed him
capable of resolving problems and helping them out, the more
prestige the *mafioso* enjoyed. Genco Russo gives a clear description of the process:

> If you live in a certain way, things come along one after another. Once
> one person has come along and I've done them a favour, once another
> person's come along and I've done them another favour, then things
> get into that pattern, it becomes a sort of habit. And that is how my
> reputation spread.[9]

If the character of the *mafioso* and the action of the mafia
played a central part in traditional society, this can be traced to
the variety of functions they performed, their ability to move on
different planes and integrate contradictory impulses. The 'func-
tional necessity' of the *mafioso*'s power and mode of behaviour lay
in the fact that these satisfied at one and the same time demands
for order and demands for mobility, the need for cohesion and the
impulse towards competition. In his chapter on the mafia in
Primitive Rebels, Hobsbawm emphasizes the endogenous, inter-
class aspect of the mafia phenomenon—the fact, that is, that

---

[7] A. Cutrera, *La mafia e i mafiosi*, Palermo 1900, p. 51.
[8] Ibid.
[9] Dolci, op. cit., p. 69.

nobody imposed or imported it, and that it expressed the needs of various rural groups, even if it served their interests unequally:

> For the weak . . . it provided at least some guarantee that obligations between them would be kept, some guarantee that the usual degree of oppression would not be habitually exceeded; it was the terror that mitigated traditional tyrannies. And perhaps, also, it satisfied a desire for revenge by providing that the rich were sometimes fleeced, and that the poor, if only as outlaws, could sometimes fight back . . . For the feudal lords it was a means of safeguarding property and authority: for the rural middle class a means of gaining it.[10]

If we neglect this public aspect—if we forget that, while seeking to preserve and extend his personal power, the *mafioso* was at the same time representing threatened collective interests —then we shall understand very little about the traditional mafia. The reasons why the phenomenon of the mafia has lasted so long have to be sought in the way the men of honour have exercised several important functions of social, economic and political integration. Some of these were carried out within the traditional local culture and society, while others were connected with the relations between this local world and the external economic and political system.

Protection

By the term 'protection', we denote those functions to do with the protection of established interests that the *mafioso* carried out within the society where he had his origins. Since in the conditions typical of the local community, there was very little security of property, wealth or person, anyone who owned anything had to entrust its protection to the leading *mafioso* of the area. Those who refused to pay protection-money against theft, or to come to some agreement with the mafia chief, found their property suffering from fires, robberies, and acts of vandalism. Should the injured party persist in standing out against the racket, then his personal safety would be threatened, and he would be the target of increasingly serious attacks, until in the

[10] E. J. Hobsbawm, *Primitive Rebels: Studies in Archaic Forms of Social Movement in the 19th and 20th Centuries*, third edn., Manchester 1974, p. 41.

end his life would be at risk.

This form of income—specific to the mafia, and consisting in the exaction of tribute in return for 'protection'—belongs to Weber's category of '"predatory" incomes', involving 'appropriation by force'.[11] Officially, the mafia offered protection against thieves and bandits, but in reality this represented a system of public taxation, parallel to (and more efficient than) the system operated by the State. Around the early decades of the present century, in the area of western Sicily studied by Blok, the portion payable to the *mafiosi* was called the *pizzu*, and amounted to two *tumoli* of grain for every *salma* of land under wheat:

> The territories of the various communes in the area were divided into districts, each of which consisted of several large estates controlled by a single *cosca*. The *campiere* was the guardian of the estate, and it was under the cloak of this role that he imposed and collected the tribute, half of which he kept for himself while the other half went to the *capo-mafia* of the district . . . *Campieri* not only extracted tributes from the peasant sharecroppers but . . . also imposed themselves upon the manager of the estate . . . They sought through more or less veiled threats to induce the manager or owner to employ one of their company. Though these 'men of confidence', as *campieri* were called, made themselves 'respected' by keeping rustlers and petty thieves away from the farm, their presence often proved a burden to the manager or owner.[12]

In protecting property and persons within a given jurisdiction, the mafia set up a regime that was—with some qualification—defensive; they safeguarded dominant positions and interests. The *mafioso* defended established positions, and was a member of the local power elite. However, the way in which he intervened to safeguard the economic status quo hardly ever brought him to identify altogether with the perspective of those who held official power and wealth. A contractual element always persisted, an element of alliance rather than fusion. In all the workings of 'protection', the *mafioso*'s role was kept clearly distinct from that of any patron or client. Mafia power was an independent power,

[11] M. Weber, *Economy and Society*, ed. G. Roth and C. Wittich, Berkeley and London 1978, vol. 1, pp. 204–205.

[12] A. Blok, *The Mafia of a Sicilian Village, 1860–1960: A Study of Violent Peasant Entrepreneurs*.

with its own autonomous bases of legitimation, and the agents through whom it operated were never too restricted in their scope. Even when it was most obvious that some private interest was being pursued, the intervention of the mafia always had the aspect of something undertaken in the name of order and of the overall stability of things.

Repression

The *uomo di rispetto* liked to take upon himself the preservation of order, and he found a second extensive field for the exercise of his power within the local community in the *repression of non-conformist behaviour*. By taking on this function, the *mafioso* was enabled to present himself to the local society and to the State authorities as a guardian of public order. Thieves and robbers, vagabonds, homosexuals, bandits and prostitutes were all subject to some varying degree of opposition from the mafia. Everyday crime and wrong-doing were tolerated by the mafia chief only within very well-defined limits, limits that allowed him to justify his own position. Should any ambitious deviant try to scale the heights of honour, the attempt was violently and savagely put down by the mafia, whose first concern was always to maintain full control of all illegal activities taking place in its territory.

The mafia did not carry out this repression of local deviance (any more than it carried out its other fundamental activities) in direct opposition to the duties and functions of the State organization—except, that is, when the official authorities were taking a particularly hard line. Weber's definition of the State as the 'monopolist of violence' within a given territorial area operates at a high level of abstraction, and in interpreting it one must take account of the concrete mediations through which the need to maintain the social order is realized in any given system and situation.

In mafia areas, it was in fact evident that the *mafiosi* and the organs of the State, for all their theoretical antagonism as rivals for the monopoly of violence, collaborated, using very similar methods, to repress the most serious threats and disturbances to the established order. Even though mafia ideology exalted opposition to the official judicial system and proscribed collaboration with the State authorities, there were innumerable episodes of banditry and common criminality in which the intervention of the mafia's armed might, on the side of the forces of law and order, was decisive in securing the capture, killing or neutralization of the deviants.

Perhaps the most important episode of full-blown collaboration against banditry and crime between the mafia and the official authorities took place in Sicily, immediately after the end of the second world war. In 1947, the central government decided to begin a determined campaign against the Sicilian bandits:

> The results were discouraging: in 1947 alone, 46 *carabinieri* died in fights and ambushes, while 734 were injured through the same causes. Many received commendations and decorations for military valour: two gold medals were given, thirty-nine silver medals, fifty-eight military crosses. But the bandits were killing the *carabinieri*, and the *carabinieri* were unable to kill the bandits . . .
>
> It was at this point that Ettore Messana, the Inspector-General of Public Safety in Sicily, found himself in a difficult position: the mafia came to his assistance. In fact, they eliminated (by killing them) those bandits from whom they feared compromising revelations, . . . while they handed the lesser bandits over to the police. . . .[13]

These 'compromising revelations' had to do with the temporary accommodation in the years 1943–46 between some mafia groups and some groups of bandits and criminals. Compromises of this kind were by no means infrequent for brief periods and at particular times. However, this hardly negates the fundamental opposition between the power of the mafia, which is repressive and conservative by nature, and the typically anomic, rebellious and utopian charcter of the various primitive forms of social revolt and deviant behaviour. The story of Salvatore Giuliano is very much to the point here: beginning his career as a bandit of the people, opposed to the mafia, he next becomes a bandit-chief, and an ally of the mafia. Ending up as a classic Sicilian bandit, Salvatore Giuliano is finally eliminated through a renewed alliance between the mafia's forces of order and those of the State.[14]

In the province of Caltanisetta alone—an area under the control of Calogero Vizzini—the *mafiosi* disposed of no

[13] M. Pantaleone, *Mafia e politica*, Turin 1972, p. 127.
[14] See Gavin Maxwell, *God Protect me from my Friends*, London 1956.

fewer than sixty-three bandits in the period immediately following the war.[15]

In responding to extra-political deviance, the mafia may use compromise, and enter into arrangements of temporary convenience. Their opposition to organized political and trade-union 'deviance' is far more coherent and unwavering. From the unification of Italy until the period after the second world war, the Sicilian peasants' movement was almost always up against an alliance between the power of the mafia ar.d the power of the State and the bosses. The official authorities virtually paid public tribute to the *persone di rispetto*, emphasizing their merits and the support they had given in carrying out political and social repression:

> The Caltanisetta Chief of Police, at a meeting held in June 1949 with a number of peasants together with two members of parliament (La Marca and Colajanni), was amazed to hear their protests against the acts of violence committed by the mafia of the former domain of Pescazzo. He went on to exonerate the mafia (who were, he claimed, benefactors of public order and guardians of social peace): the *mafiosi*, he insisted, were 'statesmen of remarkable ability'.[16]

As recently as 1953, the Mayor of the most important city in Calabria issued a testimonial to the merits of the mafia chief Donato Pagliara because the latter had intervened—at the 'simple desire' of the Prefect, the Police Chief and the Mayor himself—to put a stop to a strike by the city's bakery workers (see p. 32).

It is of some significance that in those areas of the traditional Italian south (*Mezzogiorno*) where the mafia are present, neither modern mass political parties nor class-based organizations and movements have been able to establish a really consistent presence.

These areas have been only marginally involved in the most heightened moments of class struggle in Italy from unification to 1950—as happened, for instance, during the land agitation in southern Calabria in the period 1943–50; and when they have been involved, the popular forces have invariably suffered defeat at the hands of an alliance between mafia terrorism and the ruling

[15] P. Chilanti and M. Farinella, *Rapporto sulla mafia*, Palermo 1964, p. 38.
[16] G. Montalbano, 'La mafia ad occhio nudo', in *Il Mondo*, 9 December 1958, p. 73.

classes. This happened with the *Fasci* in late nineteenth-century
Sicily, and again—on an even larger scale—in western Sicily
after the end of the second world war, when the leading mafia
figures of the day had themselves appointed to the tenancies of
vast agricultural holdings so that they could bring order to the
rebellious countryside.

Calogero Vizzini got the Princess of Trabia to give him the
lease of the domain of Micciché, which a peasant cooperative was
seeking to obtain by expropriating the Princess. Vizzini at once
set up another cooperative, with his nephew as president; and this
led to the dissolution of the first. Giuseppe Genco Russo obtained
the domain of Polizzello, in the Mussomeli region: in that area,
peasant unrest came to an end. 'The same methods were used, to
the same effect, in other places: in the Parrino domain, let to
Vanni Sacco; in the lands of Ficuzza; in the territory of Godrano,
in the domain of Strassotto, and in the territory of Corleone,
which was leased to a young mafia entrepreneur, Luciano Liggio.'[17]

Mediation

This third function of mafia power was by far the most important.
The traditional *mafioso* spent much of his everyday life in the task
of *mediating* in conflicts within the local society, and mediating
that society's relations with the outside world.

The mediation of the mafia in horizontal conflicts between
individuals and groups did in fact meet a very pressing demand,
and one keenly felt by the local population. The traditional mafia
chiefs were quite aware of the importance of their role. Calogero
Vizzini spotlighted the problem when he declared, in a famous
interview, that 'the fact is that in every society there has to be
some class of people who put things to rights when they get
complicated.'[18]

What kinds of 'complication' required the mafia to intervene?

In practice, they included every failure to respect any of the
traditional norms of behaviour, and every one of the numerous
cases of actual or potential conflict between individuals and
groups, whether arising from economic or social relations or from

[17] S. F. Romano, *Storia della mafia*, Milan 1966, p. 318.
[18] Montanelli, op. cit., p. 182.

D I C H I A R A Z I O N E

Dichiaro che PAGLIARA Donato è gestore di due
importanti forni a vapore in Reggio città, con una
rilevante produzione giornaliera.

Dalla sua attività ne ritraggono sostentamento
la madre vecchia ed ammalata, la di lui moglie con
figlio, la nipote, orfana di entrambi i genitori,
la sorella Maria, vedova con tre figli, nonchè il
fratello Luciano con moglie e cinque bambini.

Per le prove date di capacità e di onesto lavo
ro, merita ogni benevolenza e considerazione.

Va segnalato, per debito di lealtà e di coscien
za, che il Donato PAGLIARA si è reso utile alle Au
torità e alla cittadinanza sventando per due volte
le manifestazioni di sciopero, promosse dai pani=
ficatori con l'appoggio della locale Camera del La
voro.

Tanto è avvenuto a semplice desiderio espresso
dal Prefetto Dott. Rotigliano, tramite il Questore
Polimeni, e dal sottoscritto, Sindaco di Reggio Ca
labria, e ciò al fine, oltre che di garentire alla
cittadinanza il pane, anche per evitare speculazio
ni di carattere politico.

La presente dichiarazione si rilascia in omag=
gio alla verità ed a richiesta dell'Avv. Angelo
ZAPPIA.

Reggio Calabria, 11) marzo 1953

IL SINDACO

(Giuseppe Romeo)

the competition for honour. The *mafioso* acted in such cases as a
veritable justice of the peace; his intervention ensured that order
would be restored—or in other words, that the dominant socio-
economic system would be maintained. Since the society where the
mafia thrives lacks any 'traditional' dominant elite properly so
called, being instead a ceaselessly mobile collection of groups,
families and client-groupings, it is very rare that the ruling values
are those of the dominant elite of any given moment, and this
greatly strengthens the 'impartiality' of the mafia's authority.[19]

A creditor might make use of the mafia's power to persuade a

DECLARATION

I hereby declare that Donato PAGLIARA is the manager of two important steam-ovens in the city of Reggio, which produce each day a significant quantity of bread.

Through his activity as a bakery manager, he supports his old invalid mother, his wife and son, his niece (who is an orphan, having lost both parents), and his sister Maria, a widow with three sons, as well as his brother Luciano with his wife and five children.

The proof he has given of his abilities and honest workmanship entitles him to the fullest favour and consideration.

In the name of conscience and honesty, we must make it known that Donato PAGLIARA has been of use to the Authorities and the citizenry, twice foiling the attempts of the bread-bakers to organise a strike in concert with the local Trade Union (*Camera del Lavoro*).

This he did at the simple desire of the Prefect, *Dottore* Rotigliano, as conveyed by the Chief of Police, and also of the undersigned, to wit, the Mayor; his end being not only to ensure that the citizens would be supplied with bread, but also to avoid political complications.

The present declaration has been made in deference to the truth and at the instance of Angelo ZAPPIA, Advocate-at-Law.

> Reggio Calabria, 3 March 1953.
> Giuseppe Romeo, MAYOR.

debtor to pay up. A debtor might turn to the *mafioso* and ask him to intervene on his behalf. In this way, those involved avoided turning their conflict of interest into a legal conflict or a conflict of honour, so saving both time and human and material resources:

If you go to law, do you know how much you lose?—because without money, you can't speak up in the verbal examination, you can't answer the lawsuit and the lawyers. But with an intermediary, things

[19] Arlacchi, op. cit., pp. 97–105.

are sorted out cheaper all round. People have every faith in him, because he's a man who can set things straight.[20]

When goods were stolen, the owner found it more convenient to turn to the mafia than to the police: in return for a certain sum, generally roughly equivalent in value to a third of what had been stolen, he would soon get his goods back. The organs of the State were virtually incapable of carrying out their functions in such circumstances. The Prefect Cesare Mori wrote that the State authorities obtained nothing in 75 per cent of cases, found the culprits in 15 per cent, and only in 10 per cent succeeded also in locating the stolen goods.[21] By contrast, the mafia (again according to Mori) were successful in 95 per cent of cases where they mediated.

Because it was speedy and effective, mafia mediation became a substitute for official justice: describing the authority exercised by Don Ferdinando Ambesà, Familiari tells us that 'in that area, he was the judge, and against his sentences there was no appeal. . . . There was a court at Forio, and a magistrate, but he was seldom troubled.'[22]

Furthermore, there was a whole range of controversies in which it would not be technically possible to turn to the state authorities, since no official laws existed concerning the point in question. Such were the cases in which one party demanded that the other should behave in accordance with traditional norms that the State's legal system did not recognize or provide for—the classic example being a man's obligation to marry a girl whom he had seduced. Here is Hess's summary of an episode recounted by Lo Schiavo in his novel *Gli inesorabili* :

Peppino Bellía, having seduced Rosina dell'Aira, is refusing to marry the girl. Rosina, an orphan, asks the help of a relative who is a client of Don Salvatore Sparaino, the old mafia chief of Gangi. Don Salvatore summons Peppino and his father, Disma Bellía. Disma, asked what a father should do if he believes that his daughter has been seduced on the strength of a promise of marriage, replies with an oath, 'I'd blow the man's brains out if he didn't make amends within two days!' Sparaino then reveals the real state of affairs to him, adding a discreet

[20] Dolci, op. cit., pp. 63–64.

[21] C. Mori, *Con la mafia ai ferri corti*, Verona 1932, p. 98.

[22] P. Familiari, *La vera storia del brigante Marlino Zappa*, Vibo Valentia 1971, p. 25.

threat . . . 'Rosina is an orphan, and I am everybody's father.'[23]

The power of mediation possessed by the *mafioso*, and the fact that he could give speedy and coercive effect to his decision, were one barrier against the uncontrolled development of the disruptive tendencies that arise from the competition for honour between families. The local population particularly dreaded feuds (*faide*), because of the general social disruption that stemmed from their duration and their intrinsic tendency to involve ever wider circles of relatives and family groups. Familiari describes a case in which the local police authority directly asks the mafia to step in and resolve matters:

> Two families had been slaughtering one another for ten years, with one vengeance-killing answered by the next. Four people had already died on one side and four on the other, and each time the marshal had been driven into a fury, because when he looked for a culprit he found twenty—and then the judge had to acquit them, because twenty people can't get their hands round one dagger at the same moment.
> One day he said to Don Ferdi, 'You sort it out.' Next Sunday the two families met up, eighty people in all, in an outdoor clearing . . . They brought along roast lambs, dried figs, . . . fruit, wine, . . . They made speeches full of the most sincere cordiality. Then came the kiss of reconciliation: the men kissed one another, and so did the women. During the next few months, marriages began to take place between the young people of the two families.[24]

The *mafioso*'s activity as a mediator was not confined to socio-economic relations within the local society, but extended also to the relations between the local world and the great external agencies of economic and political life. The authority of the mafia tended to control contacts with the city, the State and the national market. The official occupations of the great majority of men of honour were advantageous for their relations with the outside world. They dealt in grain, oil, wine and citrus fruit; they were butchers, they owned haulage companies, they were lawyers and doctors; they held leases on small or medium-sized farms; they were the proprietors or presidents of small banks and rural co-operatives.

[23] Hess, op. cit., p. 190.
[24] Familiari, op. cit., pp. 23–24.

In the course of their daily life, they met scores of people from
all sectors of society. They received and exchanged information
on a far greater scale than was available to anybody else. In the
event of their holding public office, as they sometimes did in the
local administration, then their relations with those who represented the power of the central government were also much more
extensive than was normal in their area.

The particular 'endowments' fitting the traditional *mafioso* for
his office of mediation consisted in the network of 'friendly'
relations linking him to influential people both in other towns and
districts and in the city. The Anti-mafia Commissioners wrote of
the position enjoyed by one important man of honour of the
'thirties: 'Among the inhabitants of the village of Giardini,
Giuseppe the Greek enjoyed particular influence, due both to his
striking personality and to the friendship he kept up with certain
people in neighbouring Villabate and in Palermo itself.'[25] 'If
you've got money and friends, you keep the law up your own
arse,' according to a typical mafia proverb quoted by Alongi.[26]

Among the various occupations that the traditional *mafioso*
might follow, special mention must be made of the activities of
the cattle-raisers and dealers and the agricultural lease-holders
and excise-men (the *gabellotti* of Sicily). Continually moving
between the country and the city, continually involved in business of the most varied kind—today some episode of cattle-
rustling, tomorrow a marriage to be 'arranged', and the next day
political propaganda on behalf of a faction-leader in the city—
these figures, with their unparalleled knowledge of facts, people
and places, represented the connective tissue of a socio-economic
world dominated by insecurity and fragmentation. In their study
of western Sicily, Jane and Peter Schneider have given a vivid
description of the lives and activities of those people, whom they
term 'rural entrepreneurs':

> Animal rustling . . . [was] one of the most important . . . commercial
> activities . . . It was organized and financed by rural entrepreneurs . . .
> Rural entrepreneurs also dominated the animal markets, or fairs,
> held in the late summer and early autumn in one interior town after

[25] Anti-mafia Commission, *Commissione parlamentare d'inchiesta sul
fenomeno della mafia in Sicilia*, vols. I–IV, Rome, Tipografia del Senato, doc.
XXIII, n. 2–IV, p. 137.
[26] G. Alongi, *La mafia*, Palermo 1977, p. 57.

another . . . Before they ever owned trucks or cars, livestock owners and dealers attended fairs within roughly a 50-mile radius of their respective home towns. Mediators, brokers, wholesalers and butchers also went to these fairs. In transit these men used routes of transhumance that were little known to the population at large and sought lodging and pasture for their animals at *massarie* [the complexes of buildings housing the estate offices, storerooms and so on of the great Sicilian estates] along the way. Their close ties to this institution protected them against banditry and theft, which ordinary people greatly feared. Peasants who wished to make some transaction at a fair outside their own town usually traveled in the company of rural entrepreneurs who could arrange the necessary protection and sustenance for them . . .

The ability of rural entrepreneurs and their associates to command the routes of transhumance, the rural places, and the people of the interior gave them a considerable advantage over other social groups. People who were based in town depended on them for help in transactions that occurred beyond its borders. In Villamaura artisans told us that their forerunners acquired supplies through the carters who regularly visited Palermo. They themselves rarely went to the city. One of our friends, a tailor, did go regularly to buy cloth and other supplies, as his father and grandfather had done before him. What seemed remarkable to us, however, was the relative poverty of this man's network compared with those of the rural entrepreneurs. He went always and only to Palermo. Along the way, he knew only one person, the host of the inn where he stayed en route. For his supplies he visited the same firm that had provisioned his father and grandfather, and he always stayed in the same pension in Palermo, owned by an ex-Villamaurese. Rural entrepreneurs had more friends and contacts in the city, and many more along the way.

Even the landowners were significantly less mobile in the interior of Sicily than rural entrepreneurs. Because of their class position, the landlords' networks were extensive, yet many of them were quite ignorant of the countryside.[27]

The traditional *mafioso* thus inclined strongly towards those institutions that offered control over wide areas of the community's collective life. Through them, he could safeguard and enhance his own rule. Since the end of the nineteenth century, a multitude of small rural savings-banks and cooperatives has sprung up in western Sicily. A whole circuit of associative

[27] J. Schneider and P. Schneider, *Culture and Political Economy in Western Sicily*, New York and London 1976, pp. 70–71.

institutions has gradually come into being, extending into virtually every commune in western Sicily. In their operations, we can see quite clearly how the power of the mafia came to mediate the community's internal and external financial affairs: in the 1940s, for example, the *Cassa Rurale* (rural or agricultural savings-bank) of S. Giuseppe di Mussomeli was under the control of Genco Russo and his followers. In 1940, it had 1500 investors and a considerably larger number of clients. The access of the population of Mussomeli to the money market was thus in part mediated by the mafia.[28]

Mediation by the mafia was not just one among the many ways in which any local entity might be connected with the national political and economic world. Mediation of the mafia type was distinguished by its characteristic tendency to monopolize any channel where it once gained a footing. The *mafioso* tolerated no rivals in his sphere of influence, and found additional reason for this attitude in the fact that his excess *legal* profits depended upon his having the monopoly of some resource or some professional specialization.[29]

The *Mafioso* as a Proxy for the State

In his aggressive reaction to any threat to his monopoly of these functions of mediation, the *mafioso* was also motivated by the conviction that he acted in the name of legality. This conviction was confirmed by the facts. Since 1860, with the exception of the fascist period, the State authorities have to a considerable extent acknowledged the mafia's authority. This has resulted from the interplay of two different needs. For its part, central government has needed the collaboration of the mafia in maintaining public order, at minimum cost in men and money, in large areas of Sicily and Calabria. After the unification of Italy, the administration of public order was guided by the principle of leaving things in the hands of local elites, except during particularly severe crises, when there would be military intervention. In areas where the power elite was made up of *mafiosi*, it was to them that central government turned when recruiting the personnel of the

---

[28] Anti-mafia Commission, op. cit., doc. XXIII, n. 2–IV, pp. 604–605.
[29] Algoni, op. cit., pp. 106–108.

local police.

In June 1875, a leading legal authority who had just returned
from Sicily twice addressed the Italian Parliament (*Camera dei
Deputati*), denouncing the connivance he had observed between
the departments of the Prefect and Chief of Police in Palermo, on
the one hand, and the mafia chiefs of the hinterland on the other.
'The area around Palermo', declared Attorney-General Tajani,
'contains a number of towns full of *mafiosi*, who surround the city
like a crown of thorns.' Obliged to 'do something' about growing
problems of public safety in these towns—above all in Monreale
—the authorities, said Tajani, had taken the following steps:
'They summoned the thorns, the biggest thorns in Monreale.
There were six of them, all notorious criminals. Nonetheless, the
first was given the rank of commander in the *guardie campestri*
(rural police), the second was given the rank of commander in a
kind of suburban national guard, and the other four *mafiosi* were
made captains in the National Guard.'[30] The Bourbons had
already begun the practice of recruiting the best-known offenders
into the local police, but this became more systematic and extensive under the government of the newly unified nation, especially
during the first four decades after 1861.

Meanwhile the man of honour, for his part, obviously had an
interest in establishing as securely as possible the position he had
attained through a difficult selection process. He sought the
maximum degree of legalization for his powers: these rested
ultimately on his ability to use physical force, but acceptance as
an actor on the political scene was a necessary condition of long-
term survival.

Any really successful *mafioso* had to be an indubitable member
of the power elite. Certain compromising relations—those con-
necting him with blatant law-breakers—were broken off, and
new links forged in their place. It was necessary to 'get in with
policemen, mayors, judges, provincial doctors, officials and
deputies. It is worth his while just to get acquainted with such
people, who may perhaps come together as a party some day.'[31]

He is constantly in contact with priests, priests go to his place, and he
goes to the bank—which is always run by priests—the bank director

[30] N. Colajanni, *Nel regno della mafia*, Palermo-Milan, 1900, pp. 68–69.
[31] Hess, op. cit., p. 91.

is a priest, the bank has always been the priests' affair. Spending time with this sort of person has changed him, and now the police treat him with great respect, they greet him when they see him and go out of their way to show their regard for him. He wears better clothes today, and the marshal goes up to him and takes him by the hand, calls him *Cavaliere*. . . . At the end of May, during the election campaign, he went and had dinner with Zacagnani, the Minister, and with Lanza, the Deputy—the three of them together—they had dinner and then they came out arm-in-arm.[32]

This is how a Mussomeli peasant described relations between Genco Russo and the official authorities. Far from putting themselves in the State's place or constituting a State within the State (as they have repeatedly been alleged to do), the traditional *mafiosi* actually depend upon the State insofar as their power derives in part from the privileged access they enjoy to the levers of State power.

The legalization of the mafia's power took place by way of innumerable official acts. It even reached the point where the offices of the mafia and those of the judiciary coincided, as happened when the *mafioso* Di Carlo was appointed Justice of the Peace for the Raffadali area, and provided with a special safe-conduct valid with every police authority throughout the province of Agrigento.[33]

The fact that the power of the mafia is at bottom complementary to the power of the State was demonstrated nicely at a time when the latter was in the throes of a grave crisis. Between 1943 and 1945, the Allied military government appointed *mafiosi* as mayors of a considerable number of the communes of western Sicily and Reggio Calabria province.[34]

This same complementarity of powers was given explicit theoretical recognition by one of Italy's highest legal dignitaries on the occasion of Calogero Vizzini's death. Giuseppe Guido Lo Schiavo, Attorney-General in the Supreme Court of Appeal, wrote then in a legal periodical:

It has been said that the mafia despise the police and the magistracy, but this is incorrect. The mafia has always had respect for the

---

[32] Dolci, op. cit., p. 60.

[33] Anti-mafia Commission, op. cit., doc. XXIII, n. 2–IV, p. 282.

[34] Romano, op. cit., pp. 301–303.

magistracy and for Justice; it has submitted to its sentences, and has not obstructed the judge in his work. In the pursuit of bandits and outlaws . . . it has openly sided with the forces of law and order . . .

Today, Don Calogero Vizzini's successor is making his reputation, and in time he will succeed to his predecessor's authoritative position in the counsels of the secret conclave. May his labours increase the respect in which the laws of the State are held, and may they be for the social betterment of all.[35]

In making *mafiosi* its proxies in offices of civil and judicial administration, the central State also achieved a considerable measure of political integration. Through the *mafiosi*, a good many elements of local political life participated in the national political system. In pursuit of votes, the 'system of notables' turned to the mafia for help in those areas immune to the usual electoral strategies. The mafia chief was almost always a major local elector, whose support was needed by any candidate for political or administrative office. Many Sicilian politicians and administrators, from unification up until the 'fifties, owed a good part of their electoral success to their links with mafia groups.

In return for their support at elections—support guaranteed quite 'legally' through the maintenance of clientelistic relations, as well as by means of threats, corruption and even sometimes the kidnapping of electors[36]—government politicians granted favours to the *mafiosi* and their associates: a gun-licence issued, a police report altered, an over-zealous official transferred elsewhere, the process of legal rehabilitation made smoother, and so on. Romano argues that this function of the mafia, the function of integrating the local political sub-cultures into the national political system, has grown constantly in importance since the 1880s, when the historic left-wing parties first set out to win power and when (in 1882) the franchise was first significantly extended. During this phase, 'the *real power* of the mafia groups tended to seek a closer and closer identification with legal power in the locality, and with those who represented it; and, by way of the hierarchical connections that link systematically legal power with national power, it thus tended to become one of the elements that sustained national power.'[37]

[35] G. G. Lo Schiavo, 'Nel regno della mafia', in *Rivista Processi*, 5 January 1955.

[36] Familiari, op. cit., pp. 30–33.

[37] Romano, op. cit., p. 190.

After 1912, when universal male suffrage was introduced, the support of mafia groups in election campaigns became one of the most important prerequisites for the capture of parliamentary seats by candidates of the government parties.

Thus the career of the traditional *mafioso* could be divided into two clearly distinct phases. While he was struggling to establish his position among the men of honour, and hence committing the gravest breaches of the State's judicial norms, his behaviour was quite *anomic*; but then, once he had gained a place at the top, a progressive rapprochement with the representatives and institutions of the State gave his activity an increasingly *legal* character. For the classic *mafioso*, there came a certain point in his life—generally around the age of 45–50—when he no longer clashed with the judicial system. At this point, a reverse process begins. The case of Genco Russo is typical. Between 1920 and 1942, he was accused of ordering or carrying out eleven murders, several attempted murders and a great many robberies, thefts and extortions. In 1944, Genco Russo obtained a decree of rehabilitation from the Caltanisetta appeal court, repealing the one fixed-term sentence that had been imposed on him: 'His rehabilitation marked an important moment in Genco Russo's life . . . He had unexpectedly re-endowed himself with moral and social virginity, and was even gaining sufficient respectability to allow him eventually to engage in political activity.'[38]

From this time on, Genco Russo was to face no more criminal charges. Police files described him as a 'man of order' (*uomo d'ordine*), and his integration into the official power elite proceeded by rapid strides. In 1946, the Deputy Pasquale Vassallo conferred upon him the honorific title of *cavaliere della corona d'Italia*, the same honour bestowed upon such other mafia chiefs as Michele Navarra, Calogero Vizzini and Santo Flores. At the wedding of his eldest son in 1950, the witnesses included two of Sicily's leading personalities: Don Calogero Vizzini of Villalba, and Rosario Lanza, from Barrafranca, the President of the Sicilian Regional Assembly.[39]

In the traditional situation, mafia chief and politican had a clientelistic relationship of the classic kind: the exchange of mutual favours took place within the context of a code of honour

---

[38] Anti-mafia Commission, op. cit., doc. XXIII, no. 2–IV, p. 45.
[39] Ibid.

and chivalry. The relationship's contractual aspect was 'submerged' in a network of apparently disinterested actions and social graces. This ideology of friendship was clearly to be seen in a letter written by Vittorio Emanuele Orlando to Francesco Coppola, the chief elector of Partinico. Orlando, a member of the Constituent Assembly and a veteran of Sicilian politics, was connected with the mafia and with *mafiosi* from beginning to end of a parliamentary career during which he rose at one time (immediately after the war) to the Presidency of the Council of Ministers. The letter thanks Coppola for a gift of wine (see over). And when the eminent lawyer whose views on the complementarity between the mafia and the power of the State were quoted above received a visit from Calogero Vizzini in 1953, the introductions went as follows:

'How do you do, *commendatore* Vizzini? I am . . .'
'To you, I am not *il commendatore*. I am *u zu Calò*—uncle Calogero.'
'Welcome to my house, *zu Calò*.'[40]

One very important index of the existence of a clientelistic relationship of the diffuse kind is that the favours exchanged are not limited to any particular sphere of the beneficiary's needs and interests. Favours asked may concern grave violations of the penal code, or insignificant problems of everyday life. In these latter cases, the fact that there is a mafia-type patron-client relationship may be revealed by the disproportion between the particular assistance asked and the level of authority to which the request is directed. As a rule, we might suppose, the Director-General of the Ministry of Transport would not get personally involved in the search for five trunks of household goods lost by a Sicilian soldier in transit during World War II. However, when the request came from Sig. G. Palozzolo, MP, who had been approached in his turn by the *mafioso* F. Coppola, he not only had to intervene, he had to register his intervention in writing, as can be seen in a document reproduced by the Anti-mafia Commission (see p. 47).

[40] D. De Masi, 'Sopraluogo nella Sicilia della mafia', in *Nord e Sud*, 46, 1963, p. 20.

ASSEMBLEA COSTITUENTE
—

Roma,lì II Luglio 1948

Caro Coppola,

mi è pervenuto il fusto del
Suo vino eccellente. Al ringraziamento
orale aggiungo quello scritto e conto
di portare meco lo squisito liquore nel
la mia villa di Campiglioni per bere al
la Sua salute.

Mi creda cordialmente

Sig. FRANCESCO COPPOLA
PARTINICO (Palermo)

The *Cosca*

Contrary to the impression given in most literary and journalistic treatments of the theme, there does not exist—and there never has existed—any secret, hierarchical and centralized criminal organization called the *mafia*, the *'ndrangheta* or the *onorata società*, its members bound to one another by sinister and solemn oaths of mutual loyalty and assistance.

We have been attempting to show that the term *mafia* denotes, rather, a particular kind of behaviour and power, traceable in the actions of a particular group of people called *mafiosi*, *'ndranghetisti* or *uomini d'onore*. We must now emphasize that the activities of these people are not the work of solitary individuals, but result from their collaboration with a more or less extensive group of blood relatives, friends and family members, which is called a *cosca*. The second fundamental meaning of the expression *mafia* can thus be defined in terms of the aggregate of various family and kinship groups that co-operate or struggle with one another to gain control of a given territory and its resources. Every such *cosca* tends to mediate a very wide range of honorific, political and economic competitions, as a means to confirm and extend its own position of power.

Constituent Asembly
Rome, July 11, 1948

Dear Coppola,

The cask of your excellent wine has arrived. To the
spoken thanks I have already given you, I must now add
this note of gratitude. I look forward to taking the
exquisite liquor with me when I go to my villa at
Campiglioni, where I shall be sure to drink your health
in it.

Please believe me,

Yours cordially,

Vittorio Orlando

The *cosca mafiosa* is a simple organism, but a solid one,
without formalism or bureaucracy. Within it there are neither
statutory ordinances, initiation rites nor courts of judgement:

> There are no presidents, no elected secretaries of any kind whatever,
> and no membership lists. Those who reap the profits and direct the
> affairs of the association are almost always three, four or five people
> whose authority derives from their age, their intelligence, their social
> position, the deeds they have accomplished, the offences they have
> been convicted of—and above all, from their experience and greater
> expertise in the difficult art of breaking the law with impunity. Should
> one of these members excel the rest in all these attributes, then he
> becomes the effective supreme head.[41]

The amount of territory which any *cosca* controls depends
directly upon the power it wields and the prestige attributed to its
leader or leaders. The *cosca*'s power depends in turn on the
number of its active members. During the period for which our
ideal type of the traditional mafia holds good—that is, between
1860 and 1950—each *cosca* would seem to have had a rather
limited number of effective members, hardly ever exceeding

---

[41] G. Mosca, *Uomini e cose di Sicilia*, Palermo, Sellerio, 1980, p. 11.

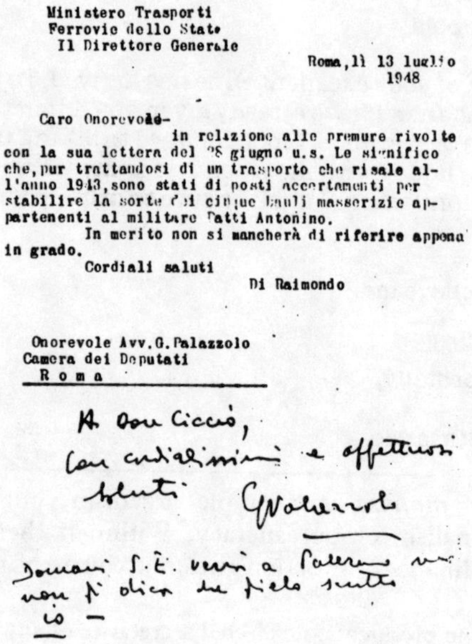

Ministero Trasporti
Ferrovie dello Stato
Il Direttore Generale

Roma, lì 13 luglio 1948

Caro Onorevole-
in relazione alle premure rivolte con la sua lettera del 28 giugno u.s. Le significo che, pur trattandosi di un trasporto che risale all'anno 1943, sono stati disposti accertamenti per stabilire la sorte dei cinque bauli masserizie appartenenti al militare Fatti Antonino.

In merito non si mancherà di riferire appena in grado.

Cordiali saluti

Di Raimondo

Onorevole Avv. G. Palazzolo
Camera dei Deputati
R o m a

A Don Cicciò,
con cordialissimi e affettuosi saluti G Palazzolo

Domani S.E. verrà a Palermo ma non si dica che glielo scritto io —

15–20. The important *cosca* studied by Blok, in inland Sicily, had a dozen members, some belonging to the Cassini family and others linked with it through friendship or through kinship acquired by marriage. G. Mosca estimates that the average *cosca* comprises 12–15 people.[42]

No mafia *cosca* was likely to grow much beyond this threshold, given the nature of the bonds between its members. At a certain point it became impossible to manage the group: internal conflicts would break out, splits arise from the formation of new family or kinship units within the parent-group, and at its outer limits the

[42] Ibid., p. 100.

Ministry of Transport, State Railways
from the Director-General
Rome, 13 July 1948

Dear *Onorevole*,

With reference to the inquiry accompanying your letter
of 28 ult., I am able to inform you that, although the
journey in question took place as long ago as 1943,
inquiries are under way to ascertain the whereabouts of
the five trunks of household goods belonging to the
soldier Antonio Patti.

We shall let you know immediately we have any further
information.

With all good wishes,
Di Raimondo.

to: *Onorevole Avv.* G. Palazzolo
Camera dei Deputati
Rome

(There follows a handwritten superscription in which G.
Palazzolo sends his good wishes to 'don Ciccio' Coppola, to
whom he forwarded the letter)

---

cosca itself become looser and more fluid. Thus no single group
ever controlled the wide physical and economic space of a whole
city or region. Control was shared by a series of groups in
relations of precarious alliance or open conflict.

Within certain limits, even mafia groups were subject to the
continual fluctuations of social stratification characteristic of the
mafiosi's native society. Only the inmost kernel of the *cosca* —
that is, the biological family from which the *cosca* takes its
name — remains unchanged over time. All the other circles of
friends, relatives and clients experience some turnover in their
personnel as the years pass. This fluidity is due in large part to the
unceasing ebb and flow of social mobility, but it also owes

CAMERA DEI DEPUTATI

Roma,lì 13/4/1951

Carissimo Don Ciccio-

L'ultima volta che ci vedemmo al-
l'Hotel de Palme Lei mi diceva giustamente
che a Partinico occorreva un Deputato Re-
gionale giovane svelto ed amico ed a portata
di mano degli amici. L'amico Totò Motisi
risponde a tutti questi requisiti ed io ho
deciso di aiutarlo con tutte le mie forze.
Se a Partinico mi aiutate lo faremo diven-
tare Deputato.

Con affettuosi saluti

mi creda

(Giovanni Palazzolo)

Sig.Francesco Coppola
Partinico

---

something to the logic of coalitions and splits that typifies the world of the mafia.

The *cosca* is not a clan or a 'survival of tribalism'. Within it, different interests are distinguished and different positions are coordinated in a way that assures its various members some degree of flexibility and freedom of action. We are not dealing with a static conspiratorial association, but with a group of friends and relatives who, just like any other such group, often meet together to play cards, go hunting, celebrate a birth or a marriage, or enjoy a *skiticchio* (a banquet for men). 'Like any group of friends who get together often . . . the *cosca* gave rise to instrumental coalitions but was not, as a rule, itself such an instrumental group.'[43]

Franchetti, in *Inchiesta in Sicilia*, likewise observed that the mafia unites 'people of every degree, every profession, and every

---

[43] Schneider and Schneider, op. cit., p. 187.

Camera dei Deputati
Rome, 13.4.1951

Dear *Don Ciccio,*

Last time we met at the Hotel de Palme, you rightly told
me that there was an opening for a Regional Deputy at
Partinico, and that what was needed was a friendly and
quick-witted young man, who would be amenable to our
friends. Our friend Totò Motisi satisfies all these
requirements and I have decided to give him all the help
that I can. If you help me at Partinico, we shall have him
made a member of parliament.

With affectionate good wishes,

I remain,

Giovanni Coppola

To: Sig. Francesco Coppola
Partinico

---

kind, who—although *there is no obvious, continuous or regular
link between them*—are continually coming together to further
one another's interests.[44]

Hess agrees with the Schneiders that relations between the
leadership and the other individual members vary widely in
nature from *cosca* to *cosca* : blood relationship, adoptive or
artificial kinship (*comparaggio*), friendship and clientelistic
relations are all found, their differing proportions dependent on
circumstances and on the kind of people involved. According to
the Schneiders, relations of friendship, and the forms in which
these are expressed, have a particular importance in maintaining
the internal cohesion of the *cosca* and enlarging its sphere of
influence (and that of its individual members):

As far as we know, the local *cosca* held no formal meetings. Neverthe-

[44] L. Franchetti and S. Sonnino, *Inchieste in Sicilia*, Florence, Vallecchi,
1974, p. 38 (italics added).

less, it served as a context for making contracts and generating trust over food and drink. The leader, or leaders, at least, were available to others in certain localities on a regular basis. A leader's house, a local tavern, the back room of a shop was a place where friends gathered, perhaps every evening or on Sunday afternoons. Such informal gatherings resembled a scaled down version of . . . banquets . . . in that men raised their wineglasses in toasts of friendship, and friends of the host entertained visitors with much clowning around. As at the banquets, at these gatherings decisions were made, not by the collectivity, but by various coalitions within it. Nor was the collectivity constant or clearly bounded. Regular participants brought semi-regulars and guests. Strangers who sought the intervention of a particular member came and then left. Perhaps a local *cosca* had as semi-regular members a nucleus of friends from a nearby town . . . and [these] gatherings were occasions for entering coalitions with individuals from other towns. The *cosca* placed its seal of approval, as it were, on members and their clients, who then became known to mafiosi elsewhere as potentially reliable and trustworthy business partners.[45]

However, the role of the mafia *cosca* is not simply to provide the setting and the opportunity for coalitions to be formed and for relations of friendship or clientship to be established between people in general or between men of honour of different origins and talents. The *cosca* offers protection and security to those of its members who find themselves most exposed to the rigours of the law, and is ready to offer these services to anyone. The head of the *cosca* will make use of his relationship with the official authorities or with the member of parliament whose client he is in an attempt to manipulate the course of justice to the advantage of the *picciotto* ('lad'—that is, young *mafioso*) who has been arrested. Meanwhile, he will arrange for financial and legal assistance to be provided for the man's family—which will also strengthen the vertical relations of obligation within the mafia group, and ensure that the arrested man says nothing to the police or the legal authorities about whatever crimes (thefts, contract killings, attacks, and so on) he may have carried out on the orders of the *cosca* chief himself.

The rest of the *cosca* will then cooperate to give false alibis and false evidence at the trial. At the same time, they will bring concerted pressure to bear on public opinion, designed to favour

---

[45] Schneider and Schneider, op. cit., pp. 188–189.

the accused man by presenting him as a victim, an innocent man slandered by his enemies.[46]

The 'Type' of the Traditional *Mafioso*

In the preceding pages, we have offered an analysis of the behaviour of the 'classical' *mafioso* and of the way his power was exercised. This has created a quite precise sociological profile of the figure of the *mafioso*. There does exist an 'ideal type' of the traditional *mafioso*, which can be defined on the basis of a series of criteria, including: a) popular origin; b) membership of the middle classes; c) the possession of a precisely defined territorial power.

All the most important Sicilian and Calabrian *mafiosi* of this century have come from the lowest social classes. Vito Cascio Ferro and Calogero Vizzini were the sons of poor peasants, and themselves began their careers as peasants. Before becoming one of the most widely-feared business dealers in the Plain of Gioia Tauro, Don Mommo Piromalli was a cowherd. The great majority of *mafiosi* described in novels, stories and memoirs are *braccianti* (farm-hands), poor peasants, shepherds or illiterate carters. In the mafia areas, subaltern classes never developed either their own ideology or any autonomous network of institutions designed to stabilize and justify their own position. These areas showed almost no trace of the 'culture of poverty',[47] and there was no stable cultural stratification within the social structure. In their quest for some release from distress and poverty, deviants and those dissatisfied with their lot were therefore guided by the values of the well-off, values focused entirely on the concept of honour. For this reason, it was precisely the members of the least 'honoured' classes who felt most impelled to enter the competition for honour—all the more so in that success as a man of honour very often meant riches too, since it was usual for the *uomo di rispetto* to acquire wealth through his activities as a *mafioso*. For the *mafioso*, increasing honour went along with rising social status for himself and his family. 'Mafia chiefs,' wrote Cutrera, 'are always to be found among the *gabellotti* (lease-

[46] Alongi, op. cit., pp. 33, 108–110.

[47] Oscar Lewis, *La Vida. A Puerto Rican Family in the Culture of Poverty—San Juan and New York*, London 1967.

holders) and land-owners—people whose economic condition is better than that of others of their own social status.' And Hobsbawm has emphasised that by far the most important characteristic of the traditional mafia was that '*all* the heads of local *Mafias* were . . . men of wealth, . . . overwhelmingly men of the middle class, capitalist farmers and contractors . . .'[48]

Nonetheless, whether in the popular scale of values or in that of the mafia, honour and wealth *went together* but were not *identical*.

Even if a man of honour was normally also wealthy, cases did occur in which we can perceive a quite clear-cut hierarchical difference between these two criteria of social stratification. Someone of great wealth might lack a correlative degree of honour: in the Plain of Gioia Tauro, for instance, large-scale export trade was monopolized until the 1940s by dealers from Amalfi, Apulia and Genoa, but although these dealers (together with the area's landed proprietors) made up the local economic elite, their social position was in no sense an esteemed or 'honoured ' one.[49]

Because honour was the structural foundation of mafia activity, social relations and social position never fell entirely under the control of purely economic motives (whether the vulgar thirst for gain, or the 'religion of accumulation'). Having reached a certain level, which was indeterminate and to a certain extent conventional, the *mafioso*'s accumulation, and especially his *concentration*, of wealth would slow down and stop: for beyond a given limit, he found wealth and its associated power an *encumbrance*, difficult to defend and justify.

To own land might be the consequence of a good position in the hierarchy of honour, and it might be a source of honour in itself. But the *scale* on which it was owned could not exceed a certain threshold, beyond which it grew difficult for the *mafioso*-proprietor to maintain his honourable position. To protect himself against his numerous aggressive challengers, he had to hire a corps of armed guards, form a binding alliance with the local and national power elite, and give up most of his functions as a mediator within his own cultural world. In the particular circumstances of the mafia areas, all three of these conditions and

[48] Cutrera, op. cit., p. 96; Hobsbawm, op. cit., p. 37.
[49] Arlacchi, op. cit., pp. 78–84.

consequences of large-scale land-ownership were highly anti-honorific, and they required the traditional *mafioso* to abandon a style of life he found gratifying and to substitute new values for those he knew of old—which he had no incentive to do.

This *imperfect conversion* between honour and wealth had a considerable influence on the aspect and dimensions of mafia power. It in fact almost always figured as a concrete, local power, within a given village, quarter or district, and never wore the guise of an abstract impersonal power of the regional or national type. Vito Cascio Ferro, Calogero Vizzini and Giuseppe Genco Russo lived most of their lives in places like Bisacquino, Villalba and Mussomeli. Michele Navarra was born, lived and was killed in Corleone. Their estates never amounted to more than a small or middling fortune, and the scope of their ambitions always remained consistent with their economic position: after the First World War, Calogero Vizzini bought three *poderi* (land-holdings) near Villalba, divided them into lots and let them at modest rents to the local peasants. 'It's not true that Don Calò gave his land away; but he had rightly calculated that the whole affair would bring him enormous popularity. When it had all been completed, he could have stood as a Parliamentary candidate, if he'd wanted to, and would have been sure of a triumphant victory. But when such offers were made to him, Don Calò declined them with thanks, and contented himself instead with "advising" the electors'.[50]

Michele Navarra applied successfully for the medical director-ate of the commune of Palermo, a post filled by competitive examination, but he turned it down at the last moment. When he died, Navarra left his widow a few plots of land and part of a dwelling-house. The Anti-mafia Commission remarked that 'the small size of his estate shows that Navarra had always aimed at power, rather than at money for its own sake . . . He often spent more than he brought in, both in his medical activities and in his career as a *mafioso*.'[51]

The *mafioso* thus occupied a middling social position, neither at the bottom nor at the very top of the social pyramid. The true vocation of the traditional *mafioso* was neither proletarian/peasant nor aristocratic/grand bourgeois. The *mafioso* often directed his

[50] C. Guarino, 'Antologia della mafia', in *Nord e Sud*, 1955, no. 11, p. 74.
[51] Anti-mafia Commission, op. cit., doc. XXIII, n. 2–IV, p. 85.

hostility against both these extremes, although his skirmishes with the upper classes were obviously less frequent and more cautious.

II

The Crisis of the Mafia
During the
Great Post-War
Transformation

3.

Honour, Wealth and Political Power in the 1950s and 1960s

The Identification of Honour with Wealth

The traditional mafia is separated from the mafia of today by the 'great transformation' of the post-war years, a powerful structural upheaval which has shattered the entire former social and economic order (in both Northern and Southern Italy), replacing it by a new dispensation.

In the *Mezzogiorno*, the twin 'motors' of this great transformation were emigration and public intervention. Together, these brought about a profound crisis in the forms of mafia power and behaviour in Calabria and Sicily. The emigration of the 'fifties and 'sixties had a disruptive effect on the structure of mafia groups, depleting the human 'resources' on which they drew and interrupting the process of renewal from one generation to the next. Many middle- and lower-ranking men of honour joined the rapid flow of emigrants to Northern Italy, and for the first time in the mafia's history the recruitment of new members became a practical problem.

During this same period, unusually extensive employment opportunities became available in the Italian secondary and tertiary sectors. The major industries of the North sought labour, and in the urban areas of the *Mezzogiorno* new public sector jobs arose. In consequence, gaps appeared in the ranks of young men of honour, and the competition for control of local resources grew less intense. Even before departing, emigrants largely assimilated the cultural norms of the areas where they were bound, in accordance with the phenomenon of 'anticipatory socialization';[1] and aspiring *mafiosi* were no exception in this regard. Those who remained behind usually became part of a client-group from which they obtained a 'position' in the public administration, and this too lessened the number of potential rivals in the mafia arena.

That the great transformation of the 'fifties and 'sixties had affected mafia groups' composition in terms of age became clear in the famous Catanzaro trial of 1968, which involved all the leading Sicilian *cosche* of the 'sixties. Although there was much talk at the time about the 'new mafia' and its 'urban gangsterism', the 117 *mafiosi* on trial at Catanzaro turned out to have an average age of over fifty. Only two of the accused were younger than thirty, while thirty-one of them (around a quarter of the total) were over sixty.[2]

Furthermore, the great transformation gave rise to a process of general cultural change, which took different forms in the different environments of Italy as a whole and of the *Mezzogiorno*. In the mafia areas of Sicily and Calabria, it found expression in an identification between *honour* and *wealth*.

On a national scale, a cultural mutation was taking place: in fundamental collective values, in habits of consumption, and in the perspectives of social action, there was a progressive 'substitution' of new for old. Everywhere, power, wealth and economic success became the goals of the group's 'existential projects'.[3] This new scale of values had a very powerful effect on the mafia elite and on its social position. As mafia areas became integrated into the wider national community, so accumulated wealth increasingly took the place of the traditional symbols as evidence of prepotency and success.

In the changed conditions of the local society, mafia behaviour of the classic kind no longer made much sense. The traditional mafia enterprises—extortion, demanding money with menaces, fraud, the assassination of rivals—began to lose their unquestioned status as forms of action meritorious in themselves and as

[1] F. Alberoni and G. Baglioni, *L'integrazione dell'immigrato nella società industriale*, Bologna 1965.

[2] Catanzaro Assize court, *Sentenza a carico di La Barbera Angelo più 116*, Cantanzaro 1968, pp. 3–6.

[3] See R. K. Merton, *Social Theory and Social Structure*, New York and London 1957, pp. 225–384.

passports to progress along the scale of honour. Almost until the end of the 'fifties, a man might still attain to the highest honours by showing—in certain specific situations—that he had an exceptional capacity to make his power tell and to defeat his rivals in the struggle between families and individuals. But anyone aiming at a stable and established position in the community was more and more obliged to base his reputation on the accumulation of wealth, rather than on these traditional grounds (and also to direct his 'traditional' activity towards such accumulation).

In the years that followed, wealth became the most readily recognized proof of success, independent of feats of violence and of the honour that these might bring. Wealth became the basis of reputation, and to possess wealth became imperative for anyone who wanted to gain any kind of position of respect:

> Up until the end of the war, it didn't take much to become *un'uomo di rispetto*, in these parts. As soon as people got to be afraid of a young *mafioso*'s courage and his bloodthirsty nature, then a group of followers would collect around the man, and they would set about extorting money from the landowners, collecting people's votes . . . And then they would act as 'go-betweens', too, if there was a dispute between families. But it was difficult for any *mafioso* to get so rich that he could outdo the biggest landowners, or the Baron Trimboli [*a pseudonym*], in the size of his estate.
>   . . . [*The mafiosi*] used to waste no end of time arguing and fighting about which of them was the most powerful . . . They were ignorant and they took more notice of a man's name, perhaps, than of his money.
>   After the war, everything changed. The politicians arrived, the *Cassa* arrived [the *Cassa per il Mezzogiorno*, the regional investment agency]. Televisions and cars arrived. To get respect, you started to need money. The more money, the more respect. The same as it is today, for that matter.
>   Lots of the *uomini di panza* [*mafiosi* : literally, 'men with belly'] were unprepared. Just imagine, for example, that even the B——, of the Plain of Gioia Tauro, found themselves in economic difficulties around 1960. I remember people saying that to get hold of money, they had been forced to organize robberies.[4]

Once accumulated wealth has become the universal sign of power, we move to a more abstract level, one reached by the

[4] Interview no. 4.

mafiosi only in the most recent period. The possession of wealth, regarded by the traditional *mafioso* as *one among* the proofs and results of a man's capacity to make himself respected, becomes, in the public opinion of the 1960s and 1970s, meritorious in itself. Wealth, in a word, becomes intrinsically honourable, and confers honour on its possessors.

During the period of national economic development, this transformation of collective goals took place throughout the *Mezzogiorno*, but different social groups were not all uniformly involved in it. Those who were most exposed to outside influences, and most concerned to establish their social supremacy, were under far greater pressure to accept the new goals. Given their position, the *mafiosi* were thus virtually compelled to 'reorient' the whole meaning of their behaviour, and to become 'different from themselves' in a brief period.

To maintain one's supremacy meant, henceforth, to have at one's disposal a growing quantity of wealth and consumer goods. Competition had shifted to a new plane; fundamentally, it was a matter no longer of individual and family honour, but of the possession and conspicuous consumption of the new symbols of consumer affluence. Analysis of the most serious episodes of violence in Calabria between 1950 and the 1970s shows particularly clearly how the old forms of conflict, based exclusively on grounds of honour and family, have fallen off. Research carried out by the Department of Sociology at the University of Calabria into the incidence of murder in Calabria during the last thirty years reveals that the classic crime of honour went into a real decline between the early 'fifties and the early 'sixties: there were thirty-six cases in the three-year period 1950–52, and only twelve in the three-year period 1960–62. An almost identical trend can be observed in the case of blood-feuds and revenge-killings, which gave rise to twelve deaths in 1960–62 as opposed to thirty-eight in 1950–52.[5]

Internal conflict within the mafia milieu declined alongside the shrinking power-base of the traditional mafia: the decade 1950–59 saw 126 deaths in inter-mafia struggles, compared to 64 in the following decade. In the same period, homicides

[5] *Indagine statistica sugli omicidi avvenuti in Calabria dal 1950 in poi,* ed. P. Arlacchi and A. Tucci, Department of Sociology, University of Calabria, 1978–82.

occasioned by intra-family conflicts halved in number. There was also a fall in the overall annual murder rate for Calabria, which stood in the late 'forties and early 'fifties at the exceptionally high average figure of 6 per 100,000 inhabitants, but fell to 3.1 per 100,000 during the 'sixties. A similar trend was apparent in Western Sicily, where the number of people charged with murder fell from 258 in 1951 to 132 in 1959.[6]

The extent and depth of cultural change can be gauged from the figures for violent crime in the mafia areas of Calabria and Sicily. By comparison with other parts, these zones show a still more pronounced decline in the incidence of forms of horizontal conflict bound up with the old scale of values. In one of the classic seats of mafia power, the Southern Tyrrhenian region of Calabria, the 'crime of honour' virtually disappeared in the space of ten years, eighteen cases being recorded for the three years 1950–52 and just two cases for the period 1960–62.[7] According to the data supplied to the Anti-mafia Commission by the Commandant-General of the *carabinieri*, murders of the mafia type in Sicily declined from twenty-seven in 1963 to one in 1968.[8]

The Crisis of Legitimation of Mafia Power

This general falling-off in conflicts and episodes of violence meant that one of the main traditional functions of mafia power, mediation in internal conflicts within the local society, was diminishing in importance. At the same time, its other functions were also gradually becoming less necessary. As the post-war revolution broke up the mechanisms by which the mafia had played a part in socio-economic integration, and as the men of honour forged a new identity for themselves, certain consequences followed—in particular, the loosening of all those bonds that had been imposed on the *mafiosi* by their role as mediators, protectors and judges. The post-war transformation of the mafia phenomenon coincided with the virtual demise of the *legitimacy*

---

[6] ISTAT (Italian national statistical digest), *Annuario di Statistiche Giudiziarie; Bolletino mensile di statistica; Sommario di statistica*, 1951–1959.

[7] Arlacchi and Tucci eds., op. cit.

[8] Anti-mafia Commission, *Commissione parlamentare d'inchiesta sul fenomeno della mafia in Sicilia*, vols. I, II, III, IV, Rome, Tipografia del Senato, doc. XXIII, n. 2–VII, p. 311.

of mafia power.

Two circumstances, one inside and one outside their own particular frame of reference, further hastened the separation of the *mafiosi* from their traditional bases of legitimation. On the one hand, the growth in the importance of economic power and success as collective goals was accompanied by the simultaneous development, in the *Mezzogiorno*, of modern mass parties and movements, which proved tough opponents when they came up against the mafia; and in consequence, the mafia—deprived of support, of recruits, and of opportunities for action—found itself hampered in its own pursuit of those goals. As the PCI (Italian Communist Party) grew in Calabria, and particularly in the Ionian part of the region, a number of former men of honour even joined its ranks, rapidly becoming antagonists of their former colleagues. Nicola D'Agostino is the symbolic representative of this trend. The traditional chief of Canolo, the small town in Ionian Calabria, D'Agostino became a trade-union organizer and then, throughout the post-war years, the town's communist mayor. The powers and functions of the rural mafia groups were undermined by the new form of social integration and political mediation represented by the institutions of the national workers' and peasants' movements: in 1959, Hobsbawm wrote of the Calabrian *Onorata Società* that:

> the Society has in many places gradually faded out as modern left wing movements have taken root . . . In Gerace it is actually reported to have dissolved itself; in Canolo—thanks to the influence of the converted D'Agostino—it became bad form and slightly ridiculous to be a member; and even in those left wing villages in which it survives, it does so—or so it is reported—as a relatively somnolent local form of masonry.[9]

In Sicily, the development of the parties of the Left was not accompanied by any incidence of 'conversions' among former mafia chiefs such as happened in Ionian Calabria, but there too it played an important role in the decline of the men of honour's popularity and power. The *mafiosi* struck back, with heavy blows: the period 1945–59 saw the murder of at least forty trade

---

[9] E. J. Hobsbawm, *Primitive Rebels. Studies in Archaic Forms of Social Movement in the 19th and 20th Centuries*, Manchester 1974, p. 52.

unionists and left-wing militants who had resisted the mafia's attempts to retain control of the labour market and the 'market' in politics.

On the other hand, the State proceeded, during the 'fifties and 'sixties, to claim the monopoly of physical violence throughout the territory of Italy, withdrawing from the local elites of the South their almost immemorial proxy powers over the maintenance of public order. This threatened one of the cornerstones of the mafia's power. Campaigns to repress the mafia began in the late 'forties and continued over the next twenty years, and in 1956 a new law was passed giving fresh powers of custody to the police. This disrupted the power of the mafia for longer, and to greater effect in the short and medium term, than had the efforts of Prefect Mori in Sicily between 1926 and 1936.

The culmination of this establishment of an effective State monopoly of force came in 1962, when a Parliamentary Commission was set up to inquire into the phenomenon of the mafia in Sicily. The Left had been calling for such a Commission since immediately after the war, and it did have a big impact on the anti-mafia clampdown, especially in the first years after its setting up: between 1963 and the end of the decade, all the leading figures in the mafia found themselves in prison, in compulsory exile, or on the wanted list.

The activities of the Anti-mafia Commission also had a notable effect in altering the relations between political power and mafia power. During the 'sixties, the latter ceased to enjoy official recognition and legal immunity, which meant a further loss of support and general legitimacy:

Before 1963, many *mafiosi* openly paraded their relationship with politicians and local administrators—and vice versa. At polling-stations, *mafiosi* were obviously and aggressively present. It is a rarity nowadays to see such open manifestations of links between *mafiosi* and politicians.

The last blatant instance of such links was the case of the Christian Democrat Regional member of parliament Dino Canzoneri, which actually took place a few days after the Ciaculli massacre.* During the

* *Massacre of Ciaculli:* On 30 June 1963, a car bomb exploded at Ciaculli, in the territory dominated by the *cosca* of the Grecos, killing seven policemen. It had a sensational impact at national level: within a few days the Anti-mafia Commission had been set up.

23 August 1963 sitting of the Sicilian Regional Assembly, Deputy Rossitto, a Communist, denounced the support given by mafia *cosche* to certain Christian Democrat candidates. In particular, he referred to the links between Luciano Liggio and Deputy Dino Canzoneri.

At the time, Canzoneri was impudent enought to reply by claiming that Liggio was the victim of judicial persecution because of false accusations . . . put about by the Communists. In fact, Liggio had been a fugitive from justice for many years, but thanks to the complicity of politicians he was able to move about freely and to organise his criminal network. Following the Ciaculli massacre, and the arrest of Liggio and other well-known mafia bosses, Canzoneri retired for good from the regional political scene.[10]

Taken together, the cultural, political and economic factors we have been outlining marginalized the *mafiosi* and turned them into deviants. During the 'fifties, and still more during the 'sixties, the men of honour underwent a deep crisis: what was their identity, where did they fit in, if they were no longer official proxies in the mediation of conflicts and the repression of non-conformist behaviour, and if public praise and flattery from the authorities had given way to speeches at meetings and sentences in courts that denounced them as enemies of order and progress? Their prestige began to waver among large sections of the population. In 1963, De Masi wrote:

> Today, a *mafioso* is regarded, not as a 'man of honour', but as a criminal; he does not excite the old admiration, even among the humblest social classes . . .
>
> *Omertà* is disappearing, *mafiosi* are far less 'accepted'. If today a Sicilian refuses to give evidence against the likes of Bontade, Greco, or Di Peri, this is not out of loyalty to traditional norms . . . but simply because he wants to save his skin from their reprisals . . . The authority the *mafiosi* used to enjoy is also in decline, . . . undermined by their backwardness and illiteracy, as well as by the general change in economic conditions . . .
>
> It would be possible to cite dozens of almost pathetic cases of this decline, in which many *mafiosi* who were at first feared, and then tolerated, now find their activities greeted with disregard or mockery.[11]

---

[10] Anti-mafia Commission, op. cit., doc. XXIII, n. 2, p. 581.

[11] D. De Masi, 'Sopraluogo nella Sicilia della mafia', in *Nord e Sud*, no. 46, pp. 22–23, 1963.

And Chilanti adds that:

> Young people—from the city and from the countryside—talked out
> loud about the mafia; in shows and cabarets, *mafiosi* were unmasked
> and made fun of. In a word, the 'sixties saw the beginning of a great
> change in people's attitude.[12]

The full extent of this 'great change' became apparent in 1968,
when an earthquake struck the Belice valley in western Sicily, a
long-established mafia centre: 'The *mafiosi* of the past, the neighbourhood and village *mafiosi*, the swaggerers—they had lost their
power. Visiting the tent settlements and the barracks built as
temporary accommodation, we saw how the *mafiosi* had become
the butt of the earthquake victims' mockery, insults and threats.
They no longer frightened anyone.'[13]

During the 'sixties, the *mafioso*'s role was becoming more and
more nearly that of a mere common criminal, a modern urban
gangster who had neither popular roots nor popular backing,
occasionally supported, sometimes tolerated and sometimes re-
pressed by the authorities. The fall-off in new recruits was due,
not just to the effects of emigration to the North (discussed
above), but also to the complete collapse of the prestige of the
mafia as a 'profession'. Not even the most lucrative sectors of the
illegal economy, such as heroin-trafficking to the USA, were able at
this time to attract young people in numbers sufficient to ensure
the replacement of older generations. In 1965, ten leading Sicilian
mafia chiefs were arrested in a joint operation by the police, the
carabinieri and the customs. They included Frank Coppola,
Francesco Garofalo and Giuseppe Magaddino; four other *mafiosi*,
three of them Americans, were also declared wanted, charges
being brought against them in their absence. The fourteen defendants were accused of having organized an international
narcotics-trafficking ring. Five of them were over seventy, eight
between fifty and seventy, and the youngest was thirty-four years
old.[14]

The change in relations beween the local community and the
State on one hand, and the mafia on the other, was so marked in
the 'sixties as to encourage the view—expressed at the time by

---

[12] F. Chilanti, *La mafia su Roma*, Milan 1971, p. 47.
[13] Ibid.
[14] De Masi, op. cit., p. 47.

magistrates, journalists and scholars—that the mafia was on the verge of disappearing, to be replaced by a more modern and less alarming form of criminality. At the close of his 'On the spot in the Mafia's Sicily', the sociologist De Masi concluded that 'the mafia is in its final stages in each of the four provinces of Palermo, Caltanisetta, Agrigento and Trapani.'[15] As late as 1976, the majority Report of the Anti-mafia Commission stated that:

> The Commission has been able to see for itself, in its latest visit to Sicily, that . . . the phenomenon of *omertà* . . . is tending to grow weaker. The abuses of the mafia are met with a clearcut attitude of rejection and refusal, and this attitude is increasingly widespread and strongly felt, especially in the cities . . . The mafia's own criminal activity is tending to be transformed—gradually, but more and more markedly—into a form of ordinary organized crime . . . As the mafia has been introduced into urban and industrial society, . . . and as it has in consequence been slowly transformed into a type of gangster-ism properly so called, a noticeable alteration has resulted in its relations with the public authorities . . . On the other hand, the mafia's long-standing grip on the formal power structure is tending to loosen (if not to slacken altogether).[16]

The Gangster-*Mafioso* of the 'Sixties

The personalities who emerge from the investigations of the Anti-mafia Commission illustrate the precariousness of the men of honour's new position. The La Barbera brothers, Rosario Mancino, Pietro Torretta, Tommaso Buscetta*—these are vague and doubtful figures, disorganized in their lives and their activities, and they typify a moment of transition and crisis. Their common characteristics are an urban or suburban origin, a less 'popular' background, and a turning towards the world outside their native communities (due partly to their involvement in drug trafficking).

Not one of these men ever held political or administrative office

---

* *Tommaso Buscetta:* Buscetta was a *mafioso* from Palmero active in Sicily, in Canada and in Latin America from the 1960s onwards. After the extermination of the greater part of his immediate family and his *cosca* by the rival Greco-Corleone *cosce* between 1981 and 1984, Buscetto decided to collaborate with the investigators, breaking a long tradition of official silence and covert collaboration maintained by all the Sicilian bosses.

[15] M. Pantaleone, *Mafia e droga*, Turin 1966, pp. 103–105.

[16] Anti-mafia Commission, op. cit., doc. XXIII, n. 2, p. 256.

and not one of them ever succeeded in building up sufficient wealth to obtain any real influence on the political life of Sicily or Palermo. The Anti-mafia Commission does report that the La Barbera brothers 'knew Salvatore Lima, the ex-mayor, and their relations with him were such that they could ask him favours', and it is true that they were always in very close contact with political power, but this is a far cry both from the levels of prestige enjoyed by the traditional mafia chiefs and from the economic and political autonomy that marks out the *mafiosi* of today.

In their relations with the leading figures of the Christian Democratic party, the La Barbera brothers, like the other 'sixties *mafiosi*-gangsters, were in a position of constant and marked subordination. *Mafiosi* formed part of the client-network dependent on City Council and regional administrators, and on members of parliament—a network whose function was to mediate and establish connections between the political milieu and other circles. The construction company director Annaloro stated in evidence to Judge Terranova* that he had given five million lire to Tommaso Buscetta in return for the latter's having 'used his authority with the then mayor of Palermo, and with certain members of parliament, to obtain approval for a construction project.'[17]

Many other entrepreneurs sought the intervention of the *mafiosi*-gangsters at this period, and it was then that the mafia first took an interest in the construction industry. The rebuilding of Palermo in the wake of its wartime devastation, and its expansion as immigrants moved in from the hinterland, coincided with the inauguration of a vast programme of public works in Calabria (the completion of the *Autostrada del Sole*, the double-tracking of the Naples-Reggio Calabria railway line, infrastructural work connected with road-building and civil engineering, and so on); and all this gave a big boost to the construction market.

Mafiosi were heavily involved in construction activities all through the 'sixties, though their involvement took different forms in Calabria and in Sicily. In the former region, it was

---

* *Cesare Terranova:* Head of the prosecutor's office in Palermo and an ex-member of the Anti-mafia Commission, he was shot in September 1979. The man who authorized the murder was Luciano Liggio, who later claimed he was being persecuted by investigating magistrates.

[17] Anti-mafia Commission, op. cit., doc. XXIII, n. 2–IV, p. 193.

chiefly a matter of intervening—through various rackets and systems of extortion, and through the imposition of 'guardians' and 'protectors'—in dealings between the outside contracting companies and the local economy. On the island, however, the mafia played a larger part, with well-known *mafiosi* taking direct entrepreneurial control of commercial and industrial activities.

The real scope of these activities should not however be over-estimated. In the great majority of cases, they always remained subject to the considerable limitations imposed by the rigid monopoly that the political leaders themselves exercised in person over virtually every aspect—legal, financial, and even technical —of the construction works.

Moreover, the *mafiosi*-gansters, with their disorganized and provisional life-styles and financial interests, were never able to decide where their priorities lay among the wide range of activities that they pursued, and never showed themselves to be bent on capitalist accumulation in the true sense. When Buscetta decided to press a legally recognized construction company to accept him as a partner, the firm failed soon after. The La Barbera brothers owned a goods vehicle agency, but this never got off the ground, and disappeared with the disappearance of its owners. The money they made in the illegal sector of their activities was never channelled into the legitimate sector and transformed into productive investment; instead, it went almost entirely to finance their need for conspicuous consumption.[18]

Their irregular and unstable life-patterns prevented these figures from building up the homogeneous fortunes and family empires, large and small, typical—as we shall see in the third part of this study—of the Sicilian and Calabrian mafia groups of the 'seventies and 'eighties.

No expansion of the mafia's legal entrepreneurial activity could in any case have made much headway, given that the construction industry and the financial system of western Sicily were control-led by a lobby of politicians, speculators and professional men—a lobby quite as ruthless as the *mafiosi*-gangsters themselves, and a great deal more powerful and cohesive.

---

[18] Ibid., doc. XXIII, n. 2–IV, pp. 131–241.

Political Power and Mafia Power in Western Sicily

The true leading figures in the western Sicily of the 1950s and 1960s were not the *mafiosi*-gangsters to whom the newspapers devoted so much space, but an elite of activists in the Christian Democratic party, whose successful remodelling of the Sicilian political system allowed them to gain control of all the fundamental levers of political and economic power in the region. This transformation of Sicilian Christian Democracy—which turned it from a party of 'notables' into an organized cadre party—was guided by the *fanfaniani di Palermo*, a group of professional politicians headed by Lima, Gioia and Ciancimino who belonged to the modernizing tendency, led by Amintore Fanfani, within the Christian Democratic party nationally. This group broke with, and so to speak 'internalized', the transformative tradition that had characterized relations between the ruling political forces on the island.

From the end of the war until the mid-'fifties, political power in Sicily continued to be exercised through a complex play of alliances that sprung up and dissolved between various groups, each with its own political tendencies and its own electoral and client base. Precarious relations, now of conflict and now of cooperation, prevailed between the various factions—monarchists, *qualunquisti*, liberals, fascists, former separatists, Christian Democrats of differing hues. Regional Governments were formed on the basis of temporary convergences between heterogeneous political and client groups, each maintaining its own independence and its own autonomous power base. So fissiparous was the texture of politics that a group of ex-fascist and *qualunquisti* regional members of parliament was even formed (under the name CESPA) to give direct support to the Christian Democratic Regional President.

This state of affairs was brought to an end by Giovanni Gioia and the group around him:

> After the Naples conference of 1954, at which the Fanfani line was victorious, the accent fell on integration: in the province of Palermo, Deputy Giovanni Gioia moved beyond . . . his previous policy of making purely electoral and power-sharing pacts with right-wing forces that were the organic expression of mafia *cosche*, but which remained separate and distinct from the Christian Democrat party.

The aim henceforth was to absorb these forces into the body of Christian Democracy itself . . . Gradually, the monarchists and the liberals saw their representatives, their local councillors and their Deputies at both regional and national level going over, together with all their camp followers, to the ranks of the Christian Democrats. Those involved included Ernesto Di Fresco, the current President of the province of Palermo; Domenico Arcudi and Giuseppe Cerami, who are still state Senators; the brothers Vito and Gaspare Giganti, respectively City and regional councillors; Giuseppe Pergolizzi; and many others . . . The same thing happened in dozens of communes in the province.[19]

This influx of pressure groups into the Christian Democratic party took place at a moment when the Sicilian public administration had at its disposal a growing and unprecedented quantity of economic resources. The privileged access enjoyed by the *fanfaniani* leadership to the channels along which these resources were distributed hastened the full integration of the new recruits, who soon became beneficiaries of and participants in the new dispensation of power. By the mid-'sixties, Christian Democracy in Palermo and in the chief towns of the province already bore more resemblance to a modern urban political machine than to the federation of heterogeneous client-groups that had characterized the immediate post-war period.

In seeking to incorporate representatives of the mafia, and mafia groups, into the new system of power, the *fanfaniani* adopted very similar means to those employed in their dealings with right-wing and centrist political and client groupings, except that when it came to the *mafiosi* there was also an element of threatened force. For the repressive apparatus of the State played an active part in integrating the men of honour, with their varying backgrounds and positions, into the political machine. Prefect Vicari (later to become the national chief of police) directed the operation, which involved a canny application of the anti-mafia provisions of the 1956 law. Many *mafiosi* were faced with the choice of falling in with the Christian Democrats' power-system or 'appearing in a bad light' before the authorities of the judiciary and the police, who were at this time particularly prodigal in their issue of internment orders, cautions and arrest warrants.

Through their merger with the power-bloc headed by the *fanfaniani*, the men of honour gained considerable advantages, even if these involved the loss of all real autonomy and any independent power-base. Many of them accepted the new situation, and *mafiosi* crowded the ranks of the fledgling regional administration along with former *mafiosi*, and the friends of *mafiosi*. The fact that the *fanfaniani* retained a monopoly of power for an exceptionally long period—about twenty years, from the mid-'fifties to the mid-'seventies—is not explained simply by its small size and its remarkable internal cohesiveness,[20] but was a matter also of the control it exercised over a very significant expansion of the public administration and the tertiary sector.[21] No real understanding of the relationship between the mafia and the political system in post-war Sicily can be gained unless we take full account of the fact that a regional government which controlled a sizeable budget and enjoyed extensive powers of economic intervention was set up during this period. An administrative apparatus comprising several thousand clerks and officials was brought into being *ex nihilo*, as were a range of public economic agencies and institutions whose purpose was to intervene in every major sector of Sicilian industrial and financial life: and all this placed in the hands of the political 'mediators' an unrepeatable concentration of power. To get some idea of how wide this power was, we need only recall that the organs of the regional government were responsible for appointing the administrators of the two principal Sicilian banks, as well as of twelve other agencies that played roles of strategic importance in the region's economy. As the Anti-mafia Commission noted:

> It was also within the power of the Regional Government to investigate the need for bank branches, and often to authorize their establishment; to put up sureties; to advance loans to Communal and City Councils; to convert registered stock to stock to bearer; to appoint revenue agents; to make contributions (in the form of capital, interest payments and low-interest loans) to building cooperatives, regional staff savings funds, and industrial enterprises; to buy up real estate; to take bus lines into municipal ownership; and to acquire rural property in order to carry out agrarian reform and reforestation.[22]

[21] J. Schneider and P. Schneider, 'La dissoluzione delle elites nell Sicilia del ventesimo secolo', in *Incontri Meridionali*, no. 3, 1981.

[21] Judith Chubb, *Patronage, Power and Poverty in Southern Italy: a Tale of Two Cities*, Cambridge 1982, pp. 62–80.

[22] Anti-mafia Commission, op. cit., final majority report, doc. XXIII, n. 3, pp. 124–125.

The actual exercise of these considerable powers—which might have been sufficient, under other circumstances, to stimulate a real take-off of the regional economy—was entrusted to a staff of officials and clerks recruited almost without exception on a clientelistic basis. The point we are making can be given quantitative illustration by way of the percentage figures for those appointed to the Regional Government and its associated agencies by *chiamata diretta* (that is, appointment by direct nomination) as against those recruited by the usual open public competition—figures that provide a measure of the presence of client relations. Table 2 gives details for seven leading regional economic agencies: it will be seen that more than 90 per cent of appointments were by *chiamata diretta*:

Table 2

Appointments of Staff to Seven Regional Economic Institutions

Name of agency	Percentage of officers and staff appointed by 'chiamata diretta'
ESE (Sicilian electricity agency)	90%
AST (Sicilian transport agency)	100%
ESCAL (Sicilian workers' housing association)	100%
SOFIS (Sicilian financial society)	95%
Regional forestry agency	90%
Upper and middle Belice Valley land reclamation consortium	100%
ERAS (Sicilian agrarian reform agency)	99%

Source: Derived from data given in Anti-mafia Commission, doc. XXIII, no. 2, p. 205.

In the period immediately after the setting up of the Sicilian Region, the practice of taking on employees without any competitive examination was officially justified by the argument that, since the central State administration refused to transfer or 'lend' personnel to the new institution, it was necessary to recruit staff quickly. However, time revealed the true function of the practice, for it continued to flourish more widely than ever many years after 1946. The figures in Table 3 give the overall picture,

covering the whole eighteen-year period from 1946 to 1963 and
the entire administration (both central and local) of the Region:

Table 3

Overall Appointments to the Sicilian Region, 1946–63

Administrative branch	Officers and salaried staff	Number taken on by 'chiamata diretta'	%
Central Regional Administration	2,627	2,138	81.4%
Branch Regional Administration	6,260	6,100	97.4%
Total	8,887	8,238	92.7%

Source: See Table 2, above.

In the competition for jobs in the Regional Government, those
who were members of the best-established client networks came
out on top. This is why the 'mafia' provinces of western Sicily,
and mafia-type friendship and family groups, were over-
represented in terms of their geographical and demographic
importance in the island as a whole. Although the population of
western Sicily is roughly equal to that of eastern Sicily, no less
than 73.2 per cent of the personnel of the Regional administration
came from the former area, as against 16 per cent from eastern
Sicily and 10 per cent from the rest of Italy. Official institutions
playing a key role in Sicily's economic and political life appointed
whole mafia and client coalitions, giving their members vital roles
in the structure. 54 per cent of those employed by the central
Regional Government were taken on in the single province of
Palermo, and in some particularly important sectors the figure
was as high as 80 or 90 per cent.

Many were appointed despite having been found 'guilty of all
sorts of crimes', or despite being 'related to *mafiosi*'. Some were
even *mafiosi* themselves, like the Riesi mafia boss Giuseppe Di
Cristina, who returned from custody to become an official of
SOCHIMISI (the Sicilian chemical industries agency). But this did
not signal any change in the relations between mafia groups and

political power. The closer integration of the *mafiosi* into the official political structures that took place during the 'fifties and 'sixties was marked by the subordination of the *mafiosi* to the patrons-politicians themselves.

The new power elite that established itself in Sicily in the early 'fifties was not of a kind to allow much independent space to the subordinate elements of the clientele structure. Up till the end, the *fanfaniani di Palermo* kept tight control of all the intermediate staff of the political machine, obstructing by a series of shrewd strategems any moves towards autonomy. The point is brought out in this description of the most important public office in Palermo:

> When, in 1956, Salvo Lima took over the Office of Public Works, he revolutionized the alliance system underpinning DC [Christian Democrat] power. The doors of the *assessorato* were closed to the privileged clientele of the old CD notables, and all decisions passed directly through the assessor himself or his personal secretary, eliminating the petty trafficking by department functionaries that had been rampant under the old regime. What Lima did was to transform the essentially episodic operations of favouritism of the notables, undertaken without any broader strategic vision and limited to a restricted social elite, into a comprehensive strategy of urban expansion and of DC power, managed directly from key posts of power within the city administration.[23]

Thus we must not over-estimate the influence that the *mafiosi*-gangsters of this period had over the holders of administrative power. The Lima-Gioia-Ciancimino group, being made up of men whose birth and social background were very similar to those of Torretta, Mancino, La Barbera and their likes, were well aware that if the mafia elements were allowed to gain any real space for independent intervention, this might give rise in time to a dangerous pluralism of powers. In their view, a free-for-all contest for political and social power could be avoided only if they themselves took control of the city's principal economic and political institutions. Their great achievement was to centralize what had been a disjointed congeries of powers, an operation that hinged on their taking control of four fundamentally important markets: a) the construction market; b) the credit market; c) the

[23] Chubb, op. cit., p. 133.

market for appointments to jobs in public agencies and institutions; d) the general markets of the city of Palermo.

We have already discussed how client relations shaped the employment market in the public agencies. The fact that a small group of people controlled the construction market became generally known in 1964, when the Anti-mafia Commission requested the Prefect of Palermo to inquire into the issue of building permits by the City Council. The Bevivino report showed that out of 4,025 construction licences approved by the department of public works between 1957 and 1963, some 80 per cent had been issued to five individuals—men of straw, behind whom stood the city's most powerful political-entrepreneurial elites.

It was likewise the investigations of the Anti-mafia Commission that revealed how every one of the forty-two stalls in Palermo's wholesale agricultural produce market had been allocated to *mafiosi* or to people linked with the mafia, all closely dependent on the mayor and the City Council.[24] Almost twenty years later, the former mayor, Salvo Lima, himself admitted that the Palermo general markets had been under mafia 'protection', an arrangement justified by the argument that competition must be regulated.[25]

The control of the credit market by those who held political power was especially important in the emergence of a stratum of building entrepreneurs, made up of mafia elements, who received favourable treatment when it came to the granting of unsecured loans, contracts, sub-contracts, and licences of all kinds. The best-known example was Francesco Vassallo, a modest carter whose first step on the road to wealth and fortune was taken when one of the two leading Sicilian banks, the Vittorio Emanuele Savings Bank (*Cassa di Risparmio*), made him an enormous loan:

> Vassallo's life-story is well-known in Palermo. He came from a very humble background; from being a carter in the village of Tommaso Natale, . . . he entered the world of contracts and contractors when he obtained a little position of power: the sewage contract . . .
>
> One fine day, the *Cassa di Risparmio* lent this unknown man some thousand million lire, paid into his current account—a thousand

[24] Anti-mafia Commission, op. cit., doc. XXIII, nn. I–VI.
[25] G. Micali, 'La mafia? Non so cos'è', interview with Salvo Lima, *Oggi*, 7 February 1981.

million, without his putting up any surety.

The *Cassa di Risparmio* is currently financing Vassallo's entrepreneurial activities to the tune of 715 million lire . . . How can it have been that the *Cassa* gave a loan of such size to someone nobody knew? And what has been taking place in the area where Vassallo has been active as a constructor?

715 million lire obviously do not represent the building of one or two mansions. They represent financial backing for a whole economic enterprise, backing sufficient for the construction of more than 100 flats . . . Everything leads us to conclude that Vassallo is a front for certain particular interests, upon which light needs to be thrown, which can be traced back to the Construction Committee of the City Council.[26]

However, Vassallo—and all those like him—nonetheless remained subordinate to the architects of his fortune. It was elsewhere that the entrepreneurial mafia came into being, created by a different sector of the mafia elite at a different time and amidst different institutions. In Palermo, the *fanfaniani* dominated city politics for twenty years. Their control of the four markets we have mentioned, and the share they took of the profits made by the construction, commercial and financial enterprises which they protected or established, enabled them to acquire considerable wealth and power.

How—concretely, in day-to-day life—did such a wide-ranging series of interests come to be controlled by such a small number of individuals? How did they overcome the difficulties involved in the setting up of a specialized bureaucratic apparatus, able to intervene rapidly to resolve the many problems that sprang up in the various sectors dominated by members of the *fanfaniani*? How were the most important decisions taken, and how were internal conflicts of interest resolved?

The answer to these questions is not to be sought in any conspiracy theory or any exercise of sociological ingenuity. What is needed is an analysis of the anthropological character of the Palermo power elite—in which the phenomenon of the 'manipulation of kinship',[27] typical of the mafia areas of Sicily and Calabria, is crucially relevant. Cohesion and unity of purpose, as

[26] Anti-mafia Commission, op. cit., doc. XXIII, n. 2, pp. 844–846.
[27] Pino Arlacchi, *Mafia, Peasants and Great Estates: Society in Traditional Calabria*, trans. Jonathan Steinberg, Cambridge 1983, pp. 106–110.

well as efficiency and speed in decision-making, were guaranteed
by the fact that all the group members were bound together by a
dense tissue of kinship and friendship relations. The interests of
the group, and of its constituent parts, were discused in day-to-
day meetings between brothers-in-law, cousins, brothers and
friends, all of whom would come to hold some share of official
power:

> . . . And in the same way, we find that Giuseppe Brandaleone is a
> City Councillor while his brother Ferdinando is a Provincial Council-
> lor. Vito Ciancimino is a City Councillor, and his brother-in-law
> Filippo Rubino is a Provincial Councillor. The Gioia family is
> particularly 'well-placed': Gioia and Sturzo are brothers-in-law,
> having married two daughters of the late Senator Cusenza, ex-
> president of the *Cassa di Risparmio*: one is a member of parliament,
> the other a Provincial Councillor. Barbaccia, brother of the parlia-
> mentarian, is a Councillor on the Tourist Board. There is 'full
> employment' in the Guttadauro family—one brother is on the City
> Council, while another, Egidio, represents the Province on the Pro-
> vincial Tourist Agency; and Guttadauro's son is a Provincial Coun-
> cillor, yet another Christian Democrat to have 'joined forces' with the
> Reina group. Then there is Vito Giganti . . . and his brother,
> Gaspare, who represents the Province on the Board for Professional
> Training.
>
> Thus anyone who is not a Councillor can be made a delegate or repre-
> sentative, or put onto a committee. And this is how they run the city.[28]

Any conflicts that arose within these complex coalitions of
friends and relatives were resolved at informal meetings, where
the traditional virtues of loyalty and family solidarity were osten-
tatiously upheld. All the members of the elite realised how important kinship relations were in maintaining their own power. This
led to a strong inclination to multiply mutual links, to meet
together, to set up profit-sharing schemes, and to hold obligations
in common.

There were accordingly very severe sanctions against those who
infringed any of the numerous rules that governed relations
within the principal coalition (or any of its constituent units).
The example given below offers some idea of how great a part
relations of mutual trust and confidence—relations based on an
obsessive respect for 'undertakings' and 'promises', and on a
precise reckoning of each member's 'duties' and 'failings'—played

---

[28] Anti-mafia Commission, op. cit., doc. XXIII, n. 2, pp. 842–843.

in defining the standards of 'morality' and 'correct behaviour' that prevailed in these coalitions. The anecdote is related by the mafia chief Nick Gentile, in his life story as told to the journalist F. Chilanti:

> . . . In the elections, I had promised to give my support to Peppino La Loggia. At Rome, Tano Di Leo was told by an informer that I had undertaken to work on La Loggia's behalf in the elections. He came to see me in my shop in Palermo . . . He was furious. He said that I absolutely must not support La Loggia. I replied that I had given La Loggia an undertaking, because his brother-in-law had give evidence in my favour when I had been arrested under the Fascists. At the time, he was *podestà* of Agrigento. Calogero Volpe, too, agreed with Tano Di Leo that I had been wrong to give my word. I was summoned by Senator Cusenza to the *Cassa di Risparmio* . . . I told Cusenza how worried I was that no-one understood my position, and Cusenza suggested that everybody involved should go for a trip into the country, to smooth things out. This trip was meant to include me, Cusenza, Di Leo, La Loggia and Calogero Volpe. I myself told Tano Di Leo about this expedition that Cusenza had suggested, but he immediately refused to go. I informed La Loggia about this refusal but he told me, '*Zio Cola*, tell Tano, Volpe and Cusenza, and all our other friends, that I will be counting on the trip to find out about any failings of mine, and if it should turn out during the trip that I have failed in anything then you can dig a grave for me and leave me in it.'[29]

The people Nick Gentile refers to represent the top power elite of Sicily. Giuseppe La Loggia was President of the Region for many years, Calogero Volpe was a member of parliament and an Under-Secretary, and Cusenza was Rector of Palermo University as well as being President of the *Cassa di Risparmio*.

Towards the Entrepreneurial Mafia

We have been analysing the long crisis of mafia power that occurred during the great post-war transformation. The integration of the *mafiosi* into the client networks set up by the new generation of politicians is itself part of this same crisis. As we have repeatedly emphasized, the power of the mafia lost not only

[29] Chilanti, op. cit., p. 60.

its legitimacy, but also its autonomy and its sovereignty. Through the State's reclamation of control over public order, and in the ensuing law-enforcement campaigns, the men of honour found themselves unable to make free use of the most important weapon in their armoury of power—physical violence directed against the person.

During the 'fifties, and still more during the 'sixties, any upsurge in crime that could be traced back to the mafia led to a wave of arrests and confinements, with results that had become far more damaging to the mafia groups now that these were smaller in number and less able to find new recruits.

Their integration into the State's administrative apparatus, through their appointment to the newly-formed public agencies, helped in many ways (especially in Sicily) to neutralize the element of lawlessness and violence that the *mafiosi* had embodied, and thus also to make them less 'visible' to public opinion. However, the significance of the crisis of mafia power in the 'fifties and 'sixties is not just a matter of this double process of socio-cultural marginalization and political integration, for its longer-term effects on the position and outlook of a certain sector of the men of honour are also crucially important. If we are to gain any proper understanding of the situation today, we must analyse how these combined effects operated in the changed institutional conditions of the 1970s.

III

The Mafia
as
Entrepreneurs

4.

The Mafia in Business
in the 1970s

The 1970s: Collapse of the State's Monopoly of Violence

Both in Italy as a whole and in the *Mezzogiorno*, the great transformation came to an end at the beginning of the 1970s. The next decade was to see the overthrow of the balance that had prevailed for the previous twenty years. From 1972–73 on, the flow of migrants from South to North grew weaker, dwindling to a trickle and before long actually reversing, until there was (as there still is today) a net inflow of immigrants to the South. This meant the closing of the channel that had united the Italian South, not just with northern Italy, but with European society in general.

At the same time, the nature of State intervention was changing, and its effects on the economy and society of the South were becoming disruptive rather than unifying. Gradually, fresh inputs of public spending lost their power to strengthen internal integration and promote market fluidity, until the situation was reversed and State intervention began to create all kinds of tensions—above all, territorial tensions, within the *Mezzogiorno* itself, between those who had 'got something out of it' and those who had not. Public resources were distributed, during the 'fifties and 'sixties, in very partial fashion and along clientelistic lines. This led to widespread discontent when, at the beginning of the 'seventies, attempts were made to concentrate these resources and 'put them to work'. There was a flood of complaints and of sectional and local claims, which affected a host of localities and institutions all over the South.

These tensions, stemming from the changed direction of public intervention, exacerbated the conflicts that arose when various problems built up over the previous twenty years came to a head—problems that had already surfaced in 1970, with the revolt in Reggio Calabria.*

The tendencies that emerged during the 'seventies were the opposite of those prevailing during the great transformation. What had previously been brought together and integrated now lay open to strong disruptive impulses. A whole range of particularisms, which seemed to have been cancelled out once for all by the homogenization of Italian society and the Italian economy, now reasserted themselves.[1]

Italy, it was discovered, differed from many other countries of the industrialized West in that neither its economic system nor its territorial system were truly unitary.[2] Numerous layers were to be found within the business sector ('assisted' businesses, family firms, out-working, 'hidden' enterprises, and so on), within the labour market (split up, it was found, into a series of more or less independent sub-markets)[3], and within the social structure, where, in place of one single proletariat, a whole range of different 'proletariats'—'young', 'external', 'marginal', 'central', and so on—was now identified.

It was in the context of this changed overall scene, dominated by a tendency towards economic and social disintegration, that the entrepreneurial mafia came into being. We have seen how as the power of the *mafiosi* lost its legitimation during the 'fifties and 'sixties, the man of honour's position became in many ways like that of the common criminal. This merging of the roles of *mafiosi* and of deviant is the necessary starting-point for any understanding of the changes which the mafia phenomenon was undergoing, for the *mafiosi* now found themselves, for the first time in their history, impelled to act and think outside the bounds of the traditional culture.

---

* *The Reggio Calabria 'Revolt':* During the whole of the year 1970 the largest city of Calabria was in more or less open rebellion against the Central Government because of the decision of the administration to elevate the rival town of Catanzaro as the seat of the new Regional Government.

[1] P. Arlacchi, 'Verso gli Stati Uniti d'Italia', in *Società rurale e società urbana in Italia*, ed. G. Elia and F. Martinelli, Milan 1982.

[2] A. Bagnasco, *Tre Italia. La problematica territoriale dello sviluppo Italiano*, Bologna 1977.

[3] M. Paci, *Mercato del lavoro e classi sociali in Italia*, Bologna 1973; M. Salvati, *Sviluppo economico, domanda di lavoro e struttura dell'occupazione*, Bologna 1976.

A certain proportion refused to accept the subordinate and marginal place to which the new economic and political order was consigning them, and tried to develop an innovative response. One section of the Sicilian and Calabrian mafia reacted to the loss of their position of supremacy by throwing all their energies into the accumulation of capital. Here once again we must note the close link between deviant status and the rise of an entrepreneurial outlook. This is a *locus classicus* of Sombart's and Veblen's sociology:[4] as with the Jews, heretics and foreigners of early capitalism, it is their marginal position that impels the *mafiosi* to act ruthlessly with a view to the maximum profit. In so far as they are 'excluded' from society, the *mafiosi* attach more importance than do other groups of the population to the pursuit of wealth, since for them money and accumulation offer the only way back to power and honour.

In this 'conversion' of the *mafiosi* to the religion of accumulation, the economic and institutional disintegration of Italy during the 1970s played a catalytic role. The crisis of the State's monopoly of violence—a monopoly established, as we have said, during the previous two decades, which, while it helped turn the *mafioso* into a deviant, at the same time, *restrained* him in that role—was crucially important in opening up new possibilities of action to the *mafiosi*.

If we take the annual homicide figures in a given society as the most comprehensive index of the degree to which the State holds the monopoly of violence there, then the situation in Italy in the 1970s takes on a truly exceptional character by contrast not only with the preceding twenty years, but with an entire phase of national life. For the boom in murderous violence that marks the 'seventies breaks a more or less secular trend of constantly *falling* homicide levels.

According to the summary of historical statistics (*Sommario di Statistiche Storiche*) published by the Italian statistical bureau ISTAT, the annual rate of murder and attempted murder fell by more than four-fifths between the decade 1881–1890 and the decade 1961–1970, from 13.0 to 2.6 per 100,000 inhabitants (see over). The number of murders and attempted murders declined with great rapidity, and there were only two marked interruptions to

[4] W. Sombart, *The Quintessence of Capitalism*, trans. and ed. M. Epstein, London 1915, pp. 286–307; T. Veblen, *The Theory of the Leisure Class*, London 1957, pp. 188–245; A. Pagani, *La formazione dell'imprenditorialità*, Milan, pp. 274–92.

86

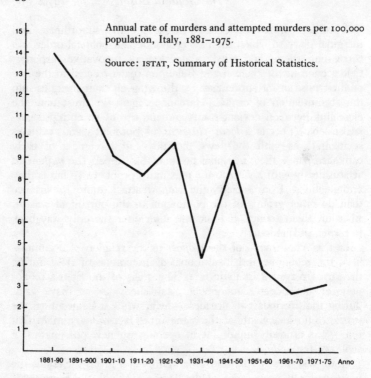

Annual rate of murders and attempted murders per 100,000 population, Italy, 1881–1975.

Source: ISTAT, Summary of Historical Statistics.

this trend, associated respectively with the two world wars. There is a steep rise in the graph between 1943 and 1945, with the rate per 100,000 inhabitants climbing from 3.3 to 26.9, but the gradual fall then resumes until in 1969 the lowest recorded of 2.2 is reached.

Between 1970 and 1975, the number of those charged with murder in Italy rose by 28 per cent. 1975–76 saw a further leap of almost 40 per cent; the 1,000 mark was surpassed, and for each of the six years from then until the time of writing, the level has remained between 1,000 and 1,200. This means that during the last decade both the gross total and the rate of violent death in Italy have doubled—from 600 in 1970 to around 1,200 in 1981.[5]

[5] ISTAT (Italian national bureau of statistics), monthly statistical bulletin, various years.

This loss by the State of its territorial monopoly of violence has indeed been (after a certain date) both a cause and an effect, not just of the mafia's growing power in the economic and political fields, but also of the increasing threat posed to that monopoly by competitors and adversaries of the State, such as terrorist groups and the forces of national and international organized crime. The crucial point here is that it has become more and more possible to make use of violence even in areas of collective life from which it is normally banned.

In the case of the Calabrian and Sicilian mafia during the 1970s, the collapse of the State's monopoly of force meant that violence was transformed into an economic power, a tool by which existing property and production relations could be altered. Murder, no longer a taboo enforced by the State, began to become an increasingly risk-free and inexpensive way of resolving conflicts. The mafia's power began to expand once more because economic competition, and conflicts between individuals and pressure-groups of the most diverse kinds, began to involve the formerly forbidden weapons of assassination and physical violence. The crisis of the State's monopoly of force redoubled the power of the *mafiosi*, allowing them to pursue the goal of accumulation by resurrecting the whole repertory of overbearing and violent behaviour that had been the stock-in-trade of the man of honour thirty years ago. In entering on a massive scale into industrial competition, the *mafiosi* were doing something radically new, but this innovation was at the same time marked by a resurgence of many of their most archaic traits.

To obtain the very large sums of money needed to purchase goods, machines, buildings and labour-power, old forms of violence were given new and harsher life. Kidnapping, with all its ferocious accompanying ritual, was once again employed. The case of Paul Getty, Junior, showed, within the new entrepreneurial *mafioso*, the return of the most barbaric impulses: the victim's ear was sent by post to his family, while the 1,000,000,000 lire ransom was used by the *mafiosi* of the Plain of Gioia Tauro to buy the trucks they needed in order to establish a transport monopoly in the construction of the industrial port.

The *mafioso*-entrepreneur is the outcome of an astonishing cultural mutation, in which many old-established individual qualities are put to fresh use. A taste for risky undertakings, lack of scruple, the ability to close his eyes to the immediate consequences of his actions—all these typical characteristics of the old man of honour are found once again, appropriately modified, in this new figure. In consequence, the *mafioso* is not held back by the legal and cultural checks that restrain his fellow entrepreneurs: for him, even more than for them, personal considerations count for little when it comes to business.

The industrial use of mafia power constitutes an innovation of a particular type, in which values that typified the traditional society undergo a continuous process of adaptation and selection. In central Italy and the Veneto, during this same period of ten or twelve years, features inherited from peasant society (institutions such as the rural family, anthropological characteristics such as work-based socialization) allowed the development of small businesses and of domestic out-working.[6] In the same way, the road to capital accumulation in the mafia areas followed the path marked out by the pre-existing culture, altering it at some points and deepening it at others.

The Mafia Enterprise

This phenomenon of *mafiosi*-turned-business operators is much more problematic than may at first appear. Is it not a little rash to define as *entrepreneurs* a group of individuals who may indeed own companies and manoeuvre capital, but in whom we have not hitherto discerned any innovative character, any capacity to combine its elements in new ways and so transform the whole economic system in which they operate? Are we not rather dealing with a transitional stage in a process leading to the ownership and management of industrial and commercial enterprises, a stage in the formation of a class of speculators and 'venture capitalists',[7] who lack the particular *culture* that distinguishes the true capitalist entrepreneur?

In our view, many present-day *mafiosi* can in fact properly be called entrepreneurs even if we take the narrowest and most precise definition of the concept: the definition proposed by

[6] *Famiglia e mercato del lavoro in una economia periferica*, ed. M. Paci, Milan 1980.

[7] M. Weber, *The Protestant Ethic and the Spirit of Capitalism*, trans. Talcott Parsons, new edn. with intro. by A. Giddens, London 1984, pp. 56–58.

Schumpeter, who identifies the entrepreneur with the innovator.[8] The *mafiosi*-entrepreneurs have indeed introduced innovations in the organization of their firms. The most important of these consists, precisely, in the adoption of mafia methods in the organization of work within the company and in the conduct of its external business. By incorporating mafia methods into the production of goods and services, a whole category of firms has been (and still is) able, like any other innovatory company, to enjoy a profit which it monopolizes to the exclusion of other economic units.

We thus need to study the interesting theoretical object that has come into being through the encounter between the mafia and entrepreneurialism—the *mafia enterprise*. How does such an economic unit function? What endows it with its market success and its growing capacity to expand? In just what respects is it 'new', and different, by comparison with the normal competitive enterprise described in economic handbooks? Our hypothesis, based on the results of research on the ground, is that the mafia enterprise does constitute a definite type of enterprise, whose economic superiority over other firms is guaranteed (*ceteris paribus*) by three specifically different features, which constitute its particular *competitive advantages vis-à-vis* a 'normal' firm.

The Discouragement of Competition

The first competitive advantage consists in the setting up, within the market where the mafia enterprise is trading, of an umbrella of protection. In making sure of goods and raw materials at favourable prices, and in obtaining orders, contracts and sales markets, the mafia enterprise achieves its ends without being exposed to the competitive pressures other firms must take account of. Mafia methods, with their power to intimidate, actually erect what amounts to a tariff barrier. FS is the proprietor of a wood and timber company in the Aspromonte, which has successfully monopolized a good proportion of raw material supplies. The following comments were made by the

[8] J. Schumpeter, *The Theory of Economic Development*, trans. R. Opie, Cambridge (Mass.) 1959, pp. 125–156.

examining magistrate during the trial of the sixty mafia bosses of
southern Tyrrhenian Calabria:

> Because of the greater power of s. and his group, other wood and
> timber merchants had ceased to compete for supplies of coppice-wood
> and in the timber-working business . . . The concrete proof of s.'s
> mafia predominance is to be found in the innumerable tenders for
> contracts and private auctions of wood-felling rights . . . in which,
> although nominally there were dozens of contenders, the one and only
> bidder was in fact s.[9]

The mafia chief of Cittanova, an important town in the Plain of
Gioia Tauro, began his entrepreneurial career in the transport of
citrus fruit and construction materials. According to the magistrate just quoted, he for his part 'drove all the competitors away,
by his mere presence', from his chosen field of activity.

In instances such as these, the power of the mafia is already
well established and recognized: violent intervention, and overt
intimidation and threats, are not normally necessary. Other cases,
where competitors ignore the authority of the mafia or refuse to
acknowledge it, call for direct discouragement:

> At Polistena [another town in the Plain of Gioia Tauro], there is a co-
> operative firm, a building co-op of masons and labourers. Last
> Saturday the management committee met to consider a contract to be
> carried out at Varapodio, which involved the building of an aqueduct.
> We were discussing whether or not we should tender for the contract,
> when the 'phone rang.
> —Hello, I'd like a word with the chairman.
> The chairman asked who was speaking.
> —Never mind, just somebody.
> —But what do you want?
> —I want . . . it's about this contract at Varapodio, this aqueduct
> . . ., we've already had a word with all the other firms that want to
> bid, but none of them are going to take part, because a friend of ours
> needs this contract. We are requesting you not to take part either.[10]

---

[9] Buying up raw materials and acquiring a monopoly in them offered favourable opportunities, in this case, for a verticle extension of business activity: s. in
fact reinvested his profits in the same sector, further downstream, buying a large
sawmill at Gioia Tauro. See Reggio Calabria court, *Ordinanza di rinvio a guidizio
del processo contro Paolo De Stefano più 59* (henceforth: *Ordinanze . . . contro
Paolo De Stefano più 59*), compiled by Dr. Cordova, 1978, p. 187.

[10] Interview no. 9.

The power of the mafia may intervene to 'protect' markets in a whole variety of ways, from simple threats to dynamite attacks and even to the murder of rivals. There is a plant in the Gerace river-bed, near Locri in Ionian Calabria, where aggregates are extracted and concrete is produced:

> The plant is run by Antonio Jemma, brother-in-law of the Cataldo brothers [the Locri mafia chiefs], whose sister Adele he married . . . The owner of a rival plant situated in the same stream-bed, a certain Leonardo Zucco, was killed by persons unknown on 26 August 1974: it seems that he had received all kinds of threats . . . After this criminal episode, the plant's trade fell off very rapidly—which was all to the advantage of the Cataldo firm, to which the big buyers turned.[11]

There are many seemingly inexplicable cases on record which become clearer when considered in the light of an analysis of how the mafia enterprise works. The example of the two North Italian truck drivers killed in 1979 in the Plain of Gioia Tauro[12] is very instructive in this respect. Their deaths can be seen as a savage instance of the discouragement of competition. The two drivers were employees of the Eva company of Verona, which had come to a mutually advantageous agreement with certain groups of citrus producers in the Gioia Plain. This had threatened the power of the mafia enterpreneurs and mafia-linked exporters, who monopolize the citrus trade in Reggio Calabria province, buying up the produce at prices up to 30 per cent or 40 per cent below the market average.

In 'normal' conditions, however, where the mafia's power is established and has taken root in the area, violent intervention is not always necessary, since the *mafiosi*'s capacity to coerce is generally acknowledged.

Through this discouragement of competition, the enterpreneurial mafia has come to enjoy a series of local monopolies in sectors of economic activity and in raw materials and commodities. These have taken the place of the territorial monopoly of

---

[11] Reggio Calabria Carabinieri, *Legione Carabinieri di Catanzaro. Gruppo di Reggio Calabria. Associazione per delinquere a sfondo mafioso di 101 più 19 persons operanti nel versante jonico della provincia di Reggio Calabria e di altre del Nord e Centro Italia*, vols. I-II, 1979, p. 31. (This document henceforth: Report on Ionian mafia.)

[12] See *La Gazzetta del Sud*, 5–6 January 1979.

violence that typified the traditional mafia. Wood and timber, grazing-land, quarries, building-plots and buildings, agricultural and commercial activity, industrial and tertiary businesses— during the 1970s, all these sectors were gradually monopolized by former men of honour and their families.

The most powerful mafia *cosca* in Calabria, the Piromalli *cosca* of Gioia Tauro, holds a monopoly in five key industrial and commercial areas and enjoys an important share of the market in four others.[13] The second most important *cosca* in the region, the Mammoliti-Rugolo *cosca*, which operates in the hinterland of Reggio Calabria province, owns property worth billions of lire and has a monopoly of the olive and citrus trade in three communes: the profits its members have made from drug-trafficking, jewel-smuggling, robbery and extortion have been invested in building a string of modern olive-processing factories, which buy up the produce of the olive-groves, at the lowest of prices, from every oil-producing estate.[14] Their profits are then further swelled by EEC subsidies for olive-oil production, which are of course supposed to be payable to individual producers to guarantee their competitiveness in the European context.[15]

In the country town of Rosarno, in Tyrrhenian Calabria, it is the Pesce clan that controls the chief source of wealth: 'shrewd and intelligent criminals, they have won a monopoly of the citrus trade, and with it a power over the townspeople whose influence extends even into political activity.'[16] After terrorizing potential rivals with dynamite attacks and other threatening actions, 'the Cataldo *cosca* gained a monopoly of the construction sector and the haulage trade, either directly through its own operations or by taking a large share of the profits made by the owners of various firms.'[17]

[13] Reggio Calabria Carabinieri, *Legione Carabinieri di Catanzaro. Gruppo di Reggio Calabria. Associazione per delinquere a sfondo mafioso di 260 persone operanti nel versante tirrenico della provincia di Reggio Calabria e di altre del Nord e Centro Italia*, vols. I, II, III, IV, 1980, pp. 50–51. (This document henceforth: Report on Tyrrhenian mafia.)

[14] Ibid., pp. 372–393.

[15] Reggio Calabria court, *Sentenza del processo di I grado contro Paolo De Stefano più 59* (henceforth: *Sentenza . . . contro Paolo de Stefano più 159*), compiled by Dr. Giuseppe Tuccio, 1979, p. 278.

[16] Reggio Calabria Carabinieri, Report on Tyrrhenian mafia, vol. IV, 1980, p. 1587.

[17] Reggio Calabria Carabinieri, Report on Ionian mafia, vols. I–II, 1979, p. 29.

The clearest demonstration of the mafia enterprises' power in the market was given in the famous episode of the contracts for the building of the Gioia Tauro port. In the competition for sub-contracts, mafia entrepreneurs came out rather well, taking direct control of 70 per cent and indirectly controlling the remainder by taking an 8 per cent quota on the value of all sub-contracts carried out by non-mafia firms. Judge Cordova's reconstruction of all the official payments made to haulage firms by the two large consortia of prime contractors (COGITAU and Timperio Spa) allows us to identify an important characteristic of the workings of the entrepreneurial mafia: the latter achieves internal order and stability when the hierarchy of economic power comes into line with the hierarchy of prestige and military power among its constitutive elements.

Table 4, showing the value of the various sub-contracts allocated to various mafia *cosche*-firms, explains the *pax mafiosa* that marked the construction of the port of Gioia Tauro.

Table 4

Value of Sub-Contracts Allocated to Various Cosche

Name of cosca	Value of sub-contract (millions of lire, 1974–75)	% of total business won
Piromalli	1,384,187,765	55%
Mammoliti-Rugolo	455,697,550	18%
Crea	235,849,522	9%
Pesce	180,398,654	7%
Avignone	117,066,981	5%
Mazzaferro	77,005,400	3%
Sigilli	28,026,760	1%
Franconieri	25,000,000	0.9%
Bruzzí	23,059,000	0.9%
Total	2,526,291,632	99.8%

Source: Indictment ('ordine di rinvio a giudizio') in the trial of P. De Stefano and 59 others, 1978, p. 226.

As can be clearly seen, the amount of business carried out by the different *cosche* corresponds to their respective positions in the hierarchy of mafia power:[18] the top mafia groups in the Plain of Gioia Tauro got the top sub-contracts, the smaller groups got the smaller ones. No conflict was involved in the fixing of this hierarchy: there were no disagreements between the haulage operators, inasmuch as they themselves shared out the work, which meant that anyone coming to ask for work had already been authorized to do so by the group as a whole.[19]

The league table of mafia power and prestige, already largely established, was consolidated by an agreement between the most powerful groups—an agreement reached all the more readily in that one particular group, the Piromalli, was especially predominant. So clear were the advantages of accepting this criterion for sharing out sub-contracts that, at times when fewer of them were available, the smaller enterprises proved ready to stand aside, and only the biggest firms remained in the market.[20]

By 1982, at the end of more than a decade of continuous growth in the mafia's economic power, mafia entrepreneurs found themselves in control of all construction work in southern Italy's second largest city. According to Judge Giuseppe Falcone,

> mafia organisations completely control the construction sector in Palermo—quarries where aggregates are mined, site clearance firms, cement plants, ferrous metal depots for the construction industry, sanitary ware wholesalers, and so forth . . . Either the entrepreneurs are *mafiosi*, or else they have to follow the orders of the mafia organizations in any case. It is significant that during the present mafia war we have seen changes in company administration within the construction sector, as firms have passed into the control of 'winning' families.[21]

The entrepreneurial mafia, in gaining very considerable power in the construction and transport markets, has done so by especially rapid strides—because of the rather high profits that can be

---

[18] Reggio Calabria court, *Ordinanza . . . contro Paolo De Stefano più 59*, (compiler: Dr. Cordova), p. 217.

[19] Ibid., p. 227.

[20] Ibid.

[21] G. Falcone and G. Turone, 'Techniche di indagine in materia di mafia', paper given at the conference on the mafia organized by the *Consiglio Superiore della Magistrature*, Castelgandolfo, 4–6 June 1982, pp. 37–38.

made in these sectors, and also because they have grown at a faster rate than have the more traditional branches of economic activity. As new rapid-growth sectors have emerged between the mid-'seventies and the early 'eighties, mafia investment has at once flowed into them. For several years now, the tourist industry has been seeing an influx of mafia capital and mafia firms, which enjoy the same immunity from outside competition there as in the sectors where they have become more traditionally established.

Capitalist *mafiosi* have now monopolized whole stretches of the southern Calabrian coast, both Ionian and Tyrrhenian. They have bought up hundreds of acres of building land, built or planned bathing establishments, laid out campsites, and opened up hotels and restaurants, sometimes of considerable size. The Mammoliti-Rugolo group, for instance, have attempted to intervene as speculators and entrepreneurs in such a way as to affect tourist activity throughout the vast area between the *marina* at Palmi and the *marina* at Gioia Tauro—and, despite the opposition of Palmi town council, their attempt has largely succeeded.[22]

The security of the mafia's tourism investments is guaranteed, because outside investment has been discouraged by the progressively worsening image that Calabria and Sicily have acquired during the 1970s, with national and international public opinion increasingly alarmed by the escalation in mafia-type murders, kidnappings and extortions. In fact, outside capital has even today established only a very small number of large-scale tourist establishments in the two mafia areas. This leaves ample space for the entrepreneurial activities of the local mafia, even if the deteriorating image of Calabria and Sicily may in future prove a major handicap to the profitability of the mafia's own investments.

The Holding-Down of Wages

The second competitive advantage enjoyed by mafia enterprises is that *wages are held down* within them, while their labour force is more *fluid*. Wages are squeezed, generally, by evading social security and insurance contributions and by not paying overtime. After all, few labour officials are likely to visit mafia firms to

---

[22] Reggio Calabria court, *Sentenza . . . contro Paolo De Stafano più 59* (compiler: Dr. Giuseppe Tuccio), 1979, pp. 106 ff.

—

check up on their observance of the law. This is especially harmful to construction and agricultural workers, who face big fluctuations in job availability (for seasonal reasons and because of the varying demand for labour) and whose work involves rather high risks of injury, and who thus have a particular interest in seeing their occupational status regularized.

The mafia firm's control over the job market is particularly evident in the case of female agricultural workers. During the 'seventies and 'eighties, the old phenomenon of the *caporalato* (recruitment through a middle-man, the *caporale*) has reappeared, in a new, mafia guise. Rita Comisso, regional director of the PCI (Italian Communist Party), has explained what this means for the flow of labour between the Calabrian hinterland and the three coastal plains:

> This phenomenon has started to crop up in Calabria once more, and now involves several thousand women, being especially marked in a few particular cases . . . Here, the phenomenon can now be seen in its most typical form: the labourers are not recruited through employment offices, but by the *caporale*, who arranges their terms of pay, their days of work, and even their transport (often, the labourers do not even know who their employer is). This leads to systematic evasion of insurance and welfare payments, and also to systematic violation of wages agreements (amounting to around 8–10 thousand lire, of which, however, part is payable to the *caporale* for transport) . . .
>
> There exists a real 'parallel market', beyond any kind of control . . . In Calabria, the problem of the *caporalato* has a darker aspect, because the mafia is spreading its tentacles into this area, too: in fact it has been established that *mafiosi* often either themselves run, or else lease out to subcontractors, the lorries in which the women are transported.[23]

It is well known that the Nirta *cosca*, from S. Luca, has played a dominant role in the system by which seasonal labour is recruited to the State Forestry Corps: 'in their capacity as gang-leaders, the Nirta family had control of when the workers began work, and of the issue of documents showing that they had been on site'.[24] In guaranteeing an elastic and above all *regular* supply

---

[23] Interview no. 8.

[24] Reggio Calabria Carabinieri, Report on Ionian mafia, vols. I–II, 1979, p. 162.

of labour-power, mafia methods have proved especially convenient given the contemporary scarcity of agricultural and construction workers. Control of the labour market is thus a more important element of mafia power than may at first appear. This alone can explain why the mafia react so strongly to any threat, however small, to their power in this field. Emanuele Godone, an architect, is the owner of a Ligurian construction company that tendered the winning contract for the building of the hospital at Locri a little while before the Cataldo family-firm got involved in the carrying out of the work: 'His car was damaged by persons unknown on 14 September 1970 . . . During inquiries, the architect admitted that he had received various threats, and that the carpenters to whom he had allocated the woodwork had been replaced by others from the Jemma company [a mafia firm belonging to the Cataldo group]'.[25]

The *mafiosi* of the Bianco area, on the Ionian coast of Reggio province, opposed the construction of a large tourist centre, which was intended to include 400 family maisonettes for employees of the UN in Vienna. The project was backed by Filippo Velonà, a local entrepreneur: he was kidnapped as a punishment, and his partners fled Calabria. The mafia's opposition to the project sprang from their fear of 'losing their hegemony as employment recruiters, which allowed them to remain the sole providers of work for the local builders' labourers.'[26]

The typical medium-sized or small mafia firm is organized along authoritarian lines, with a special staff (watchmen, overseers and so on) to ensure that the workers' lives, even outside working hours, are subject to constant checks and interventions. This actively discourages the workers from making any kind of protest. They must accordingly put up with lower wages, and with highly uncertain and irregular availability of work. Olive-pickers are paid up to 50% less than the contractual rate for the job.[27]

When (as happens with increasing frequency) an agricultural or industrial company passes from the hands of a non-mafia entrepreneur into those of a mafia entrepreneur, trade union struggle in that firm soon slackens off:

[25] Ibid., p. 34.
[26] Ibid., p. 161.
[27] Interview no. 8.

The new management of the Finetti company [a pseudonym], an industrial firm operating in Palermo, resolved to rid the company of all traces of trade-union organization. Since the new mafia owners took over, there has not been a single meeting. The reason is quite simple. A number of the workers and clerks were made to resign their jobs, and their places have been taken by members of the *cosca* which the new proprietors belong to.

One of these is the foreman, another is the store-keeper, another is the overseer, and still another—who has a diploma—is the book-keeper.[28]

The presence of mafia power in the company's relations of production increases the enterprise's productivity: heightening the pressure on the workforce makes it possible to extract a larger surplus. The Palermo mafia family-enterprise led by Matteo Citarda set up the TAMIC company in order to build a large *palazzo*:

The huge building (which had 108 rooms and three entrances) was completed in the record time of two years. One contributory factor, according to the *carabinieri*, was that the job of site foreman was taken by Giuseppe Albanese, one of the partners and the son-in-law of Citarda. His mafia background was well known, and his prestige guaranteed that things went on at a good pace in all areas of the work.[29]

To ensure the conditions typical of the mafia enterprise—low wages, and a mobile and productive labour force—direct repression is not always necessary. In many firms, a good proportion of the company personnel consists of common criminals, people bound over by the police, those under special surveillance, and ex-convicts: these people are either members of the same *cosca* as the *mafioso*-entrepreneur, and thus share close bonds of mutual interest, or they are linked to him by the fact that only he will give them work.[30] Moreover, we must also note that in one mafia-dominated sector, the haulage business, the personnel are bound to the proprietors and entrepreneurs by very strong clientelistic relations, experienced in terms of the 'loyalty' and 'respect' felt

[28] Interview no. 7.

[29] M. Cimino, 'Familiari prestanome', in *L'Ora*, 9 September 1980.

[30] *Ordinanza . . . contro Paolo De Stefano più 59* (compiler: Dr. Cordova), p. 148.

towards the boss. This client relationship offers the employees substantial opportunities for upward mobility:

> If the driver behaves himself, the boss will help him to acquire the lorry that he normally uses, so allowing him to join the ranks of the formally independent 'little bosses'. In the last few years, there has been a considerable growth in the number of these small proprietors of trucks, bulldozers, mechanical excavators and so on in Reggio Calabria province.[31]

The mafia firm, then, being very often a cohesive rather than conflictual group, is very well adapted to compete in the market and in society, benefiting from a particularly docile and flexible labour-force. Other firms are quite aware of the especially favourable position that mafia enterprises enjoy in the labour market, and they appreciate what this means. This is one reason why the practice of sub-contracting is so widespread:

> Let's give an example. Some public agency has given out a contract for work to the value of 100 million lire. The contracting company has to include in this 100 million all the contributions paid on behalf of the workers—holiday pay, pensions, insurance, in a word all the workers' entitlements, which might come to 30 millions. This firm then sub-contracts the 100 million lire job to another firm—this time, a mafia firm, which doesn't bother to make these payments because the workers are under its control and can't make any protest. At the outset, this 100 million lire job costs the mafia firm 30 per cent less than it would cost other firms . . . and it can make the money because it doesn't pay the workers all that it ought to pay them.[32]

It is not only local firms that perceive, and exploit, the advantages that flow from the mafia's presence in a productive organization. The most dynamic multi-national companies operating in mafia areas do the same: and here, as ever, Coca-Cola has distinguished itself by its timely judgement, employing Sicilian and Calabrian *mafiosi* in its factory on the outskirts of Reggio Calabria from as early as 1971. In the prosecution case for the imprisonment of the defendants, case no. 3562/2, the Reggio Calabria chief of police wrote that

---

[31] Interview no. 10.
[32] Ibid.

It can be stated that the Coca-Cola factory at Pellaro is in the hands of the mafia . . . One of the *mafiosi* who has managed to establish his power in this factory is the Filippo Marchese to whom reference is made above [Marchese, a *mafioso* from Palermo, had taken up residence at Pellaro].

Marchese was regarded as one of the most feared hit-men in the mafia *cosca* headed by Vincenzo Chiaracane, which had close links with the notorious Greco family that used to rule over the Ciaculli quarter of Palermo . . .

The accused had formed a close relation with Vincenzo D'Ascola, and with Giuseppe and Francesco Ficara, who are all bound over; and with Giuseppe Costantino, who was formerly bound over—all of them employed in the Coca-Cola factory . . .

On the occasion of the savage murder of the Palermo Public Prosecutor, Dr. Pietro Scaglione, the commandant at the Pellaro police station reported by telephone that Marchese had been away during the particular few days in question; but according to the company's records, which were subsequently checked, he was present —which naturally occasioned considerable perplexity.[33]

During the trial that followed this indictment, the Pellaro Coca-Cola factory predictably issued a testimonial in favour of the *mafioso* Filippo Marchese, declaring that 'he has hitherto carried out the work assigned to him in the most willing and zealous fashion, to the profit and entire satisfaction of the Company' (see facing page).

Access to Financial Resources

The last of the mafia firm's three competitive advantages is the greater *access to financial resources* that it enjoys compared to a normal small or medium-sized industrial enterprise. The money needed for the ambitious investment programmes that mafia capitalism has planned—and, as yet, only partly carried out— does not come, as in the 'normal' capitalist case, solely from the ordinary accumulation of company profits. The mafia entrepreneur does not save up to acquire the wealth he needs, nor does he accumulate wealth before he sets production going. Like the entrepreneur studied by Schumpeter, he invests resources that

[33] Reggio Calabria court, *Sezione per le misure di prevenzione di Pubblica Sicurezza*, 'Procedimento a carico de Marchese Filippo', 1971.

SOCIB
SOCIETÀ CALABRESE IMBOTTIGLIAMENTO BEVANDE GASSATE S.p.A.
VIA NAZIONALE · PELLARO · REGGIO CALABRIA · TELEFONO PBX 26901
C.C.I.A. n. 57722 · CASELLA POSTALE 168 · TELEGRAMMI: SOCIB · CIC POSTALE 21/6486
CAPITALE SOCIALE INTERAMENTE VERSATO L. 1.000.000.000
DEPOSITI: COSENZA · CATANZARO · CASTROVILLARI · VIBO VALENTIA

Reggio Calabria 6/9/1971

La sottoscritta S.O.C.I.B. S.p.A. con Se-
de in Reggio Calabria Via Nazionale Pellaro dichia-
ra che il Sig.Marchese Filippo nato a Palermo il
11/9/1938 è alle dipendenze di questa Società sin
dal 27/10/1967 con la qualifica di operaio e le man-
sioni di meccanico.
       Dichiara inoltre che sin oggi ha svolto
il lavoro affidatogli con piena volontà,attaccamen-
to e profitto lasciando la Società pienamente sed-
disfatta.
       Si rilascia la presente su richiesta del-
l'interessato e per gli usi consentiti dalla legge.
                                    Il Direttore Amm.vo
                                    (Francesco Ninfa)

SOCIB
Calabrian Mineral Water Bottling Company, Ltd

Reggio Calabria, 6 September 1971

The undersigned SOCIB company, Ltd., based in Reggio
Calabria, in the Via Nazionale, Pellaro, declares that Sig.
Filippo Marchese, born in Palermo on 11 September
1938, has been employed by the Company since 27
October 1967 as a workman and mechanic.

We further declare that he has hitherto carried out
the work assigned to him in the most willing and
zealous fashion, to the profit and entire satisfaction of
the Company.

The present testimonial is issued at the request of the
party concerned and in accordance with the provisions
of the law.

(signed)
Francesco Ninfa,
Administrative Director.

entrepreneur studied by Schumpeter, he invests resources that come from outside his personal estate. In his case, *illegal activity* plays the part taken by the banking system in the Schumpeterian model.[34]

The considerable capital sums acquired in the course of the mafia's illegal activity do in fact tend to be transfused into its legal entrepreneurial operations. By far the greater part of these sums is made in operations conducted outside the market in which the mafia firm trades. Very often, these operations are carried out in the richest parts of Italy and the West (in the USA, Lombardy, Switzerland, and so on), and in that sense they amount to a kind of 'primitive accumulation', tending to strengthen positions that are weak in capitalist terms. The production and sale of heroin, smuggling of weapons and jewels, kidnapping with ransom demands aimed at the northern industrial bourgeoisie, clandestine export of capital: the whole massive growth in the mafia's illegal activities, national and international, that has occurred in the last fifteen years has given mafia firms access to a reserve of their own finance capital that far exceeds the firms' own present dimensions—and far exceeds what is available to non-mafia firms, which often find themselves squeezed by lack of credit and therefore subordinated to finance capital.

What distinguishes the contemporary Italian mafia from American gangsterism and mafia activity is precisely this investment in the legal sector of illegally acquired capital. Most of the profits made by American criminal entrepreneurs from the organization of gambling, drug-smuggling, prostitution and extortion rackets are put back into the *same illegal market*. The latter is so extensive that it can absorb even large investments: we need look no further than the case of Las Vegas, virtually founded and developed by a small group of criminal entrepreneurs of Italian and Jewish extraction,[35] or of Atlantic City, the mushrooming 'gambling city' of the eastern US. In the USA, moreover, there are severe limits on the extent to which capital can be transferred, as it has been by Italian mafia firms, from the illegal to the legal sector: there are specially designed institutional and

---

[34] Schumpeter, op. cit., pp. 95–115, 137 ff.

[35] D. Eisenberg, U. Dan and E. Landau, *Meyer Lansky*, New York 1979, pp. 261–270.

informal barriers[36] (laws concerning capital of suspect provenance, absence of secrecy for bank accounts, checks and interventions— some of them 'heavy'—by the police and the FBI), while the rate of profit obtainable in the illegal and semi-legal sector is far higher than can be obtained from legitimate investments. The American mafia entrepreneur who has adequate 'professional' experience and knowledge of the market thus realizes that investment in the illegal sphere of the economy is not only more profitable but even in a sense less risky, in that he will be less likely to become the target of investigations by the police, the legal authorities, public opinion, or some aspirant to political office.

In Italy, there were, until the anti-mafia legislation of September 1982, only a few, ineffectual barriers between the legal and illegal spheres of the economy. This fact, together with the small size of the market for illegal goods and services (drugs apart), led to a massive influx of 'dirty' capital into the 'clean' economy, which has contributed to the commercial success enjoyed by mafia entrepreneurs and their businesses.

In day-to-day economic competition, any firm possessing its own reserves of liquidity wields a weapon of unrivalled power. The Spatola company is one of Palermo's largest construction firms, employing some six hundred workers. It is owned by Rosario Spatola, one of the powerful Sicilian *mafiosi* now im- prisoned for heroin smuggling:

> The Spatola company took over—in very short order—a large site in the Sperone quarter, on which council houses were to be built. The site had been set up by a contractor from Trieste, Delta Costruzione. This was a very well established firm, which had always been in- volved in large contracts, and had come to Sicily because of legislation offering especially favourable financial terms for investors . . .
>
> But the workings of a public contract are lengthy and complex. To obtain the initial payments, for example, one has to present a 'pro- gress report', showing that some of the work has been completed. Meanwhile ordinary credit is needed, which means paying 25 per cent interest. All it takes is a liquidity crisis, and the firm goes bankrupt.
>
> This is precisely what happened to Delta, which had to abandon the site just when it was in optimum condition. The Spatola company came forward, paid off the debts, at once submitted a 'progress report', and—in record time—received the initial payment due

---

[36] A. G. Anderson, *The Business of Organized Crime*, Stanford 1979, pp. 136–147.

under the contract. So far as the investigators have managed to discover, the directors of Delta never received any threats or any 'advice' that they should leave. What they suffered was economic defeat, at the hands of a more solvent rival.[37]

There is currently an imbalance between the mafia firms' financial reserves and the investments they can make. We can see evidence of this in the fact that when the well-known mafia boss Giorgio De Stafano was killed in the Aspromonte in 1976, his briefcase contained a plan for industrial and property investments which, if carried out, would have tripled the already considerable scale of the economic activity of the De Stafano brothers' *cosca*-enterprise. Further evidence lies in the increasing frequency with which mafia entrepreneurs make investments without having recourse to loans: the 1976 majority report of the Anti-mafia Commission noted the 'great significance' of a series of episodes involving the business dealings of the Teresi brothers (Palermo *mafiosi*-entrepreneurs, active in drug-smuggling) in the Vittoria area of Ragusa province:

> The involvement of the Teresi brothers in the Palmero construction industry, through three companies (TAMIC, RECASI and CORES), has an interesting and unusual aspect—namely, the fact that they have built eleven large mansions, worth around 10,000 million lire, without any kind of loan or advance, not even from banks, while their account with the *Credito Italiano* stands at barely 16 million lire.[38]

However, the mafia firm's economic superiority does not derive only from such illegal sources of finance. The mafia entrepreneur also enjoys privileged access to the legal banking system, and can obtain liquid assets in case of need with an ease beyond the reach of any ordinary businessman. This privileged access is guaranteed, not just through a network of client relationships and established business connections among the small local lending institutions, but also because *mafiosi* are linked, in a complex and murky circuit of 'friendships' and contacts, with the managers of the leading national banks. In February 1978, Carmelo Cortese, an

[37] D. Billitteri, 'Il boom dell'impresa mafia', in *Il giornale di Sicilia,* 16 June 1981.
[38] Anti-mafia Commission, *Commissione parlamentare d'inchiesta sul fenomeno della mafia in Sicilia*, vols. I, II, III, IV, Rome, Tipografia del Senato, doc. XXIII, no. 2, p. 423.

industrialist with textile factories in Calabria who had managed
the property of various mafia *cosche*, was

> arrested for peculation committed jointly with Gennaro Campitiello
> and Alfredo Cognetti, the manager and deputy manager of the
> Catanzaro branch of the *Banca di Napoli* . . .
> On 17 December 1973, Angelo La Barbera, the notorious Sicilian
> *mafioso*, arrived in Catanzaro . . . to stand trial with 91 fellow-
> defendants . . . Police investigations had revealed . . . that he and
> Cortese were at the centre of a circle of previously convicted criminals
> feared throughout Sicily and Calabria. Those with whom La Barbera
> was in daily contact included Augusto Casciano, deputy manager of
> the Catanzaro branch of the *Banca Commerciale Italiana* . . . who
> lodged in the same hotel as him and whose Mercedes he drove when
> he went to Porto Empedocle in July 1974.[39]

The same indictment records that Paolo De Stefano, the Reggio
mafia chief, obtained a loan from the *Banca Nazionale del
Lavoro* although he had provided almost none of the stringent
guarantees normally required. Having commented on the 'silence
maintained by all the lending institutions', and on the 'absolute
unwillingness of the banks to collaborate with the law', the judge
went on to comment as follows on the way this loan was advanced
to De Stefano:

> In drawing up the instrument of credit, a clerk at the *Banca
> Nazionale del Lavoro* in this city noted that, 'We do not have the
> usual information about the borrower's estate, since it did not seem
> appropriate to demand this, as we are dealing with people very well
> known in the city—sensitive people, who command respect . . .
> Therefore, considering . . . what is appropriate given the particular
> environment in which we operate, where Signor De Stefano exercises
> a strong influence, we suggest that we give a favourable reply to the
> application made to us.' The manager did not dissent: 'Considering
> the question of *appropriateness* dealt with above,' he noted at the foot
> of the page, 'we agree, and authorize the loan.'[40]

[39] Reggio Calabria court, *Ordinanza . . . contro Paolo De Stefano più 59*
(compiler: Dr. Cordova), pp. 164–175.
[40] Ibid., p. 23.

Mafia Capitalism and Big Firms

The discouragement of rivals, the holding down of wages and the availability of ample finance: these are the driving forces in the expansion of the mafia firm. They explain the market strength and economic power of the present-day mafia. By the mid-'seventies, the mafia's traditional, parasitic methods in the economic sphere were already giving way to a new phase. There was a qualitative change, with the mafia now aggressively present as entrepreneurs, acting to expand rather than obstruct the working of market forces. This qualitative leap was plainly visible in the Gioia Tauro area:

> In September 1974, the three leading mafia *cosche* of the province, headed respectively by don Antonio Macrí, by the Piromalli brothers, and by the De Stefano brothers, met at Gioia Tauro to consider the projected development of the industrial port and the 'V' Steelworks. It would seem that all the participants agreed to reject the offer made by the businesses concerned, an offer of a 3 per cent payment (or 'quota') on all work carried out in return for being left in peace. It was in the mafia's interest to make sure of getting the sub-contracts, so as to make an opening for its own people and control the whole project.[41]

This change in the *mafiosi*'s position *vis-à-vis* big business reversed the pattern of the recent past. In the 1950s and 1960s, there had been conflict between mafia parasitism—which took the form of demands for 'quotas', protection money, and so on—and the point of view of the companies, for whom such claims increased the costs of production. During the building of the Salerno-Reggio Calabria motorway, quotas demanded by mafia *cosche* were among the most serious problems faced by the firms that had won contracts for the sections of the route between Rosarno and Villa San Giovanni. By the mid-'seventies, episodes of criminal damage and attempted attacks ran into hundreds, with the Reggio police department and the provincial Commissioners forced to set up special 'site squads' to keep watch on the most vulnerable installations and workers.[42] Several large companies pulled out of contracts they had been awarded, and construction

---

[41] Ibid., p. 221.
[42] Reggio Calabria court, *Atti del processo contro Paolo De Stefano più 59*, vol. XCVI 1978, p. 107 (this document henceforth: De Stefano *Atti*).

work on the motorway was appreciably delayed.

During the 'seventies, the growth of the mafia's autonomous entrepreneurial power created the conditions for a real alliance. It now became convenient for large firms from outside the local economic system to encourage the power of the mafia. To the traditional motive of wanting to get on with things in peace were now added considerations of company finance properly speaking, for mafia firms that became satellites of large enterprises were able to supply goods and services as cheaply as, or more cheaply than, other businesses. One reason why the two largest industrial companies operating in Calabria have given haulage contracts to local mafia firms is that the latter are able to do the job 'at very low rates, far lower than the nationally established rates in the sector.'[43]

During the trial of the sixty mafia bosses of the Tyrrhenian coast of Reggio Calabria province, evidence was given by the directors of the enterprises that carried out the two most important public works projects of recent times in Reggio Calabria— the building of the Gioia Tauro industrial port, and the double-tracking of the railroad between Villa San Giovanni and Reggio. This evidence stressed that the prices charged by the Gioia Tauro 'syndicate' of mafia haulage contractors, and by the Edilizia Reggina company run by the Libri-De Stefano family, were comparable to those current in the market.[44]

Given these factors, large companies have stood to gain obvious advantages, in terms of saved 'protection money' and a safe working environment, by entering into business relations with local mafia firms. The managers of the COGITAU consortium, responsible for the completion of Gioia Tauro port and of the infrastructure for the steel works there, chose to make the *mafioso*-entrepreneur Gioacchino Piromalli an official associate:

> Neither legal proceedings nor the reports of the investigators have revealed any instances of extortion aimed at COGITAU's officials, or of the infliction of damage of any kind on the agency's extensive and very valuable operations, exposed though these are to all sorts of assault— and this in an area where no less than 154 explosives attacks had taken place during the previous year.[45]

---

[43] Interview no. 3.
[44] Reggio Calabria court, De Stefano *Atti*, vol. xcvii, 1978.
[45] Ibid., 1979, pp. 264–265.

In Gioia Tauro, this alliance between large-scale enterprise and the new mafia capitalism has subsequently developed into a truly confidential and trusting relationship. This was expressed in an episode heavy with symbolic meaning, when COGITAU chose Gioacchino Piromalli to act as host at the ceremonial laying of the foundation-stone that marked the beginning of construction work —a ceremony attended by Prime Minister Andreotti.[46]

But perhaps the most important reason for the solid alliance between the big companies and the entrepreneurial mafia is that they have now established themselves *vis-à-vis* the State as a pressure group whose goal is to inflate artificially the cost of public investment in the *Mezzogiorno*. When contracts are auctioned for public works to be carried out in mafia areas, the starting prices are upped by around 15 per cent. The officially acknowledged reason is to avoid discouraging entrepreneurs, who know they will have to pay out a quote: 'what is surprising is that the "cost" of the mafia should be officially recognised, as appears from the details (which are in any case well known) supplied by the Directorate of the State Railways.'[47] Since the large companies and the mafia entered, during the 1970s, into relations based on production rather than extortion, the higher prices paid by the State amount to a geographical differential income, enjoyed by (and shared out between) both the mafia groups and the large companies; and the latter actually find it to their advantage, here, to be operating in mafia areas.

Inflated prices apart, super-profits can also be made if, with each party using its own particular methods, *joint* pressure is brought to bear on the public authorities, persuading them to offer additional payments, to vary or revise the price agreed, and so on. The contract for the double-tracking of the Villa San Giovanni-Reggio Calabria railway line was won by a company called Cambogi, whose successful bid offered an 8 per cent discount on the starting price (by comparison, an identical piece of work in a non-mafia area of Sicily, the double-tracking of the Messina-Catania line, was bid for by a different company at a discount of 39 per cent).[48] A good proportion of the work was

---

[46] *Sentenza . . . contro Paolo De Stefano più 59* (compiler: Dr. Giuseppe Tuccio), 1979, pp. 265–266.

[47] *Ordinanza . . . contro Paolo De Stefano più 59* (compiler: Dr. Cordova), p. 26.

[48] De Stefano *Atti*, vol. XIX–5, 1978.

sub-contracted by Cambogi to mafia entrepreneurs from the Reggio area; and only two years after work had begun, the overall price of the job was raised from 5,800 million lire to 12,800 million lire (in 1976). The difference between what the State paid Cambogi for a given operation (for instance, the levelling of an embankment) and what the sub-contracting mafia firms actually charged for doing the job amounted on average to around 50–60 per cent—a difference that augmented the other super profits the company stood to gain from operating in a mafia area.[49]

If, during this phase of the development of mafia capitalism, its relations with large firms have predominantly been those of allies, a very different note is struck when it comes to medium-sized undertakings from outside the local market. In this case, mafia firms have charged higher prices, while making more numerous and peremptory demands to supply goods and labour and receive sub-contracts:

At G., in Ionian Reggio Calabria province, tenders were invited for the contract to build the geriatric hospital. The successful tender came from a Sicilian firm, Spa Edilizia C. [this is a pseudonym]. Soon after arriving at G., the surveyor in charge of the works was contacted by Franco Zagara [pseudonym], a local entrepreneur, who asked for work to be sub-contracted to him, saying that he had the equipment needed to clear the site and could supply necessary materials.

After brief negotiations, a deal was struck for the supply of concrete at a rate of 16,000 lire per cubic metre, the current market price. Four or five days after they had begun, Edilizia C.'s surveyor told Zagara's workers to stop work. When Zagara went to ask for an explanation, the surveyor told him that he had received threats over the telephone, but the moment things were sorted out he would get the same firm to start work again.

A few days later, Zagara was astonished to see that the work had started up again, but was being done by a different firm, which belonged to the Bruno brothers [pseudonym], well-known local *mafiosi*. Exasperated, Zagara rushed off to the *carabinieri*, and when he got to the police station began yelling in the yard: 'Go and arrest those *mafiosi* who are working over at Rocchi [pseudonym]! I should have been doing that job! There's no State here, and no justice! Go and arrest them, they are big mafia bullies!'

The *carabinieri* made enquiries and found that Edilizia C. had been compelled to give the sub-contract to the *mafiosi*-entrepreneurs. The latter had threatened the director of works, who had felt forced to

[49] Ibid., vol. xxxv, 1978.

accept once he realised who he was up against. What is more, the Bruno brothers had set a price of 21,000 lire for every cubic metre of concrete, as well as insisting that timber should be supplied by the Bastone company, owned by a *mafioso* called Bastone [pseudonym] who was a member of the Bruno *cosca*. The price for this timber, 145,000 lire per cubic metre plus sales tax, was also above the market rate.

It seems that the threatening phone calls were made, 'in good Italian', by one of the Bruno brothers, a law student at Messina University.[50]

Property, Investments and 'the Circulation of Elites'

The competitive advantages enjoyed by the mafia firm, and their privileged relationship with the big enterprises carrying out public works programmes in the far South, have allowed *mafiosi*-capitalists to reap unusual profits. The size of their companies and the volume of their business have grown at a pace none of their rivals can match. The mafia boss of C. runs a very thriving milling business which, according to the *carabinieri*,

> has built up its trade in the space of a few years, by typical mafia methods, until it is now worth over a thousand million lire. It is one of the most economically important in the province, so much so that it has succeeded in achieving fourth place among the eight companies in receipt of AIMA facilities for the purchase of grain.[51]

In the early 1970s, Nicola Varacalli set up in legitimate trade, having been a small-time cattle-thief immediately after the war and a smuggler and extortion racketeer during the 'sixties: 'within ten years, he built up the biggest construction materials firm in the entire Locri area.'[52] Antonio Frascati is a young *mafioso* from Reggio, born in 1952. Over a six-year period from 1969 to 1975, he rose from being a simple driver to become a medium-ranking entrepreneur, with a 'respectable' economic position: 'as the accused has himself stated, he owns "about" ten trucks, a bulldozer, and a mechanical excavator (in partnership, he says, with his brother Demetrio—who is also his partner, along with others,

[50] Interview no. 11.

[51] Reggio Calabria Carabinieri, Report on Tyrrhenian mafia, vol. II, 1978, p 566.

[52] Reggio Calabria Carabinieri, Report on Ionian mafia, vols. I–II, 1979, p. 97

in the running of the Peugeot concession).'[53]

The change in the position of the *mafioso* Vincenzo Mammoliti has been described as follows by one of the innumerable landed proprietors ruined by the spectacular rise of their former tenant-farmers, herdsmen and lease-holders: 'A few years ago Vincenzo Mammoliti used to earn a paltry amount from his dishonest dealings as a watchman in the citrus orchards. Now he travels around in de luxe cars, he's bought up factories and land, and people say he's accumulated a fortune worth hundreds of millions.'[54]

Most of the *mafiosi*-entrepreneurs who have emerged in Calabria and Sicily during the 'seventies have risen from a condition of poverty or moderate prosperity to a level of wealth allowing them to own small or medium-sized industrial, agricultural and commercial undertakings. A much longer distance has been travelled, in the same brief span of time, by entrepreneurs from the Palermo 'families' active in the world-wide import and export of heroin. This small group of people—not more than a hundred or so, of whom about twenty hold the top positions—are the only ones in the whole history of the mafia phenomenon to have crossed the frontier into the world of *big* power and *big* wealth, with the ownership of money fortunes worth hundreds, or even thousands, of thousands of millions of lire. The wealth of the Spatola-Inzerillo-Gambino-Badalamenti group certainly exceeded a million million lire overall at 1982 values. From an entrepreneurial and legal point of view, this group's most important representative is Rosario Spatola—a travelling milk-salesman in the 1950s, a small-scale building contractor in the mid-'sixties, and during the 'seventies, until his arrest for drug-trafficking in March 1980, one of the leading financiers and industrialists in Sicily.[55]

This growth in mafia-type entrepreneurial activity has not taken place against a background of extensive economic development. The areas of Calabria and Sicily where it has been most marked are not among those parts of the South where investment and production have grown fastest. Thus mafia firms have not developed alongside a *parallel* development of previously existing

[53] Reggio Calabria court, *Ordinanza . . . contro Paolo De Stefano più 59* (compiler: Dr. Cordova), pp. 159–60.

[54] *Sentenza . . . contro Paolo De Stefano più 59* (compiler: Dr. Giuseppe Tuccio), 1979, p. 272.

[55] G. Falcone, *Sentenza istruttoria del processo contro Rosario Spatola più 119*, Palermo court, 1985, pp. 676–743.

firms; instead, they have in large part taken the latter's place. Already existing means of production have been put to fresh uses, rather than formerly unused productive resources being set to work. Mafia firms have grown because new techniques and arrangements have been introduced by people *different* from those who used to control the productive and commercial process. Mafia innovations took shape in new companies, which did not spring from the old ones but went into production alongside them. Once again, 'it's not the stagecoach owner who brings the railway to town': once again, the process of social change involves discontinuity, expressed in the elimination of an old elite and its (still ongoing) replacement by a new one.

This rise and fall of individuals and families is very clearly visible in Calabria and Sicily, where we are witnessing the ousting of a whole stratum of landowners, traders, businessmen and small- and medium-scale entrepreneurs who rose up the social scale during the second world war and its immediate aftermath. In the Plain of Gioia Tauro, this phenomenon of the 'circulation of elites' has taken on the unmistakable features of a transition from one kind of social order to another. The rising mafia elite has almost completely supplanted the area's two oldest existing elites —the heirs both of the indigenous landowners and commercial and industrial entrepreneurs, and of the traders from Amalfi, Apulia and Genoa who held the monopoly, from the middle of last century up until the second world war, of the large-scale export business in oil, wine and citrus fuit, as well as of the wholesale foodstuffs market:

> What has become of the *amalfitani* of Gioia Tauro? Many of the oil and victual wholesalers have disappeared. A few have married local women and become part of the community, but many have returned to Amalfi after their families had been in Calabria for two, three or even four generations.
> They have found the mafia too heavy a weight to bear . . . Some were forced into bankruptcy with big consignments of goods on their hands which they could get no payment for, or only at the lowest prices . . . Others found that the 'quotas' more or less destroyed them . . . But it isn't only the *amalfitani* who have disappeared . . . Look at the fate met by the biggest landowners and businessmen on the Plain—Baron Trimboli, for example. He had been the *padrone* of the S. Possedava district for more than thirty years, he controlled many of the resources of the place—the land, the water, even the electricity when that came along, because before nationalization he

was the owner of the electric power station. Baron Trimboli had no liking for the mafia. In his eyes, they were not much more than illiterate peasants, who thought they were dangerous types when actually they were just ridiculous . . .

The Baron held to his opinion, while the mafia changed. And in the end, he fell into the hands of a local *mafioso* bandit, who extorted a large cash ransom from him, as well as taking over much of his property. When the Baron tried to retaliate, he was tortured and mutilated by the *mafioso*, and he finished his days as an invalid. . . .[56]

During the trial of the sixty mafia bosses of Tyrrhenian Calabria, one of the most compelling indictments of the power of the Mammoliti clan in fact came from two members of the old landowning class, forced by their former dependants to submit to all kinds of impositions.

This decline of the traditional elites has also led to some murky episodes in which members of the old dominant groups have got mixed up with rising young criminals and set out to inflict further damage on the possessing classes. One of the best-known descendants of the agrarian bourgeoisie of old Calabria, Baron Francesco Cordopatri, was arrested in 1978 and charged with heading a criminal gang that had planned, and begun to carry out, a series of extortions and attacks 'directed against the *marchese* Cesare Bisogni, who owned agricultural land and campsites' and who was Cordopatri's cousin, and also against 'another relative of Cordopatri's, Cesare's brother, the *marchese* Antonio Bisogni'.[57]

As the entrepreneurial mafia have penetrated further into the most important areas of Calabrian economic life, especially in Reggio Calabria province, they have ended up by clashing even with the most recently formed sector of indigenous capitalism, the group of businessmen who emerged at the time of the 'black market' (from 1943 to 1945, when the events of the war had divided Italy in two) and immediately after the war. And the professional middle classes have suffered along with this stratum of indigenous entrepreneurs: the mafia's need to accumulate capital by extraordinary means led, after 1970, to an upsurge in cases of kidnapping, whose victims were members of the local wealthy classes. During the last twelve years, more than a hundred kidnappings for ransom have been carried out in Calabria.

[56] Interview no. 2.

[57] See *La Gazzetta del Sud*, 4 November 1978.

The kidnappers have singled out professions whose members' social status and local power have particular symbolic meaning—small-town pharmacists, head physicians of hospitals, doctors, rentiers. In certain areas of the Ionian part of Reggio Calabria province, virtually *every* pharmacist living in seven or eight neighbouring communes was kidnapped during this period. In the Plain of Gioia Tauro, a very large number of industrialists and traders were involved in the elimination of the old entrepreneurial elites:

> Because of the intolerable state of affairs brought about by the mafia, the following people left Gioia Tauro and moved elsewhere: . . . Giuseppe Sprizzi, victim of extortion, who gave up his furniture business and moved to Messina; Concetto Sprizzi, who owned a marble business, and was also a victim of extortion; . . . Giuseppe Bucca, an agricultural trader.[58]

> Luigi Gerace, after the kidnapping of his son Agostino, thought it advisable to move his business activities to Montecatini Terme. A similar lot fell to Pietro Di Giovanni: together with his cousins Rocco and Annunziato, he ran an important oil business on his Valleamena plant, in Gioia Tauro, but he was obliged to leave after selling a factory comprising six workshops and several warehouses.
>
> The Scibilia family, who had important oil and food interests in Gioia Tauro, also moved—to Civitanova Marche—to escape from the impositions and extortions that culminated in the kidnapping of Francesco Scibilia.[59]

At S. Martino di Taurianova, a few kilometres from Gioia Tauro, the Cianci *cosca* bought up 'numerous and extensive properties in the Peraino and Lofrina districts, which had formerly belonged to the Contestabile family, whose members were obliged to move elsewhere en masse.'[60]

In the same district, adjoining the Contestabile family's land, Signor Nicola Rossi owned and ran a model farm famous as one of the most technologically advanced agricultural businesses in the whole province. This, too, attracted the interests of the Cianci *cosca*: 'the property in question, whose olive grove and citrus

---

[58] *Ordinanza . . . contro Paolo De Stefano più 59* (compiler: Dr. Cordova), pp. 250–251.

[59] Reggio Calabria Carabinieri, Report on Tyrrhenian mafia, vol. I. 1980, p. 51.

[60] Ibid., vol. II, 1980, p. 814.

orchards were cultivated, until a year ago, along the most modern lines, was attacked over a long period: plants were cut down, explosives were used, and there were anonymous telephone calls . . . Rossi struggled long and hard against the pressure brought to bear by the mafia, but in the end . . . he had to abandon his land'.[61] In the same town of S. Martino di Taurianova, the same *cosca* had had its eyes since 1974 on another local entrepreneur who rebelled against mafia accumulation:

> It was only a few months ago that persons unknown killed *cavaliere* Vittorio Nasso, who had been brave enough during the last few years to identify the perpetrators of numerous extortions and episodes of criminal damage as members of the notorious 'La Bastarda' group [the largest local mafia grouping, of which the Cianci *cosca* formed part] . . .
>
> In the course of these same events, a certain Santo Fazzari, like *cavaliere* Nasso, had made repeated accusations. Immediately after his friend's murder, Fazzari accordingly made public his intention of selling his provision shop and moving away from Calabria for good.[62]

When they threaten and make use of force to acquire land, buildings or companies, *cosche* such as the Cianci *cosca* and its leading Sicilian and Calabrian counterparts are not—we must remember—simply accomplishing a transfer of wealth and property rights from an old ruling class to a new stratum of speculators and 'venture capitalists'. This transfer of property is just the first stage in a large process of accumulation, whose second stage consists in the *concentration* of the wealth acquired in a smaller number of hands, and its further valorization by means of an extensive investment programme. The seriousness of the mafia phenomenon today lies, as we have already remarked, precisely in the fact that it is no longer an unproductive, subordinate element in the economy, but has become a productive force embedded in the socio-economic structures that dominate ever larger areas of the *Mezzogiorno*.

This is confirmed by the scale and type of investments favoured by mafia entrepreneurs. In *acquiring* their wealth they may use methods typical of primitive capitalism, but their investment programmes are those of contemporary capitalism. The Cianci—

[61] Ibid., vol. II, 1980, pp. 814–815.
[62] Ibid., vol. II, 1980, pp. 815–816.

the 'fierce and bloody' Cianci mentioned above—have set out to acquire the Floricola Calabria company, worth several thousand million lire, one of the leading glasshouse floriculture firms in all Europe. The most feared Calabrian ex-*uomini d'onore*, having gained their wealth by methods not unlike those described by Marx in his account of primitive accumulation in Part VIII of *Capital*, are now putting that wealth into new and highly advanced productive ventures:

> A whole stretch of Calabria is rapidly changing its appearance. Where centuries-old olive groves recently stood, full of enormous trees, . . . there now rise model orchards, endless citrus plantations, nurseries and glasshouses as advanced as any in Europe. This truly miraculous transformation has affected a huge area covering the communes in the triangle between Sinopoli, Oppido and Rizziconi.
>
> The change has happened very fast, and it has been the work of the top *mafiosi* in Calabria. The Mammoliti family, from Castellace; the Rugolo family, from Oppido; the Alvaro family from S. Procopio, the Cianci from Taurianova—these are the new, 'modern' landed proprietors, who in a brief space of time have become the owners of hundreds of hectares. But how has this huge transfer of ownership taken place?
>
> 'Many of the area's big landed proprietors,' explains Dr. Giuseppe Tuccio, the Public Prosecutor at Palmi, 'have come and informed us that they have been forced to sell their farms at derisory prices.'[63]

The model of mafia accumulation, with its mixture of archaic savagery and advanced technology, then continues to operate in the running of the new undertakings:

> The Calabrian mafia, . . . once it has acquired a property, seeks to get the biggest possible profit from it, and turns once more to violence and illegality. But . . . it knows how to pursue other courses.
>
> 'Although it is normal practice to "milk" the labour-force, to run a large-scale *caporalato* system, and to show no mercy in crushing trade unionism,' says Dr. Tuccio, 'when it comes to modernizing and restructuring their land-holdings, and making the most of the grants on offer from the State and the EEC, the new mafia bosses turn without hesitation to agronomists, hydraulic engineers, and prestigious professional consultants . . . Several hundred people are employed in these agricultural enterprises, where considerable strides have been made in transforming the land through canalization and irrigation works.'[64]

[63] G. Manfredi, 'Cosí la mafia all'avanguardia in agricoltura', *L'Unità*, 25 April 1982.
[64] Ibid.

5.

The *Mafioso*-Entrepreneur, the 'Family' and the *Cosca*

The Culture and Lifestyle of the *Mafioso*-Entrepreneur

We can bring together several important aspects of the modern mafia phenomenon by describing the basic features of the distinctive 'lifestyle' and culture of the *mafioso*-entrepreneur.

The traditional *mafioso* had no love of ostentation. His power, like his consumption, was characteristically discreet and reserved. To say little, to keep a low profile, to disparage the extent of one's influence—these were the rules the mafia followed in its appearance in public life. The *mafioso* felt his superior and exceptional position to be sufficiently established by the fact that he led a life of leisure: even when he was not rich, the traditional *mafioso* lived like a gentleman in that he did no work and depended on nobody. In a society where the great majority of the population has to work hard every day, this freedom to use one's own time in one's one way is the clearest symbol of honour and power. His courteous manner, the breadth of his social circle, the mystery and secrecy that veiled his private life: all made it quietly clear that the *mafioso* belonged to the world of gentlefolk.

The *mafioso* made no display of superfluous consumption, because none was necessary to establish his respectability. Indeed, he would have found conspicuous consumption counter-productive, because it would have contradicted his other, populist image as 'everyman'. As we saw in the first part of the present study, the traditional *mafioso*, while a gentleman, nonetheless mixed with his fellows; in his role of man of honour, he was at the disposal of anyone who needed him. His actual prepotency and superiority were overlaid with an egalitarian veneer, and he never drew attention to them by strident or excessive behaviour and possessions. The traditional *mafioso*, aware that his was an insecure position gained and preserved through violent conflict with his peers, avoided any display of his own power that might provoke the envy of his rivals.

Now, the traditional culture no longer exists, and the *mafioso* too has changed. The horizon of his activities encompasses regional or national society, and his honour and power can no longer be left to express themselves in a leisured lifestyle directly witnessed by people in general. As the sign of his entitlement to honour, conspicuous consumption becomes more necessary than a leisured style of life. The communications media, and the horizontal mobility of affluent society, now expose the *mafioso* to the gaze of many people whose only criterion for judging what respect they should accord him is the amount of wealth he can parade before their eyes. He can no longer figure in the role of tough customer, the man who has fought and won and who is feared and respected by everyone in his country district or quarter of town. If he is not to appear ridiculous, he must develop his tastes, learn a more refined bearing, and show that he is at home in more than one world.

The *mafioso*-entrepreneur has a particular and characteristic lifestyle, in which a dominant part is played by symbols of conspicuous wealth and power—luxury hotels, luxury restaurants, the right kind of luxury car. Since 1973–74, some of the leading mafia entrepreneurs have begun to acquire bodyguards and bullet-proof automobiles. The most powerful young mafia bosses move in Roman and Milanese high society. When in Rome, they are to be found in fashionable haunts, socializing with international swindlers and speculators, French and Italian underworld personalities and members of the ruling class. Nothing in their dress or manner suggests the mafia.

The mafia entrepreneur is a talker, giving regular interviews in which he makes himself out to be a persecuted benefactor. He takes good care of his image. He has got beyond the marked distrust that the old-style *capo* felt towards newsprint, journalists and mass communications media. His ignorance of McLuhan may leave him theoretically unaware that 'the medium is the message', but he knows the value of publicity well enough to put

money into private radio stations: *mafiosi* have financed several of
these in the Plain of Gioia Tauro and in Reggio Calabria province. Indeed, we have already seen a number of attacks, assaults
and murders among private broadcasting personnel, as rivals
compete to control the radio and TV airwaves. Now that he
performs, no longer on the stage of some small market town or
southern provincial city, but before the national 'society of the
spectacle'—an audience quite familiar with his image as presented in films and on television—the *mafioso* has acquired a certain
ambiguous fascination that mitigates the effect of his notorious
clashes with civil society and the law.

In describing the mafia entrepreneur's lifestyle, we must not
lose sight of the fact that he still belongs to two distinct cultural
worlds. He may have lost his provincialism, he may differ from
the traditional *mafioso* in demeanour and consumption, but he
himself remains a traditionalist, tied firmly to the values and
institutions of the culture from which he springs. Despite growing conflicts with some sectors of local society, he has not de-
tached himself from his native background—the world of close
family ties, client relationships, honour, instrumental friendship
and adoptive kinship. Indeed, the *mafioso* has even reaffirmed his
membership of this cultural world by intensifying, in his single-
minded pursuit of accumulating wealth, the process of instru-
mentalization in which traditional relationships and institutions
are put to use.[1]

The Type of the Mafia Entrepreneur

The *mafioso*'s ideology and lifestyle have been radically transformed by his identification with market forces. For the most
articulate *mafiosi*, the adoption of modern capitalist values is
expressed in terms of a religion of accumulation whose seriousness
should not be underestimated: profit and power are regarded, not
as means to the satisfaction of material needs, but as the goals of
life. However, we must not underestimate the extent to which
this same religion has reinforced mafia behaviour:

---

[1] P. Arlacchi, 'Mafia e tipi di società', in *Rassegna Italiana di Sociologia*,
1980, no. 1, pp. 24–25 (this essay was partly translated in *New Left Review* : see
'From Man of Honour to Entrepreneur: the Evolution of the Mafia', *NLR*,
Nov.–Dec. 1979.

Even when he's wealthy, the *mafioso* isn't likely to enjoy his wealth. Take the example of De Stefano. He was supposed to have property in Switzerland, but he died in the Aspromonte with his Dupont lighter in his hand. Once he's been involved in mafia business, the *mafioso* can never get away, not even if he makes millions. He always has to live a *mafioso*'s life.[2]

His development as an entrepreneur has meant that the *mafioso* has absorbed modern notions of success and power in full measure. The mafia entrepreneur is motivated, in the last analysis, by the quest for wealth and power rather than by the desire for riches. Common criminals of every age and place, as well as a host of disparate social figures,[3] have felt the *auri sacra fames*, but this hunger has little or nothing to do with the abstract pursuit of profit and power which marks out the modern *mafioso*. Profit and power denote that the *mafioso* is an able exponent of his 'profession', and this ability is the alpha and omega of his moral universe.

Although, after the crisis of the 'fifties and 'sixties, the *mafioso* of the 'seventies and 'eighties is once again solidly integrated into the local culture, and although he has regained a measure of territorial sovereignty, he is no longer restricted to this single culture, helpless like a fish out of water the moment he leaves it. He now moves in diverse milieux and speaks diverse languages. This type, by contrast with the man of honour of the old stamp, seems able to combine the ideas and attributes typical of an industrial society with traditional values and archaic forms of behaviour. The mafia entrepreneur is at once enlightened and superstitious, at once proud of his individualism and in constant fear of not being like everyone else. Open to new conceptions of success and economic prestige, quick to adopt new patterns of consumption, he nonetheless reveals an incredible degree of

[2] Interview no. 1.

[3] 'The thirst for wealth, the ambition to gain as much money as possible, has in itself nothing in common with capitalism. This ambition is found among waiters, doctors, coachmen, artists, *cocottes*, clerks open to bribery, soldiers, bandits, crusaders, gamblers and beggars—that is to say, among "all sorts and conditions of men".' See p. 67 of the Italian edn. of Max Weber, *L'etica protestante e lo spirito del capitalismo*, Florence 1973, p. 67: this passage is not included in the standard English edn. (*The Protestant Ethic and the Spirit of Capitalism*, trans. Talcott Parsons, new edn., London 1984), but a similar point is made on pp. 53–60 of that edition.

reaction and bloodthirstiness in many crucial aspects of his life.

The post-war cultural revolution, and then the fact that he became actively involved in economic competition, meant that the *mafioso* no longer patterned himself on the old models. It was not to the agricultural and professional bourgeoisie of the *Mezzogiorno*—the local leisured classes—that he now looked, but to the industrial, commercial and financial bourgeoisie of the 'industrial triangle': on his visiting card, Gerolamo Piromalli described himself, precisely, as an 'industrialist'.

The *mafioso*-entrepreneur who has emerged from the social and institutional disintegration of the last fifteen years is a 'type' whose characteristics are very different from, and in many respects opposed to, those of the 'type' of the traditional mafia mediator. Two salient features of the modern *mafioso* are a *composite social background* and the *possession of a reasonable level of formal education*. No longer drawn almost exclusively from the lower social classes, he is increasingly likely to belong to one or another stratum or group of professional and white-collar workers, or indeed to the world of commerce and industry itself:

> The traditional *mafioso* came from the countryside . . . He was generally a peasant, a farm labourer, who had joined the mafia because it offered the hope of escaping his wretched lot and the promise of some rise in his social standing . . . Today, the *mafiosi* no longer come from that kind of social background. Today, middle-class people, and university students—lots of university students—are coming into the mafia. The boy who cut Luppino's ear off [Luppino was a young kidnap victim] was a fifth-year medical student. Paolo and Giorgio De Stefano went to university for several years. Giorgio was enrolled in the faculty of medicine, and I think Paolo studied law . . . One of the Nirta family, the ruling clan in S. Luca and thereabouts, has just qualified as a doctor . . . Lots of them are local government officers and clerks, lots of them work for the big consortia. . . .[4]

We can obtain one interesting index of the nature of this change in the mafia's social composition by examining the social status of those killed in internal mafia struggles. The following table compares the class position of those killed in such struggles in Calabria at the beginning of the 'fifties with that of their successors thirty years later, at the beginning of the present decade:

[4] Interview no. 4.

Table 5

*Social Status of Individuals Killed in Calabria
in the Course of Intra-mafia Conflicts*

Year	Lower class	Middle class	Upper class	Total
1950–51	95%	5%	—	100%
1980–81	50%	27%	23%	100%

Source: Sociology Department, University of Calabria, 1982.

It will be seen that there is a very large difference. Whereas on the eve of the post-war transformation the *mafiosi* came almost without exception from the rural working class (peasants, labourers, herdsmen), today's mafia tends to recruit members from every level of the social pyramid. The *mafioso*-entrepreneur is born into a family quite well integrated into the life of the district, commune and social stratum to which it belongs. He is not infrequently the son, or at any rate the relative, of *uomini di rispetto*, and realises as a child that he holds a special position in society: 'this is *don* A's son', 'this is *don* B's nephew'.

Other children avoid falling out with him, and his teachers in primary and secondary school avoid telling him off. He soon finds a niche in some profession or career—unlike many of his contemporaries, who under present conditions in southern Italy may face long years of youth unemployment. Mafia firms are family firms, and everyone gets a chance to play their part. From adolescence onwards, he earns—and spends—a lot. His psychological profile reveals only faint traces of the deviant and the outsider.

The head of the Locri-based Cordí *cosca* is a 29-year-old surveyor. Until the end of 1982, one of the most powerful *cosche* in western Sicily was headed by Stefano and Giovanni Bontade: the latter had a degree in law, and his official profession was that of a solicitor. Many lesser members of Calabrian and Sicilian *cosche* hold posts in public or quasi-public agencies—being appointed, very often, by way of quite irregular procedures: 'Peppino Melara was taken on in February 1973 as a specialist radiological technician with the Provincial Anti-Tuberculosis Agency in this city, even though his only qualification was a school-leaving certificate . . . His contract was periodically renewed, and in 1978 his post was made permanent.'[5] One in ten of those accused in the Reggio Calabria trial of the sixty Tyrrhenian mafia bosses was educated to secondary or university level, and one of these was actually a secondary school headmaster. Of the sixty, a good forty-five could be categorized as upper middle class in terms of their income and type of work.

As the *mafiosi* have come to occupy positions at the nerve-centres of economic life, their culture and ideology have been transformed, until their 'lifestyle' now offers a model for those social groups (such as university students and the young unemployed) whose members experience a strong tension between the aspirations arising from their level of education and their subculture, and their actual level of income. With the collapse of the State's power to inhibit and control violence, moreover, and with the growth of the individualistic, consumerist, competitive culture typical of mafia areas, there has been a fall in the comparative prestige of the bureaucratic professions and occupations which only fifteen or twenty years ago represented the apex of upward social mobility for the lower classes of the Italian South. Otherwise, it would be hard to explain why growing numbers of clerks, lawyers, teachers, doctors and even magistrates should abandon their lawful and well-established professions to swell the ranks of fortune-seeking *mafiosi*. Recently, a judge from the Palermo court was removed from the upper Bench because he had been bringing heavy pressure to bear on his colleagues in favour of the defendants in international drug-trafficking cases.[6] A few years earlier, in Calabria, another judge, Guido Cento, was struck from the Bench because he was 'at the centre of a network of unacceptable dealings and friendships . . . He was involved in a marketing concern registered in the name of the Mazzaferro brothers, . . . mafia bosses specializing in speculation.'[7]

[5] Reggio Calabria court, *Ordinanza di rinvio a giudizio del processo contro Paolo De Stefano più 59*, (henceforth: *Ordinanza . . . contro Paolo De Stefano più 59*), compiled by Dr. Cordova, 1978, p. 154.

[6] See *L'Ora*, 13 July 1982.

[7] 'It is true that the Judge was later rehabilitated by the State council, and a new post assigned him "in the North" . . . But we should still take note of his business dealings, friendship and association with the Mazzaferro family, which show . . . how legal officials working in mafia areas come to think in mafia ways, so that they are no longer fully independent when they deal with mafia matters' (A. Madeo, *La nouva mafia*, Bologna 1976, p. 134).

The attraction that the *mafioso*'s way of life offers to members of the middle classes lies in the prospect of getting rich and gaining social power opened up by the mafia route to social mobility. The *speed with which he rises in his 'career'* is another feature distinguishing the *mafioso*-entrepreneur from his traditional precursor. In the old days, many years usually passed before the small-time side-kick in a *cosca* became a fully-fledged *uomo di rispetto*. The accompanying table, giving the classification by age and the average age of the defendants in the four most important mafia trials of the last fifteen years, shows that there has been a progressive lessening of the time needed to attain a middle- to high-ranking position in the mafia hierarchy.

The way new generations have entered mafia groups can be seen especially clearly from the growing percentage of those accused who belong to the age-group 21–30: the figure rises from 1.7 per cent in 1968 to 16.7 per cent in 1978–79 and to 30.6 per cent in 1980–81.

A further important difference between the *mafioso*-entrepreneur and the traditional *mafioso* lies in the former's different relationship both with other *mafiosi* and with the judicial system. Nowadays, the distinction outlined in the first part of the present study—the distinction between a lawless or anomic phase of the *mafioso*'s career, marked by frequent brushes with his peers and with the State authorities, and a subsequent, legitimate phase, in which his position of command receives formal and *de facto* acknowledgement—no longer obtains. The career of the *mafioso*-entrepreneur seems to be marked by *continuous conflict with the judicial system and with competitors*. He can expect to spend long periods in prison and on the run, interspersed with short spells of liberty, to live under constant tension, and to go in fear of a violent death.

Of the three most important mafia chiefs in post-war Calabria, only Gerolamo Piromalli died a natural death (and he was in confinement). Antonio Macrí was killed in an ambush in 1975, and Mico Tripodio was murdered in prison. Even figures like Angelo La Barbera and Luciano Liggio, who represent a transitional period, never enjoyed fully legitimate status, and spent many years in prison or on the run: Liggio was in hiding for sixteen years (from 1948 to 1964), and after his arrest he took flight once more, escaping from the Roman clinic where he was convalescing. Arrested again in 1976, he was in jail once more in

Table 6

Classification by Age and Average Age of the Defendants in Most Important Mafia Trials (1968-1981)

Trial	Number of defendants	Average age of defendants	Classification by age (in years)					
			up to 20	21-30	31-40	41-50	51-60	over 60*
Trial of 117 Sicilian *mafiosi* at Catanzaro, 1968	117 100%	50	—	2 1.7%	32 27.4%	27 23%	25 21.4%	31 26.5%
Trial of 60 *mafiosi* from Tyrrhenian Reggio Calabria, 1978-79	60 100%	39	—	10 16.7%	24 40%	18 30%	8 13.3%	— —
Trial of 230 *mafiosi* from Tyrrhenian Reggio Calabria, 1981	230 100%	38	5 2.2%	61 26.5%	77 33.5%	63 27.4%	22 9.5%	2 0.9%
Trial of 124 *mafiosi* from Ionian Reggio Calabria, 1981	134 100%	37	3 2.2%	41 30.6%	49 36.6%	27 20.2%	10 7.4%	4 3%

*Of those over 60, 23 were aged from 61 to 70; 7 from 71 to 80; and one was aged 83.

Source: Court Records.

1982. His whole career as a *mafioso*, which began when he murdered an estate guard at the age of twenty, has involved conflict with the institutions of the State.

Today, scarcely any of the most important mafia bosses in Sicily and Calabria is at liberty or enjoys unchallenged leadership and peaceful relations with his fellow-*mafiosi*. Giuseppe Piromalli has been in hiding for more than ten years. Saverio Mammoliti and Paolo De Stefano are in prison. Giuseppe Nirta is out on parole, after being sentenced to four years imprisonment in 1981 for membership of a criminal organization. In a period of barely more than a year, between spring 1981 and summer 1982, the members of the four most powerful mafia families of western Sicily were decimated, along with their chiefs, in a war that was still raging late in 1982 and which had claimed more than 150 lives.

The 'Weltanschauung' of the Modern *Mafioso*

The *Weltanschauung* of the modern *mafioso*, like that of the denizen of Hobbes's 'state of nature', is dominated by an anguished sense of danger. Pessimism, fatalism and a feeling of persecution fill the memoirs, autobiographies and court statements of the *mafiosi* and their circle. 'I advise you to keep your wits about you, because the world is rotten all through', wrote the old mafia chief 'Mimmo' Tripodio to the young Paolo Equisone, in a letter intercepted by investigators. In the lengthy petitions he sent to the examining magistrate, the *mafioso* Avignone expresses his constant resentment against a social order thick with traitors, spies and jailers.[8] The interrogations of *mafiosi* arrested as a preventive measure regularly reveal their vague, nostalgic idealization of family life and the domestic affections, constantly imperilled because of the ingratitude of the world at large.

Today's mafia chiefs like to picture themselves as champions of justice, endowed with an especially strong sense of the traditional moral imperatives: *'uomini d'onore*, men of honour,' in Rosario Spatola's words, 'who always do good and never do harm'[9]—and

[8] Reggio Calabria court, *Atti del processo contro Paolo De Stafano più 59*, vol. xcv, 1978.
[9] G. Falcone, *Sentenza istruttoria del processo contro Rosario Spatola più 119*, Palermo court, 1982, p. 485.

Bruno, my dearest companion—

In one of your letters you told me when the time would
come for me to turn to you in person, now that time
has come and it seems right and fair and I feel that I
should let you know what you must do for me. You well
know that I find myself in prison though innocent, so I
must get out by any possible means, to manage that will
need money and as a brother you must help me by going
to the people listed below, because they will be ready to
do a great deal when they hear my name. The money
they will give you, you keep yourself, and after I will tell
you who you must hand it over to.

These are the people: Filippo Crocè, Nino Mangernea,
Ciccio Flachi, Milio Foti and others who you know, all of
them from Melito Porto Salvo. As well as this go to
Andrea Legato from Condofuri and tell him to go to
others. From Reggio there is Vittorio Canale, go to him
using the same method. Lastly go to *don* Pasqualino
Comi, from Gallico, he knows a lot of people and can do a
lot. I advise you to keep as quiet as possible and above all
don't give my brother so much as one lira.

As soon as you have been the rounds then let me know
the outcome by the bearer of this. My friend, if you have
got enough bread, like what my brother gave you, give it
back to me because I need it urgently, if you haven't got
it then get hold of it, I had already sent my brother, I
don't believe you meant any harm ... That idiot, my
brother-in-law, has lost everything for me, don't you
see? I advise you to keep your wits about you, because
the world is rotten all through. If you need to spend
time with young people, then find them for yourself,
make sure they are people you know. The crowd you
were with before were, and are, nothing but police
narks—no doubt you have realised this.

All my life I will respect you. But I am tightly bound, and
don't know when I will get a chance to prove this to you
by my deeds.

If you have any reply then go to the bearer of this, or
give your reply to my wife. As for what I told you above,

you should make it a general thing, it would also be a
way of testing the respect of some of our friends. Write
to all of them and keep what you need.

Greetings—your comrade and brother embraces you
with fraternal affection—

Mimmo Tripodi.

You'll tear this up at once, of course—*ciao*.

---

who find themselves living in a world full of risks and snares.

Here, a problem arises. As we have seen, the risks and snares
that the *mafioso* sees as always lying in wait for him are anything
but imaginary. What, then, is the fullest 'response' they have
developed to these threats? What modifications have their lives
and their conception of the world undergone as a result of this
constant danger of death?

On the basis of our research, we can say that most *mafiosi* do
not respond to the problem along any ritualistic or religious lines.
The rather 'worldly' nature of their activities and way of life does
not seem to leave much space for tendencies towards sublimation.
The *mafiosi* of the modern age seem to show no general pre-
dilection for rituals and superstitions and no tendency towards
what Veblen (who attributed them to criminal entrepreneurs and
civilisations of a predatory kind) called 'devout observances'.[10]

Nor are they habitually disposed to 'deny' or underrate the costs
and risks of the various enterprises they undertake. The mafia
entrepreneur *knows* he may die a violent death, and, like anyone
fond of life, he fears this possibility. However, since he is often in
mortal danger, he has worked out certain solutions to the problem.
The prevailing tenor of these consists, very often, in a highly
contradictory amalgam between the impulse of self-preservation
on the one hand and, on the other, a readiness to acknowledge the
extremely high risks inherent in what he does. Thus one sees a

[10] Thorstein Veblen, *The Theory of the Leisure Class: An Economic Study of
Institutions*, London 1957, pp. 293–331.

tendency to accept the full worth of life and all its pleasures (including the 'unruliest' and most 'immoral'), and a countervailing tendency to adopt a 'barbarian' type of morality that attempts some solution to the problem of death.

From observations made in a series of quite immediate contacts with representatives of the mafia, one can identify the elements of what might be called a 'heroic' and 'anti-Christian' world-view, which is unfamiliar and appears scarcely western. In fact, these elements seem to allow the *mafioso* to accept death on the basis of a qualitative distinction drawn between human beings. His frame of mind appears in many ways elitist and anti-egalitarian. Since not all men are seen as being on the same plane, not all lives have the same worth in mafia eyes. Certain men may be killed without this calling for any condemnation, in that they belong to inferior categories: they are in the category of the 'non-elect'.

Other men's lives, by contrast, have great value and must be carefully safeguarded. But this value is altogether intrinsic: it does not depend strictly on quantitative length, but on quality. The life of a superior man may already give satisfaction at a relatively young age. The question is well illustrated in the following exchange, taken from an informal discussion between an examining magistrate and a prominent contemporary *mafioso* from Palermo. The discussion turns on the death of the mafia chief 'Totò' Inzerillo:

MAGISTRATE: Totò Inzerillo was killed. He was only 37. Isn't is a shame to die so young? At that age, so many important experiences still lie before one . . . So many goals to reach, so many things to do and see . . .

MAFIOSO: Inzerillo died at 37, it's true. But his 30 years amount to 80 years for an ordinary person. Inzerillo *lived well*. He got a great many things out of life. Other people will never get even a hundredth of those things. It's not a shame to die at that age if you have done, had and seen everything Inzerillo did, saw and managed to get. He didn't die weary of life or dissatisfied with it. He died *full up* with life. That's the difference.[11]

This qualitative distinction between human beings is a fuller development of ideas already held by the *mafioso* of the classic

[11] Palermo, spring 1972.

type. However, in those times rates of violent death and conflicts with the State authorities were less unremitting and much less pronounced. Thus in Leonardo Sciascia's *Il giorno della civetta* (*The Day of the Owl*), the *mafioso* can even include his adversary, the police chief, among the highest strata of his fivefold human hierarchy:

—I know the world a bit, went on don Mariano. As for humanity, as we call it . . . I divide it up into five groups: men, half-men, sub-men, and (with all due respect) cuckolds and *quaquaraquà* . . . Men are very few; half-men are few, so much so that I'd be happy if the human race went no lower than half-men . . . But no, it sinks lower, to sub-men: they're like kids who think they're big, monkeys who imitate grown people's actions . . . And lower still, to the cuckolds—there's getting to be an army of them, nowadays . . .And at last you get to the *quaquaraquà*: they ought to live in puddles like ducks, since their lives have no more meaning or feeling than a duck's . . . Now, you—nail me down to these papers like a Christ, if you like—but you're a man . . .
—And does it seem like a man's work, to you, to kill another man or have him killed?
—I've never done anything of that kind. But if you're asking me (to pass the time of day, or because you want to talk about life)—if you're asking whether it's right to take a man's life, then I say: first you must see if he's a man. . . .[12]

It is ideas like these that encourage the *mafioso*-entrepreneur, even more than his traditional precursor, in the belief that he has the right to take other people's lives. At the same time, his fear that he may die too soon, before he has managed to reach the goals set for him by the fact that he belongs to a superior group, leads him (as we noted above) to develop a strong sense of life and its pleasures:

These people have amazing vitality. They never stand still, they're never idle. One moment they are busy over some deal, later on they're having lunch with friends, then they are working on some other business affair, then they visit one of their lovers. Then some 'situation' comes up which they have to 'control' . . . They are always on the move, and spend hours travelling from place to place in their

[12] L. Sciascia, *Il giorno della civetta*, Turin 1972, pp. 118–119.

cars . . . Then it's off to the bar, to talk. They go to see some relative, and discuss business again . . . Lots of them are polygamous, they have several families and lots of children. They eat, they drink, they have a good time, they kill. The whole thing's done with feverish intensity: never an empty space, never a slack moment. . . .[13]

The Mafia 'Family' and the *Cosca*

To be a *mafioso* is not to follow a profession, nor even, strictly, to have a fixed station or condition. Thus *mafiosi* as such do not constitute a social class in the sociological sense of the term (unlike, for instance, landed proprietors, capitalists, or workers). Some *mafiosi*, and their relatives, enjoy—in terms of social standing—something like a class position because of their mafia activity in the economy, and this may (and in fact to a large extent does) influence the lifestyle and value-system of many local communities; but in and of itself it neither denotes nor pre-supposes membership of a class.

The class position that *mafiosi* may in some cases attain is not the position *of mafioso*, but of landed proprietor, merchant, capitalist—depending on the use made of the proceeds of successful mafia activity.

The fact that these proceeds can be bequeathed to his descendants may play a part in preserving the position of the *mafioso* beyond the productive life-span of any single individual, and may also help the descendants to pursue further gains. The personal capacities and duties of the *mafioso* are not, however, directly handed down in this way. In this area, there is rather a high 'turnover', and it is very rare for the sons of *mafiosi* to succeed in keeping hold of top positions bequeathed them by their fathers. Among mafia entrepreneurs as among traditional *mafiosi*, the elite is selected on the principle of free competition. Attempts to impose candidates for the succession 'from above' almost always undermine the group's cohesion and spark off violent conflicts.

Nor does the criterion of seniority have any binding force when it comes to deciding who will be chief. There have been notable instances in which mafia *cosche* have been led by members younger, or only slightly older, than the average age of the *cosca*

---

[13] Interview no. 18.

as a whole. It can be seen from Table 7, which shows the composition by age of nine leading mafia *cosche* of southern Ionian Calabria, that only in two cases did the role of chief fall to someone of an older generation than the average for the members. In most cases the chief's age is not much greater than that of his acolytes, and in two cases he is actually younger than the average for the *cosca*.

Table 7

Average Age and Age of the Mafia Chief in Nine Calabrian Mafia Cosche

Name of cosca	Territory of cosca's *operations*	Members' average age (in years)	Age of chief
Cataldi-Marafioti	Locri-Ardore-Gerace	37	42
Nirta-Romeo	S. Luca-Bianco-Bovalino	40	67
Ursino-Jerinò	Gioiosa Jonica	34	53
Ruga	Monasterace-Stilo-Riace	31	29
D'Agostino	Canolo-S. Ilario	39	54
Mazzaferro	Marina di Gioiosa Jonica	32	38
Aquino-Scali	Marina di Gioiosa Jonica	33	36
Cordí	Locri	35	29
Macrí	Siderno	39	43

Source: Derived from data in judicial documents (Reggio Calabria Carabinieri, 1979), and elsewhere.

None of this means that the world of the mafia has adopted the methods used by formal organizations of the kind described in the sociology textbooks, which base their selection of personnel on rational criteria of mobility and special suitability for particular roles and functions. It means only that the internal hierarchy of mafia groups is not determined by the chief's transmitting or bequeathing his power, but by the extent to which members possess certain qualities needed to govern the *cosca*. Once it appears that the sons of the current chiefs will not necessarily have inherited these qualities in their genes—that they may, for instance, lack aggression, cunning, steadiness of nerve, intelligence, ruthlessness, quickness of decision—then the stage is set for intense and rapid mobility, both within the particular mafia group and among the various groups of a given area.

As the entrepreneurial mafia has established its position, however, a strategy has been evolving to deal with these vicissitudes within the mafia hierarchy. For over a decade, the modern mafia has been attempting to establish some control over internal mobility. This attempt is part of a wider pattern by which the mafia is establishing a stable presence, and individual mafia groups are preserving their identity for longer and longer periods. We are now seeing the formation of mafia confederations far more stable and permanent than any formerly known. In the chief communes of southern Calabria and western Sicily, the *mafiosi* are beginning to make up a definite social stratum, which is stable, numerous, and continually expanding. The basis of this stabilising mechanism is the phenomenon of the *maximization of descendants*, and the fundamental unit of the new order consists of the mafia family/enterprise and the *cosca* (the latter term denoting a group of families closely bound or fused together).

The power of the traditional mafia chief depended only *in part* on his ability to attract to himself a group of followers (or several groups, where there were several different chiefs)—a more or less permanent band, linked to the chief by quite a range of different relationships, and hardly ever exceeding fifteen or twenty in number. The modern entrepreneurial mafia is different, consisting of a series of very sizeable groups of people (sometimes having seventy, eighty or even more adult male members), centred on a nucleus made up of one or more unusually large biological families.

To become a leader in the contemporary Calabrian or Sicilian mafia, it is indispensably necessary to possess a large family and an extensive network of blood relationships: this is an absolute *sine qua non*. A whole variety of relationships of adoptive or artificial kinship and instrumental friendship[14] may subsequently come into being around the *cosca*'s inner nucleus, but the original clan remains its core and gives it its name.

The most important relations within the *cosca* are based on immediate biological kinship. This tends gradually to displace all other types of relationship and to become the sole internal bond in modern mafia groups. Groups built around a single individual— however adept he may be at weaving 'networks' of friendship or clientelism, however well he may carry out his role as *mafioso* and entrepreneur—have an inherent fragility, and tend to decline and disappear quite quickly. Our research into this point produced a

---

[14] P. Arlacchi (trans. Jonathan Steinberg), *Mafia, Peasants and great Estates: Society in Traditional Calabria*, Cambridge 1983, pp. 105–110.

surprising result: having examined fourteen Calabrian mafia *cosche*, taken from among those which appeared to wield the greatest power in 1979–1980, we found that *in every case their inner nucleus comprised at least three brothers* (see Table 8). Seven were centred on the four families of four brothers, and three were actually based on six family nuclei headed by six brothers.

This phenomenon may be explained in part by economic factors: the nature of mafia activity has changed, and it is based nowadays on families that are also enterprises and enterprises that are also families, which means that the domestic community is more closely involved in business decisions. However, there are also important factors of a 'military' kind, connected with the increased frequency of internecine conflict in the mafia world, which tends to increase the minimum number of adult males (and hence of biological families) needed to keep or gain a place at the top.

His adversaries are well aware how many brothers or sons any particular *mafioso* has, and they give full weight to this fact. Other groups operating in the same area or sector, and deliberating whether they should fight against a particular *cosca* or enter into alliance with it, regard the number of its militarily active members as a crucial point to which they pay particular attention.

Table 8

*Number of Brothers' Families
in Fourteen Leading Calabrian Mafia Groups*

Tyrrhenian Calabria		*Ionian Calabria*	
Name of cosca	*Number of brothers' families*	*Name of cosca*	*Number of brothers' families*
De Stefano	3	Nirta	3
Mammoliti	4	Mazzaferro	6
Rugolo	6	Cataldo	4
Cianci	3	D'Agostino	4
Piromalli	3	Ursino	6
Mazzaferro	4	Jerinò	4
Pesce	4	Ruga	4

Source: Research carried out on judicial records and registrars' documentation.

Where two or more clans have come together to form a single *cosca*, the size of their respective family units plays some part in determining the hierarchical relations between them. If he loses one or more blood relatives, the chief may find himself demoted from his commanding role to a purely titular position (as happened in the Cataldo-Marafioti *cosca*, made up of two 'clans' from Ionian Calabria):

> Giuseppe Cataldo rose to become chief, not only because of his personal qualities . . . but also because of the eclipse of Bruno Marafioti following the killing of his brother and his son. Marafioti, as the former chief, continued to play a part like that of an 'honorary president'.[15]

The power and prestige of a modern mafia *cosca* are closely linked to the number of its members. The most powerful mafia groups are those with the most members: the smallest *cosche* have from 5 to 10 adult males, the middle-ranking ones have 20 or 30, and the top positions are held by *cosche* with 70 or 80.

How is the cohesion of the *cosca*'s inner nucleus guaranteed? Neither the mere fact that they are related nor the strong 'normative' power that this may possess will in itself necessarily suffice to foster really co-operative, dependable and cohesive relations among a collection of different biological families. Moreover, a series of anthropological studies of Sicilian and other Mediterranean social systems[16] has highlighted how often relations *between families of brothers* are marked less by co-operation and solidarity than by disagreement and impulses towards mutual conflict.

Apart from these general considerations, we must remember

---

[15] Reggio Calabria Carabinieri, *Legione Carabinieri di Catanzaro. Gruppo di Reggio Calabria. Associazione per delinquere a sfondo mafioso di 101 più 19 persone operanti nel versante jonico della provincia di Reggio Calabria e di altre del Nord e Centro Italia* (this document henceforth: Report on Ionian mafia), vols. I–II, 1979, pp. 29–30.

[16] J. K. Campbell, *Honour, Family and Patronage*, Oxford 1964, pp. 103–104; C. G. Chapman, *Milocca, A Sicilian Village*, Cambridge, Mass., 1971, pp. 76–77; E. L. Peters, 'Aspects of Rank and Status among Muslims in a Lebanese Village', in *Mediterranean Countrymen: Essays in the Social Anthropology of the Mediterranean*, ed. J. Pitt-Rivers, the Hague 1963, p. 184; J. Schneider and P. Schneider, *Culture and Political Economy in Western Sicily*, New York 1976, pp. 73–79.

that mafia families are cut from a special kind of human cloth: they include people of especially strong aggressive and predatory tendencies, while prevailing modes of socialization—within the family itself—positively endorse the use of violence in interpersonal relations. Given all this, one can see that the internal cohesion of a mafia group is by no means a foregone conclusion, following automatically from the tissue of primary obligations between its members. There is a real and very concrete possibility that the aggression directed against those outside the *cosca* may turn inwards, and give rise to dangerous internecine struggles.

Many mafia groups have a special strategy for dealing with this constant threat of disintegration. This consists in: a) the further multiplication of family relationships between the group's own members, which has even led to the encouragement of intermarriage between first cousins—as in the Spatola-Inzerillo-Gambino-Di Maggio mafia families, in Sicily, which in the course of a couple of generations have become one single group; b) the creation of a very extensive network of common economic interests among the group's members, including those (such as adolescents, women and old people) who play a subordinate role in the domestic community: c) the institution of forms of outright 'family communism', based on common ownership and control—by the members of the *cosca*'s innermost nucleus—of a good part of the group's possessions and economic activities. An important mafia leader from the Plain of Gioia Tauro told the *carabinieri* that:

> With the other brothers, we are actually partners in everything we do—managing our property (citrus- and olive-plantations), running the petrol station, and owning various trucks, which were originally registered in my brother Giacomo's name for purely commercial reasons . . . We three brothers run things in common without distinction between us, and we all draw the profits. . . .[17]

This joint management of possessions, one of the oldest ways of administering wealth, has also surfaced again among the Inzerillo

---

[17] Reggio Calabria Carabinieri, *Legione carabinieri di Catanzaro. Gruppo di Reggio Calabria. Associazone per delinquere a sfondo mafioso di 260 persone operanti nel versante tirrenico della provincia di Reggio Calabria e di altre del Nord e Centro Italia* (this document henceforth: Report on Tyrrhenian mafia), vols. I, II, III, IV, 1980, p. 233.

clan of Palermo. Judge Falcone has shown how the five Inzerillo brothers, together with their father, conducted a whole range of entrepreneurial activities, using the property and liquid assets belonging to one of their number, Salvatore, who headed the *cosca*. In his account of the situation of some of the brothers, Falcone makes clear the degree to which the economic activities of the clan's various members were in fact fused together:

> Santo Inzerillo had no personal current account, which is remarkable given that he was involved in commercial and entrepreneurial activities: and this can only mean that in business matters there was no substantial distinction between him and his brother Salvatore . . . If we further consider that Pietro Inzerillo, too, had signed various paying-in slips relating to Salvatore Inzerillo's account, then it can be seen that the above-mentioned defendant was also 'in the service' of his brother, and that it was impossible to distinguish between their respective activities.[18]

These tendencies towards common ownership and control are naturally found only within the inner nucleus of the *cosca*. The other family groups comprising it enjoy considerable autonomy, running firms that operate in various spheres of economic activity.

The morphology of modern mafia groups is not just a result of the economic, military and other causes we have been analysing. It also follows from the strategy of *maximizing the number of descendants* that seems to motivate individual *mafiosi* and their families. This strategy consists, basically, in the production of as many male children as possible and the practice of an increasingly rigid endogamy within the ranks of mafia groups.

This tendency to maximize their descendants is apparent in the very high demographic growth-rate of mafia groups, which is now starting to have a number of visible consequences in terms of the ratio of mafia to non-mafia families in local communities. The table (see Table 9 over) shows the average size, and the total number of members, of a random sample of 210 mafia families living in 13 communes in the Plain of Gioia Tauro in 1980–81, with comparative figures for all families in these communes (drawn from the latest population census).

[18] G. Falcone, *Sentenza* . . .(cit.), pp. 656, 660.

Table 9

*Average Size and Number of Members of 210 Mafia Families
in the Plain of Gioia Tauro*

Commune	No. of mafia families	No. of their members	Average size	Average size all families 1981	Resident population 1981 census
Rosarno	32	155	4.8	3.6	13,845
Gioia Tauro	41	167	4.1	3.5	17,592
Taurianova	25	131	5.2	3.4	15,384
Polistena	15	77	5.1	3.4	10,699
Cittanova	9	45	5.0	3.1	10,523
Oppido	24	173	7.2	3.2	5,782
Seminara	8	60	7.5	3.5	4,214
Rizziconi	13	69	5.3	3.5	6,956
Palmi	7	38	5.4	3.2	18,705
Sinopoli	12	72	6.0	3.5	2,463
Delianuova	8	72	9.0	3.3	3,638
Cinquefrondi	6	34	5.7	3.2	5,678
S. Giorgi M.	10	66	6.6	3.4	4,150
Total for the Plain of Gioia Tauro	*210*	*1.159*	*5.5*	*3.5*	*119,629*

The mafia families have on average 5.5 members, as against an average of 3.5 for all families. In certain communes, mafia families are actually over twice as big as the average, and in some cases their members make up over 2 per cent of the total resident population. If from the 210 families in our sample we select those whose wealth can be estimated (on the basis of information derived from a series of judicial and other documents)[19] to exceed 500 million lire, then we obtain the results shown in the subsequent table (see Table 10 over).

[19] Reggio Calabria court, *Sentenza istruttoria del processo contro Paolo De Stafano più 59* (compiled by Dr. Cordova); Reggio Calabria court, *Atti del processo contro Paolo De Stafno più 59*, vol. xcv, 1978; Reggio Calabria Carabinieri, Report on Ionian mafia, vols. I–II, 1979; Reggio Calabria Carabinieri, Report on Tyrrhenian mafia, vols. I, II, III, IV, 1980; Reggio Calabria Carabinieri, *Legione Carabinieri di Catanzaro. Gruppo di Reggio Calabria. Assoiciazione per delinquere a sfondo mafioso di 120 persone coperanti nella fascia Sud del versante jonico della provincia di Reggio Calabria e di altre del Nord e Centro Italia*, vols. I–II, 1981.

Table 10

Average Size and Number of Members of 102 Mafia Families in the Plain of Gioia Tauro, Each with Possessions Valued at Over 500 Million Lire

Commune	Number of mafia families	Number of their members	Average size
Rosarno	10	67	6.7
Gioia Tauro	15	107	7.1
Taurianova	9	63	7.0
Polistena	8	54	6.8
Cittanova	3	20	6.7
Oppido	16	143	8.9
Seminara	6	50	8.3
Rizziconi	6	45	7.5
Palmi	4	27	6.7
Sinopli	7	53	7.6
Delianuova	8	72	9.0
Cinquefrondi	3	21	7.0
S. Giorgi M.	7	55	7.9
Total for Plain of Gioia Tauro	*102*	777	7.6

It will be seen that the richest mafia families seem also to be the most numerous. Tendencies towards the maximization of descendants seem to operate more strongly in mafia groups at the top of the economic hierarchy than they do either in less well placed mafia groups or in normal families in the community.

The second strategy for maximizing descendants consists in using the female side of the mafia family to enlarge the *cosca* by cementing matrimonial alliances with mafia groups in the immediate neighbourhood. Much has been written about the tendency of mafia families to make their way back into the legitimate world by marrying their descendants to the heirs of respectable citizens, which does seem to have played a very important role in the history of the American mafia;[20] but no such

[20] D. Bell, 'Crime as an American Way of Life', in *The End of Ideology*, New York 1965; F. Ianni, *A Family Business*, London 1972; A. G. Anderson, *The Business of Organized Crime*, Stanford 1979.

tendency seems to have operated among Calabrian and Sicilian *mafiosi* in the 1970s. Our analysis of some fifty marriages of members of Sicilian and Calabrian mafia families between 1970 and 1980 showed that in thirty-five cases both parties had mafia backgrounds, while ten women and five men from mafia families married spouses with no such background.

Through endogamy within their own ranks and through the production of numerous male children, the mafia groups have increased their power and influence over the local community until it has reached levels unimaginable in the past. In many small and medium-sized Calabrian and Sicilian communes, the last decade has seen two or three big family clans monopolizing a good proportion of the local economic resources, gaining control of the levers of political power, and absorbing many formerly public relations, functions and activities into their own closed world:

> The Santo group numbers about 200 people around here—some *mafiosi*, and some not; and including women, young people and children. It has members in about twenty-five or thirty family units. They are closely related to the Calvesi family, from Montegrano, and the Segesta family from Altopiano. All three *cosche* have economic interests in construction, in tourism—they run hotels and campsites—and in agriculture. You could say they make up a good half of the building industry locally. A couple of years ago, these mafia groups started to be less 'visible' in the public economic markets hereabouts . . . Perhaps this is because, after five or six marriages between young *mafiosi* and '*mafiose*' belonging to the three *cosche*, they've reached the point where their numbers allow them to do business without having to go outside the *cosca* in most cases . . .
>
> Nowadays, they do masses of business among themselves. They get contracts from a man closely related to them, a regional councillor. They go to their own quarries for much of the construction material they need. Earth-moving equipment and machinery of other kinds is constantly being lent and borrowed between members of the *cosca* . . . The market is inside the *cosca*, now . . . They even lend each other money, interest-free or at very low interest . . .
>
> In this district, you only need 100 votes to elect a councillor for the commune. Well: the Santo family elects three directly, and sees to the election of another three or four. They've reached the point now where they make up a 'little world' of their own: inside it, they meet up, do business, fix marriages, bring up children. For the rest of us in the district, it gets harder and harder to find out about their lives and their doings. They do so much inside the group, now. . . .[21]

[21] Interview no. 16.

6.

The Limits of Mafia Capitalism

Trials, Lawyers, Experts

As mafia activity has grown riskier, and as his continual clashes with the machinery of justice have spread these risks throughout the *mafioso*'s entire life, so the latter has come to adopt a new attitude to the processes of the law and to its principal agents. The easy confidence of the classical *mafioso* as to the judicial consequences of his activity has given way, now, to a keen and anxious attention. Vito Cascio Ferro may have been accused sixty-nine times and acquitted sixty-nine times, thanks to his ability (typical of the traditional mafia chief) to influence the judiciary and manipulate every stage of criminal proceedings; but the same cannot be said of the *mafioso*-entrepreneur.

Because magistrates now form a less homogeneous social and cultural group, and because criminal justice as a whole has become more complex, it is more difficult for mafia power (or political power) to manipulate the *entire course of justice* in any given case. There may, in other words, be more people and institutions through whose intervention the process of criminal justice can be obstructed or perverted, but there are also more people and institutions that present a serious danger to the *mafioso*.

In the old days, the *mafioso* had only to arrange for the witnesses to be intimidated, and he was sure to be acquitted for lack of proof (and this has been widely regarded as the true distinguishing feature of the mafia). Now, however, his relations with the judicial system are among the *mafioso*'s liveliest concerns. To protect himself effectively against the criminal law accordingly requires: a) the investment of considerable financial resources; b) plentiful opportunities to exert pressure and influence; c) a reasonable amount of legal knowledge.

This is why all mafia groups are now tending to establish relationships—both consultative meetings and *permanent* collaboration—with lawyers, fiscal experts, and judicial personnel who are in a position to provide proper information and advice. The 'counsellor', the lawyer who is part of the mafia *cosca*'s inner circle, a figure popularized in *The Godfather*, is more and more often met with in Sicily and Calabria.

This tendency to incorporate the function of legal defence into the group itself can be seen in the practice—common to all the most importance *cosche*—of engaging one's *own* lawyers in cases involving the prosecution of group members: one lawyer gradually becomes '*cosca* X's lawyer', another becomes '*cosca* Y's lawyer'. The lines of demarcation are very seldom crossed: Judge Cordova, commenting on the situation in Reggio Calabria province, has said that it is 'unknown, apart from a few rare exceptions, for a defendant thought to belong to one group to be defended (in a separate case, that is) by a lawyer who looks after the interests of people regarded as members of an opposing group.'[1]

This *need for defence* is now so extensive and frequent that any mafia *cosca* that has reached a certain size finds it economically worthwhile to incorporate one or more lawyers into the *cosca* itself, or into its most immediate entourage. Legal defence thus tends to change its character: its basis is no longer the two-way relation between lawyer and client, but the defence of the whole group. Judge Macrí has explained how the accused, in mafia cases, 'has so to speak a collective character':

Even his defence is conducted in terms of protecting the whole group of which he forms part, rather than the defendant himself. The traditional relation between counsel and defendant is turned upside down. Counsel no longer fixes on the line of defence that he believes most advantageous to his client: it is the defendant who guides the

[1] Reggio Calabria court, *Ordinanza di rinvio a giudizio del processo contro Paolo De Stefano piú 59* (compiler: Dr. Cordova), 1978, p. 49 (this document henceforth: *Ordinanza . . . contro Paolo De Stefano piú 59*).

lawyer, requiring him to adopt a line that will serve the interests of the whole group.[2]

This incorporation of the defensive function into the group itself offers other advantages besides saving expense and increasing the overall security of the *cosca* and its undertakings. In particular, it makes the *cosca* more resistant to pressures brought to bear by the judicial authorities. *Cosca* members who are *not* facing criminal charges can keep a close eye on their accused colleagues, thanks to the defence lawyers—who pass on information in violation of the secrecy supposed to govern the proceedings. In this way the *cosca* can protect itself against the possibility that defendants may betray it, 'confess' or repent—and can also take steps to counter the moves of the authorities:

> In making sure that he has access to a particular, known defendant, the defence lawyer makes it his priority to avoid negative consequences for other, unknown accused parties whom he already in fact represents. His presence during the questioning of the defendant thus ceases to be simply an irrevocable right of the accused, and becomes a source of privileged information, through which the *cosca* gets to know the results of the preliminary investigations while these are still veiled in secrecy. Nor is this all. Not only can counsel for the defence convey to the outside world the nature of the charges, together with any indications the judge may give the defendant concerning the sources of the evidence; not only is he able to hear the defendant's statements (thus allowing those defendants who are not yet known, or who are in hiding, to prearrange alibis and plan their defence in accordance with what the first defendant has stated); he is also able to confront the defendant himself with an admonitory, and therefore intimidatory, presence—a reminder that whatever he may say will get back to the other members of the *cosca*.[3]

Thus it happens that all those taken into custody 'are led to name defence lawyers drawn from a single rather small group, while others are strictly excluded—evidently because they do not enjoy the same confidence.'[4] In the monopoly they exercise over the *need for legal defence*, the leading mafia *cosche* deploy a

---

[2] V. Macrí, 'Communicazione del giudice istruttore Vincenzo Macrí al convegno sulla mafia organizzato dal Consiglio Superiore della Magistrature' (conference paper), Castelgandolfo, 4–6 June 1982, pp. 3–4.
[3] Ibid., p. 4.
[4] Ibid.

powerful weapon, enabling them to bring pressure to bear on lawyers who prove insufficiently 'flexible', or are reluctant to 'fall into line'. Such lawyers risk finding themselves without clients and being excluded from the most important trials.

Because lawyers are becoming increasingly involved in the activities of the mafia groups, they are more and more frequently drawn into conflicts between *cosche*. Cases of murder and attempted murder have multiplied in recent years, and several members of the learned profession have been arrested and convicted thanks to their over-intimate identification with their clients' interests.[5] The two cases described by Macrí are significant in this connection:

> To limit our examples to the Reggio district, we might recall the case of the young lawyer retained as defence counsel by a well-known *mafioso*, who was in hiding and faced a murder charge. During the course of the trial, when it appeared that the defendant's position was in jeopardy, this lawyer actually gave up the defence and himself became a witness so as to put forward an alibi on the accused's behalf. In particular, the lawyer stated that on the day of the crime he had met the accused in Milan, during the morning (the murder took place that same evening, in the countryside of Gioiosa Jonica). But he was unable to give any reason why he had gone to Milan; he said that he had slept, not in a hotel (where his name would have been registered) but at a friend's house—whose whereabouts, naturally, he could not recall; and he also explained that, having gone to Milan by car, he had no rail or air ticket. The Assizes found the defendant guilty (obviously dismissing the lawyer's alibi), and criminal proceedings were started against counsel for the defence, who was charged with perjury.
>
> In another symbolically important case, a lawyer was brought to trial . . . on charges of altering the documents pertaining to a civil case pending in the magistrates' court at Melito Porto Salvo, so as to summons a well-known mafia boss to give evidence. The boss in question had been banned from residing in Calabria: the summons allowed him to return to Reggio, and—by way of various requests for adjournment—to remain thre for about a month (this was at the time of the local election campaign).[6]

Because of the massive interests at stake, criminal proceedings in mafia areas now have a completely changed atmosphere. Little

---

[5] See *Questa Calabria*, no. 54, 1978.
[6] Macrí, art. cit., p. 5.

or no time is given to learned legal exposition and displays of courtesy between prosecution and defence. In many southern Italian courtrooms, neither Latin phrases nor sonorous claptrap from textbooks of precedent are to be heard today:

> Things used to be different. The proceedings, to be honest, used to be a kind of play-acting, where the parties (just two groups—the lawyers and the judges) would try out their skills in a chivalric tournament, full of bows and curtsies and *Messieurs les anglais, tirez les premiers*.
>   . . . It was all decided between the lawyers and the judges. The defendants had nothing to do with it, they didn't count. And the *mafiosi* of those days couldn't follow all the technical aspects of a trial . . . Admittedly, they weren't at all interested. Besides, there was simply no need for the *mafiosi* themselves to 'get involved' at that stage, during the legal argument and the passing of sentence. They had already done what they had to do, outside the courtroom before the public trial began—intimidating and killing witnesses, getting rid of whatever might be used in evidence . . .
>   In mafia trials . . . you could predict the outcome. And the *mafiosi* themselves knew this better than anyone . . . It's true that the lawyers got excited, raised their voices, ran through their stock of rhetoric— but at bottom it was just a 'show', which hardly anyone bothers with nowadays. . . .[7]

Modern mafia trials are conducted in a spirit of dramatic and unyielding antagonism. The lawyers' oratory is sober and aggressive. The defendants are capable of understanding everything that goes on: they grasp each nuance of legal argument, sometimes suggesting what line the defence should take, and they weigh up how everyone is behaving. In trials where there is a large number of defendants, their shouts and applause punctuate the different phases of the hearing. On occasion they are able to influence the course of the session by threatening the judge and the (few) witnesses.

The close links between contemporary *mafiosi* and their lawyers sometimes find expression in gestures and signs, as the defendants on their bench (or 'in the dock') send messages across the courtroom to the seats of counsel for the defence. They are expressed, moreover, in the way the lawyers themselves speak. Not infrequently, one hears such phrases as: 'My learned friends,

[7] Interview no. 15.

the innocence of the accused proclaims itself as loudly as a shot from a Magnum 44!' or: 'If I were you, your honour, I would not refuse the request I am making much longer.'

Because of the economic importance of the modern mafia, much greater consequences attend the court's decision than used to be the case. An unwonted 'hitch' in the course of justice—due, perhaps, to the excessive zeal of an investigator, a judge's unusual 'rigidity', or the stubbornness of a witness—may decide the course of an entrepreneur's career, or upset a dominant position in the heroin business, and this may lead in turn to the loss of tens of thousands of millions of lire, the failure of a string of companies, and the sacking of numerous employees.

Such weighty economic interests now turn upon judicial sentences and police reports that it has on occasion been decided physically to eliminate the judge, police agent or *carabiniere* reponsible for some decision of crucial importance to the mafia group.

In their efforts to get the better of the judicial system, mafia groups have developed other tactics apart from simply murdering independently-minded agents of the State. One of the commonest is to submit expert medical and psychiatric reports, issued by favourably disposed professional consultants, which allow *mafiosi* to evade the judicial process:

> No prominent mafia boss is without his sheaf of impressive-looking medical documents, confirming that he suffers from very serious illnesses—illnesses that prevent him travelling to the place where he is supposed to be held in detention, or coping with the rigours of preventive imprisonment, or attending a court hearing. In most cases, the illnesses in question are either non-existent, or they are common ailments (such as arthritis, diabetes, or liver disorders) which suddenly become severe should they chance to afflict a representative of the mafia. Several mafia bosses have been suffering for years from incurable diseases, according to their medical certificates: we must expect their imminent demise . . . There are also frequent diagnoses of mental infirmity in respect of people who keep a close and canny eye on a whole range of interests spread right across Italy . . . Nor are different diagnoses made when the judges turn to experts living in the North: there, too, favourably disposed practitioners can be found, as numerous examples prove.[8]

8 Macrí, art. cit., p. 5.

A real 'market in expertise' has grown up around the courts. It is dominated by a few pre-eminent figures offering certificates and documents guaranteed to be 'scientific'—which sometimes depend on the rediscovery of out-of-the-way eighteenth-century ailments. We see this in the case of 'Ganzer's syndrome' (so-called), supposed to consist in a state of paranoia due to prolonged *simulation* of paranoia. In other words, a healthy person who feigns madness in order to get out of some unpleasant obligation (military service, a prison sentence, or whatever) may be struck down by this syndrome and go mad in earnest. The courts of southern Italy have heard a good deal of 'Ganzer's syndrome' lately, because the psychiatrist Aldo Semerari and his school diagnosed the condition in several mafia chiefs and leaders of the Neapolitan *camorra* : in April 1982, Semerari himself was killed by a *camorra* clan. In recent years, there has been less and less room for independently-minded technical and professional experts, as a climate of terror has been created by attacks, threats and murders whose victims have been those experts who have resisted the pressure of the mafia.

Mafia Tradition, Mafia Territory

As we saw in the previous chapter, mafia groups are groups of blood-relatives, relatives by marriage, and friends. Every mafia *cosca* has its framework of brothers, friends and clients. New entrants into a *cosca* find themselves involved at once in a far-reaching circuit of artificial kinship and marriage and client relationships, which may actually include several hundred people. This forms the basis of impressive networks of primary relationships, stretching across regional and national frontiers by way of the channels created by the emigration of southern Italians in the post-war years. Journalists and superficial researchers like to speak of 'world-wide organized crime', 'the terror industry' or 'the ruthless mafia network whose tentacles stretch into every continent and every country': very often, the reality underlying these phrases is simply a web of kinship relations and established dealings, linking together small core groups of blood relatives and fellow-citizens who come from quite identifiable areas, districts and villages in Calabria and Sicily. The Barbaro-Sergi-Trimboli clan is a case very much in point.

On 15 July 1977, Donald MacKay, a candidate for the Australian parliament, was murdered in the town of Griffith. MacKay had been running a campaign against the role of organized crime in drug-trafficking. The legal investigation that followed his death ended in 1979 with a report blaming his murder on a group of *mafiosi* who came originally from Platí, a commune of 3,800 souls in Reggio Calabria province. The *mafiosi* accused of the murder belonged to a federation of six *cosche*, headed by the Barbaro and Sergi families, which have members resident in Australia, in Platí, and in various regions of central and northern Italy. MacKay's campaign had been putting serious obstacles in the way of this mafia group's illegal activities, which were based on extensive cultivation of cannabis in three areas of New South Wales, and realised a net annual profit of up to sixty million dollars.

Further investigations carried out by the Italian police established that the members of the group in question, about a hundred people all told, had financed their Australian drug production with the proceeds of a series of kidnappings carried out in Italy over the previous few years. A proportion of the profits made from the Australian cannabis plantations was returned to Calabria, where it was reinvested both in the legitimate sector (in construction, tourism, and so on) and in additional, local cannabis plantations, discovered in various parts of the region between 1977 and 1980.

The impressive network needed to conduct an illegal business of such extensive economic and geographical scope was found to consist solely in the ordinary channels of communication between two groups of families and fellow-citizens resident in different places—telelphone calls, personal visits, occasional excursions organised by the local administration, and so on.

To get an idea of the extent of the 'web' of relations—at once of kinship and of common criminal purpose—spun by this Platí-based mafia group, we need only follow the reconstruction carried out by the *carabinieri* :

> The mafia organisation now existing in Platí . . . boasts links with the leading *cosche* in the whole province—in particular, with the Nirta family in S. Luca, the Cataldo family in Locri, the Morabito family in Africo, the Ursino family in Gioiosa Jonica, the Macrí family in Siderno and the D'Agostino family in Canolo-S. Ilario . . . The

running of the organization is shared almost equally between six *cosca* heads, who represent both the older and the younger generation, . . . and the group is held together by bonds formed through numerous marriages between its adherents . . . The Platí federation of *cosche* has a theatre of operations stretching into Lombardy, Piedmont and Lazio, as well as overseas (Australia, Canada, the U.S.A.), and including the most sophisticated and modern types of activity . . . Platí is the *casa madre* [the 'mother' or parent cell], and the *mafioso* feels a traditional link with the place, to which a proportion of capital for reinvestment accordingly flows—temporarily, at least, before financing fresh activities in a kind of perpetual motion. Platí is the nerve-centre . . . One proof of this . . . is that numerous banknotes from a series of kidnappings were found in a single day's checks carried out in banks and post offices of the Locri district by the deputy public prosecutor of Locri, Dr. Alberto Bambara: on 14 November 1975, notes were found that could be traced to the ransoms paid for Paul Getty, Bulgari, Madonia, Mazzotti, Cogna Vallino, D'Amico, Malabarba, Perfetti, Maffei and others . . . The group operates from, and meets at, the following bases:

In *Rome* : the *Bottegone del Risparmio*, a food supermarket run by Antonio D'Agostino; . . . the dwelling of Francesco Gentile, the son of the lawyer Giuseppe Gentile, who was killed on 11 December 1979: here Antonio Trichilo, a native of Platí and the cousin of Domenico Papalia, used to come; . . . the AOR supermarket in the via Sacchetti di Roma, run by Domenico Papalia, in whose possession were discovered cash-registers belonging to the *Bottegone del Risparmio* ; the *Archimede* bar-restaurant, in the Piazza Euclide, where Domenico Papalia met up with other Calabrians, and other members of the Roman mafia, and where the elimination of Antonio D'Agostino was planned and carried out.

In *Genoa* : where Domenico Papalia had formed a partnership with Antonio D'Agostino to set up another import-export agency similar to the one in S. Ilario Jonico.

In *Milan* : the dwelling of Gianni Della Rocca, husband of Domenico's sister Marianna Papalia: Antonio Trichilo, Domenico Papalia and Pino Barbaro chose this as their base of operations when they were planning the Ferrarini, Scoleri, Lazzaroni, Galli and Rambaldi kidnappings.

In *Volpiano* : the dwelling of Giuseppe Portolesi . . . where Giuseppe Crea had set up his base of operations for a series of vehicle thefts and number-plate falsifications.

In *Buccinasco* : the dairy . . . belonging to Francesco Trimboli: it was here that the Bergamo and Zogno *carabinieri*, in the course of their investigations into the Bolis kidnapping, found persons later identified as (among others) Michele and Salvatore Sergi, relatives of

Paolo Sergi; the dwelling of Rocco Papalia, Domenico's brother, where Domenico Barbaro, Francesco Trimboli and Francesco Molluso met to plan the details of the Bolis kidnapping and of other serious crimes.

At *Ponte S. Pietro* : the dwelling of Rosario Mittiga, where Domenico Barbaro and Paolino Sergi met up, . . . and which became the base of operations for the kidnapping.

At *S. Martino Siccomario* : the dwelling of Pasquale Crea, brother of Giuseppe and Rocco, who had made it their headquarters together with the convict Carlo Mignemi, from Catania.

In *Australia* : . . . the town of Griffith, where Donald MacKay was murdered on the orders of the Platí mafia . . . The towns of Michelago and Yelarbin. . . .[9]

It can be seen that the carrying on of the mafia's illegal activities depends absolutely on these kinship and friendship networks. Our studies of the kidnappings carried out from bases in Calabria during the last twelve years have led us to conclude that the existence of an effective, and geographically extensive, web of traditional primary allegiances was essential in the planning and execution of all the more important cases.

Where political terrorism relies on ideology, the mafia relies on the family, on kinship, and on primary affective bonds. In either case, we are dealing with groups of men who form a 'political community', characterized—according to Weber—[10] by its ability to call on its members at any moment to sacrifice their own lives or those of others: and it is this which assures that safe houses and reliable support will be available, that messages and communications can be transmitted, and that the group's activities will remain impermeable to the investigations of the police and the pressure of public opinion.

As well as belonging to a particular culture and a fabric of traditional institutions (even as his life-style and sphere of activities takes on a more cosmopolitan or 'universalist' pattern), the mafia entrepreneur also belongs to a particular *territory*. The *mafioso* of today is not just the product of a given culture; he also

[9] Reggio Calabria Carabinieri, *Legione Carabinieri di Catanzaro. Gruppo di Reggio Calabria. Associazione per delinquere a sfondo mafioso di 120 persone operanti nella fascia Sud del versante jonico della provincia di Reggio Calabria ed in altre del Nord e Centro Italia*, vol. 1, 1981, pp. 301–307.

[10] M. Weber, *Economy and Society*, ed. G. Roth and C. Wittich, Berkeley and London 1978, vol. 2, pp. 901–940.

remains tied to a given territory—a given area, district or village. Even if his influence on the affairs of his local area is nowadays usually limited to the spheres of economic life and local illicit activity, the mafia entrepreneur stakes out his territorial claims even more precisely than did the old-style mafia chief who exercised general powers of control over collective life:

> A landslip was blocking the main road in the hills above Bagnara. The State highways agency, ANAS, gave a company the contract for the removal of the obstructing material, and this company in turn subcontracted the job to some lorry drivers . . . One of these men set to work, but when he got halfway across a little bridge that spanned a mountain stream, he stopped and would go no further. Asked why, he explained that the far side of the stream was not his territory: from that point on, someone else should be given the work.[11]

In Reggio Calabria, the division of territorial powers between the various *cosche* has created a precise political geography of the mafia:

> Every village or town has its own *mafioso*, who is free to act much as he chooses within that area. Nobody can trespass in his area, just as he can't trespass in the areas reserved for other people . . . However there also exists a larger-scale territorial division, at a higher level, in which several *mafiosi* join up under the leadership of one bigger *mafioso*: through his subordinates, he then controls a larger area. In Reggio Calabria province, this large-scale division of territory is in the hands of three, maybe four leading *mafiosi*, who control fairly large areas of influence.[12]

The *larger-scale territorial division* to which this interviewee refers chiefly concerns the more extensive sectors of economic activity, both legal and illegal. We saw above that when the Gioia Tauro contracts were subdivided, each mafia group was allotted a share corresponding to its economic and military power. Similar territorial criteria are applied in large-scale hard drug trafficking: heroin dealing—which extends across very wide physical and economic spaces, and thus impinges on the territorial sovereignty of numerous mafia groups—requires agreements, treaties and

[11] Interview no. 17.
[12] Interview no. 13.

conventions entered into at the highest level. When two American police agents masquerading as dealers asked the *mafioso* Mammoliti to supply them with large amounts of heroin and cocaine, he explained that before a deal could be struck it would be necessary to obtain the 'confidence and sanction' of three people—the other two being don Mommo Piromalli and don Antonio Macrí, mafia chiefs respectively of the Tyrrhenian and Ionian parts of southern Calabria: 'if these two gave their assent, he had any amount of cocaine available; but when it came to heroin, he would have to get in touch with contacts overseas', in other words with 'his friend Paolo Violi, a well-known Italo-American *mafioso* resident in Toronto'.[13]

An up-to-date knowledge of mafia political geography is in-dispensable for anyone involved with the economic and social life of Italy's two southernmost regions. Entrepreneurs, magistrates, businessmen, investigators, politicians, terrorists, secret agents—if they are not precisely aware of the territorial divisions in force in a given area, they will all find themselves incurring very much heavier risks and expenses in the course of their activities. The Prattícò company, doing business in Polistena commune, 'took care to entrust the haulage work to so-called "local resources", which consisted—so the company assumed—in the Polistena haulage operators.' Despite this, the firm was the target of a series of damaging attacks (explosives were set off underneath the equipment they were using, and so on), and these grew so serious that it was decided to stop work. Since Prattícò had received no demands for money, and since they were not competing with any mafia firm, they were at a loss to understand these attacks. Eventually, the real reason came out: they had followed what looked like the correct procedure with regard to the local (mafia) resources,

> but—and of this the company were unaware—although the site fell within the Polistena administrative boundaries, it lay in the territory controlled by the mafia of Melicucco [a neighbouring commune]. Once they had discovered this fact, . . . Prattícò lost no time in complying with the rules . . . that govern relations in our province between companies and the mafia: they allotted the work to the Melicucco mafia chiefs, that is, to the Franconieri family. There is no

[13] Reggio Calabria court, *Sentenza del processo di I grado contro Paolo De Stefano più 59* (compiler: Dr. Giuseppe Tuccio), 1979, pp. 302–303.

need to add that the series of attacks came to a stop and did not resume.[14]

If ordinary city criminals or 'white collar crooks' simply underestimate the mafia's territorial powers, they too can end up paying a very high price. This happened to two men who carried out a robbery from the Reggio Calabria branch of the Calabria and Lucania *Cassa di Risparmio* (one of the robbers was employed as secretary to the committee for the allocation of council houses, presided over by the city's public prosecutor). Straight after the crime, these two were 'summoned' by the mafia bosses Giorgio and Paolo De Stefano, and obliged to pay out 98% of the enormous sum stolen (507 million lire at 1976 values), as a punishment for their failure to seek authorization in advance for this crime carried out in territory governed by the De Stefano *cosca*.[15]

To accomplish the full range of their illegal activities, *mafiosi* need both a territorial base and a network of traditional institutions: and these two requirements are interdependent, for the territorial safety of mafia power could not be guaranteed without the effective information-gathering and surveillance system operated by the locally-based group of relatives and friends. This is well illustrated by the example of the mountainous Aspromonte region in southern Calabria.

The Aspromonte is a time-honoured refuge of fugitives from justice. Until a few decades ago, its shepherds and peasants gave largely spontaneous welcome and protection to people on the run. The whole area—and especially the Ionian part of the Aspromonte itself—had a rebellious tradition of conflict with the State, so it was quite easy for outlaws, whether from the mafia or from some other background, to merge with the local population. As late as the 'fifties of the present century, the famous *mafioso*-brigand Musolino was able to spend many years in hiding in the woods and pastures of the Aspromonte, thanks to the active support he was given by the inhabitants.

The modern mafia fugitive cannot rely with equal confidence on general support and protection. Both the anti-State culture and the people who kept it alive have virtually disappeared from

---

[14] Ibid., pp. 66–67.
[15] Magistrature democratica, *Mafia e istituzioni*, Reggio Calabria, 1971, p. 91.

the Aspromonte, and their place has been taken by new social groups whose culture is far more uncertain and contradictory. Today's fugitive is thus obliged to turn for protection and support to the mafia *cosche* that dominate the various areas of the Aspromonte—protection and support that will cost him a good deal, whether in cash or (more commonly) in services rendered, such as keeping guard over kidnap victims or carrying out whatever attacks and murders his protectors may from time to time decide on. The power of the leading mafia families who control this mountainous terrain and obstruct the capture of the hundred or more outlaws hidden there is based on a capillary network of friends and relatives, many of whose members are State employees: 'It is surprising,' noted judge Cordova, 'to see how many suspected persons are taken on by the public agencies responsible for forestry and nature conservation.'[16] We noted in our discussion of the Nirta group that members of mafia *cosche* have been made *caposquadra*, or foremen of gangs, in the State forestry service—a practice denounced by Marcello Minasi, a judge on the Reggio Calabria bench, at the conference of democratic magistrates held in Palermo in 1980:

> Many of these *caposquadra* are appointed simply on the written recommendation of political or religious figures, and some of them have turned out to be members of mafia *cosche* and families. This has more serious consequences than might at first appear: it is true that the *caposquadra* do no more than carry out the tasks assigned to them, but as well as keeping 'order'—mafia order—in the mountainous and isolated areas where they work, they are also issued with two-way radios, required for operational reasons. They are thus able to set up, at State expense, a first-rate surveillance network to keep watch on the police forces searching for fugitives. The fugitives are informed and warned in good time of every move the police make.[17]

Conclusion: the War of Each Against All

Cultural traditionalism and a sense of his territorial roots help to form the *mafioso* both economically and anthropologically, without coming into conflict with the cosmopolitan or 'universalist'

[16] *Ordinanza . . . contro Paolo De Stefano più 59*, p. 30.
[17] Magistrature democratica, op. cit., p. 92.

character of his lifestyle and aspirations. A good example of this coexistence of apparent opposites is the behaviour of Saro Mammoliti, the *mafioso* 'playboy': at home among the international criminal fraternity, Mammoliti—on the run at the time— nonetheless celebrated his marriage, to a local woman, in the parish church of his own village.

During a whole phase of the entrepreneurial mafia's development, its activities both legal and illegal have benefited from the *mafioso*'s close links with his local territory and its culture. Once his identification with market forces had led him to acquire monopoly positions in commerce and small industry, the *mafioso* deployed an instrument of great economic power in the sovereignty he exercised over a particular territory and in the willingness of his kinsmen and relatives to stake their own lives, and those of others, in support of whatever he undertook. The phenomenon of the mafia has regained a dominant place in the economic and political life of the *Mezzogiorno*, and of Italy, just because these classic features of mafia power have been turned to exclusively economic ends. The young men of honour born during the 'forties and 'fifties no longer aspire to concrete, limited powers of territorial and social control; they seek an economic power that is abstract and limitless.

However, it is precisely this commitment to market logic as the fundamental basis of mafia activity that has turned the *mafioso*'s territorial and cultural bonds into chains constricting the free expansion of his dealings as an entrepreneur. As the mafia accumulates capital, territorial monopolies over particular kinds of economic activity become more and more of a straitjacket. To ensure expanded reproduction of his capital, through investments which rapidly increase previous levels of activity, the *mafioso*-entrepreneur finds himself under the *permanent necessity* of encroaching on areas controlled by others. Continual conflict thus becomes inevitable, and mafia accumulation clashes with the territorial bases of mafia power itself.

Battles over territorial monopoly were one of the classic forms taken by the long-term power-struggles of the traditional mafia. Every twenty or twenty-five years, the balance of power between the various mafia groups was put to the test. The settling of accounts involved violent conflicts, arising from territorial disputes combined with more general issues of supremacy and prestige. Trespassing, fraud and breaches of territorial sovereignty would lead—if they became too frequent, and if enough families were involved—to out-and-out wars, which served to establish a new medium- or long-term equilibrium.

However, participation in these wars depended on a kind of Darwinian selection: the contending parties had to be aggressive, fierce, cunning, and so on. In consequence, they did obey a crude underlying mechanism of generational succession, which saw younger *mafiosi* rise while their elders fell. Thus the so-called 'struggle between the old mafia and the new' would take place, periodically though not at any predictable interval.[18] War and slaughter could even sometimes be avoided, if the supremacy of particular individuals or groups was acknowledged by their rivals, and if the latter were prepared to cede sovereignty peacefully.

But now that the mafia's activities obey forces tending towards a ceaseless territorial expansion of power, this balance of generational succession has been disturbed, and continual conflict between *mafiosi* has become inevitable. Many mafia entrepreneurs, embarked on apparently brilliant careers, have fallen fatally at this hurdle. The De Stefano brothers are a typical case in point. Having won a monopoly of construction work in northern Reggio Calabria, driving out the rival Tripodio group of mafia entrepreneurs from the market for contracts (with the support of the Piromalli and Mammoliti *cosche*), the De Stefano *cosca* climbed to the very peaks of mafia power and prestige:

. . . Until very recently, the names of the brothers Giorgio and Paolo De Stefano were on everyone's lips, and never out of the papers. In fact the two brothers, emboldened by the success they had achieved and confident of the support of their allies in high places, . . . had widened the scope of their interests to an extraordinary degree, seeking to extend their sphere of activities over the whole of Italy, and embarking on new and highly profitable ventures. . . .[19]

[18] The judge G. Lo Schiavo notes, in his brief study of the vicissitudes of the Monreale mafia (near Palermo) from the second half of the nineteenth century up to the second world war, that the first conflict between older and younger members of local mafia groups took place in 1872, with the struggle between the *giardinieri* ('gardeners') and the *stuppagghiara* (a name derived from the Sicilian word *stuppagghiu*, a cork or stopper). See G. G. Lo Schiavo, *100 anni di mafia*, Rome 1962, pp. 145–148.

[19] Reggio Calabria police headquarters, *Rapporto giudiziaro di denuncia n. 1780/E/Mobile a carico di Paolo De Stefano e di altri 59 mafiosi*, 1978, pp. 35–36.

The De Stefano brothers then tried to turn their accumulated profits and power to account by staking a claim in the struggle for contracts for the Gioia Tauro port: the resulting clash with the Piromalli group, whose monopoly this was, half destroyed the De Stefano *cosca* and left its leader dead.

Nor should we forget another point. The mafia firm's superiority over its rivals, deriving from the three competitive advantages discussed in chapter 4, ceases to exist once it comes up against another mafia-type firm—which enjoys the same advantages. In the clash that follows, the deciding factor is not productive efficiency but coercive power. Of the 244 mafia-type murders committed in Calabria between 1970 and 1979, some 176 (over 70 per cent) arose from conflicts among mafia groups; and of these 176, at least 141 can be traced back to clashes between mafia familes/enterprises struggling for economic and territorial supremacy.[20]

Thus mafia-type entrepreneurial activity is not constrained only by the imbalance between the rapid pace of capital accumulation and the restrictive narrowness of territorial markets. It is also limited by the particular cultural background of the *mafiosi* themselves, which tends to transform impersonal market confrontations into personal antagonisms. Traditionalism and entrepreneurial values are proving to form a most explosive mixture. Economic conflict between two firms or enterprises—whose results, in other contexts, are confined to the sphere of production and distribution—here becomes a conflict between two sovereign *political communities*, which soon escalates to war between families and clans, involving tens and even hundreds of relatives, friends and clients. One of the oldest forms of conflict, the blood-feud, which seemed until recently to have disappeared along with the most backward cultural legacies, has made a bloody comeback during the 1970s, its destructive power undiminished: in Calabria alone, feuds and vendettas claimed 166 lives in the decade 1970–1979, many of the victims children, women and old people. Conflicts of this type are now exacerbated and multiplied by the power of the mafia—which once used to hold them in check: districts and areas with a high incidence of mafia murders

[20] *Indagine statistica sugli omicidi avvenuti in Calabria dal 1950 in poi*, edited by P. Arlacchi and A. Tucci, University of Calabria, Dept. of Sociology, 1978–1982. See also A. Padalino, 'Calabria. Une regione che uccide', in *Panorama*, 7 July 1980.

also show the highest levels of feuds and vendettas.[21]

The rise of the entrepreneurial mafia has culminated in a veritable war of each against all, which has its own killed, wounded, and missing in action. This war has cost over 700 lives in Calabria and Sicily between 1970 and the end of 1982. Mafia murders have reached such a high level, and have become so ostentatious in their symbolic meaning (as *propaganda*), that the phenomenon can no longer be dismissed with the old phrase, 'After all, they're only killing each other off'. Indeed, one leading result of research undertaken into the mafia at the University of Calabria has been the discovery of a very acute state of socio-cultural disintegration produced by mafia murders.

Once they exceed a certain level, in fact, mafia murders begin to develop a powerful *multiplier effect*, which has devastating consequences for the structure of society. The mechanism by which mafia murder sparks off other murders (often quite remote in nature and in motive) is not based on any superifical imitation; it derives from a range of socio-psychological tendencies deeply rooted in collective and individual life. When murders happen again and again, within a particular, limited social and territorial context (over 300 killings—more than 25 per cent of the total for the whole of Calabria—took place between 1970 and 1982 in just five communes of Reggio Calabria province), and when it is clear that their perpetrators are going unpunished, then the social and cultural barriers that make killing taboo are gradually beaten down.

When the risks and costs of murder are regarded as common-place and insignificant, people begin to feel that they too may well end up killing or being killed. This greatly exacerbates the sense of rootlessness and sociocultural disintegration, felt especially by certain particularly sensitive segments of the population (the young unemployed, for instance). In some cases, whole groups of people have even fled, in a kind of centrifugal mass emigration— in Cimina, for example, a Calabrian town in the Ionian part of Reggio province, where a feud between two groups of mafia families and their relatives led to 35 deaths and 16 injuries in little more than a decade, where the local community virtually fell apart,and where more than two-thirds of the inhabitants left:

---

[21] A. Tucci, 'Mafia e omicidi in Calabria: 1970–1981', in *Gangsters a Cosenza* (by various authors), Cosenza 1982, pp. 191–193.

from a figure of some 2,000 at the start of the feud, the population has now fallen to around 500. And in S. Luca, a township in the foothills of the Aspromonte, the people

> are afraid to stay, afraid to come and go, afraid to work. Recent outrages have included the attempted murder of the secretary of the local branch of the Italian communist party; the burning of many private cars; bomb attacks on three homes and on the employment bureau; an arson attack on the main gate of the town hall; the sending of threatening letters to many of the inhabitants; extortion against local traders; and burglaries from private houses, from stall-holders at the Friday market, and from food suppliers. Nor is that all: the pharmacist has been frightened into closing his shop for more than a month; the doctors want to leave; and nobody wants to come and teach in the town's primary and secondary schools.[22]

The progressive social and institutional disruption that has accompanied the growth of the entrepreneurial mafia is now destroying even those few powers of self-regulation still possessed by the mafia world itself. Alliances are becoming more and more precarious, demarcation lines are becoming fluid and unstable, and the rhythm of conflict speeds up all the time. Competition between mafia groups grows more and more fragmented and atomistic, as the groups seem to shut themselves off in impenetrable isolation from the outside world and it becomes impossible to foretell how they will proliferate or who they will turn against. The 'great Sicilian war' has been going on for two years as these words are written: in its opening phases, it seemed to present a picture of rigid alliances and clear-cut rivalries, but it has since become a confused guerrilla struggle, with 'groups and men of uncertain allegiance, traitors and betrayals both real and feigned, and some chiefs rising while other bosses fall'.[23]

In conclusion: because the sphere of traditional institutions and modes of behaviour has remained to some extent in being alongside the modern, objective rationality of the market, the *mafioso*-entrepreneur has been able to expand the scope of his undertakings until he stands on the verge of breaking into large-scale manufacturing industry. Making shrewd use of the special

[22] Italian Communist Party, *Rapporto della delegazione parlamentare del PCI sul fenomeno mafioso in Calabria*, 13–15 November 1976, pp. 6–7.
[23] See *L'Ora*, 21 August 1982.

characteristics of his own culture, he has created a novel form of accumulation: mafia capital accumulation. To break out of these confines, however, this accumulation must become accumulation *tout court*—which entails an abandonment alike of traditionalism and of territorial roots. Here, Weber's admonitory comment still holds good: if extraordinary capital accumulation calls into play certain traditional, archaic cultural and personal qualities— predatory instincts, the use of violence, small-group loyalties, boldness, and so on—*ordinary* capital accumulation depends on 'formally peaceful probabilities of gain'.

7.

The Political Autonomy
of Mafia Power

The Growth of Political Competition

All struggle and competition on the social and economic plane
leads in the long run (Weber wrote in *Economy and Society*) to
the 'selection' of those best endowed with the personal qualities
needed for victory in the struggle. However, these qualities are
not given once and for all. In one situation, one set of attributes
will triumph at the expense of others: in another, the opposite
will happen:

> What qualities are important depends on the conditions in which the
> conflict or competition takes place. It may be a matter of physical
> strength or unscrupulous cunning . . . of creative originality, or of
> adaptability, of qualities which are unusual, or of those which are
> possessed by the mediocre majority. *Among* the decisive conditions
> . . . belong the *systems of order* to which the behaviour of the parties
> is oriented.[1]

Hitherto, we have attempted to single out the factors underlying the evident competitive advantage enjoyed by mafia firms
operating in the market. To make the picture more complete, we
must extend this analysis to the 'systems or order' governing
competition. In other words, we must ask which politico-
institutional changes have played the biggest role—along with

[1] M. Weber, *Economy and Society*, ed. G. Roth and C. Wittich, Berkeley and
London 1978, Vol. 1, pp. 38–39.

the crisis of the State's monopoly of violence—in the development of the mafia's power during the 1970s and 1980s.

What influences have such changes had on the phenomenon of the mafia, and what influences has it had on them? In attempting to answer this question, we must take account of two parallel phenomena—developments in 'systems of order' in general, and in the particular political character of the mafia presence: the *growth of political competition* on one hand, and the growing *autonomy of mafia power* on the other.

One marked feature of the Italian experience in the 1970s and 1980s was the intensification of competition and conflict at all levels—national, regional and local—within the country's major political power groupings. During this period, the government became less and less able to act as a coherent whole, and found itself paralysed by the proliferation of centres of power, whether institutional, quasi-institutional or illegal. The Italian political system grew ever more complex, eventually fragmenting into various constituent parts as the creation of regional parliaments led to administrative decentralization, and economic development transformed large areas that had formerly been subordinate and peripheral. Pressure groups, tendencies, lobbies, and factions of all kinds multiplied in the absence of any principle of institutional regulation capable of channelling the forces produced by social change into some wider system of conflict or consensus. In the *Mezzogiorno*, the institutional disintegration of the 1970s and 1980s took the form of a crisis in the way public resources were redistributed. From 1950 until the late 'sixties, the massive transfer of resources carried out by the central authorities of the *Mezzogiorno* remained firmly under the control of a stratum of political intermediaries, similar in type to the 'broker capitalists' of anthropological literature.[2] In the second part of the present work, we analysed the changes brought about by the Palermo *fanfaniani* in the context of Sicilian politics—changes set in motion during the early 'fifties on the basis, precisely, of the group's control over the island's public spending.

This elite of *mediators* was different from the class of petty bourgeois intellectuals who mediated consensus in the *Mezzo-*

---

[2] Boissevain, *Friends of Friends. Networks, Manipulations and Coalitions,* Oxford 1974; E. R. Wolf, 'Kinship, Friendship and Patron Client Relations in Complex Societies', in M. Banton, *The Social Anthropology of Complex Societies,* London 1966.

giorno described by Gramsci and Salvemini. It retained no vestige of autonomy in its dealings with the central power; in fact, its strength derived from its direct link with national political power.[3] Intermediaries of this kind no longer drew legitimacy from their authority as *patrons* in a clientelistic system, with their own relatively independent possessions and resources; they depended, rather, on their ability to control the flow of public money from the centre and regulate its distribution in the peripheral economy. The political mediators of the South gathered at all the major junctions of State intervention, where their activities brought them not only power but also considerable wealth and money. They made their fortunes within the margin between two sets of prices—those budgeted for by the State when it made investments in the *Mezzogiorno* and transferred resources there, and those actually paid when the investments and transfers were made operative.

This close control of the channels of State aid by professional politicians, together with their control over two of the most important markets (credit and construction) in the economy of the South, allowed a compact system of power to be built up which lasted more or less intact until the early 'seventies. Virtually every region of southern Italy came to be governed by one or two 'big mediators', possessed of seemingly unlimited powers and redistributive authority in areas such as the allocation of public-sector jobs and the granting of credits, contracts, licences, loans, pensions, and so on. This was the golden age of modern political clientelism in the *Mezzogiorno*, and these powerful mediators—the Gava family in the Campania, the Colombo family in the Basilicata, the Mancini and Misasi families in Calabria, the Lauricella family and the *fanfaniani* in Sicily— were its symbolic representatives.[4]

But since this system of mediators depended on a continuous and expanding transfer of resources, without which it could not last, its very premiss foreshadowed the coming crisis of the 'seventies. By the late 'sixties, it was already becoming evident

[3] Gribaudi, *Mediatori. Antropologia del potere democristiano nel Mezzogiorno*, Turin 1980.
[4] P. A. Allum, *Potere e società a Napoli nel dopoguerra*, Turin 1973; L. Sacco, *Il cimento del potere*, Bari 1981; G. Graziano ed., *Clientelismo e mutamento politico*, Milan 1974.

that a distended and hyperactive public sector had grown up as a result of the mediators' need to widen the network of clients on which their power was based. This was the origin of what has been called the *inflationary-clientelistic* process, which continued to develop and expand all through the 'seventies, and which consisted in a growing disequilibrium between the quantity of resources actually available for distribution, on the one hand, and the expectations of clients and the profits needed by patrons on the other—profits that must be distributed as largesse if the mediators were to retain the loyalty of their followers.[5] 'The power elite was thus rent by struggles over the division of scarce resources . . . and both its relations with the mass of the people and its electoral legitimation were put in jeopardy.'[6] As competition intensified among the various coalitions within each of the parties of government, there was less and less space for outside influences. Until the 'sixties, reference had been made to large-scale class and sectional interests, and alliances and strategies had been broadly based; but all this gradually gave way to an ever more bitter struggle for ever narrower goals, conducted more and more exclusively within the small groups themselves. In the space of not much over a decade, between the late 'sixties and the early 'eighties, the three leading lobbies or tendencies within the Calabrian Christian Democratic party alone proliferated into twelve groupings, whose relations shifted constantly from one set of alliances and antagonisms to the next.[7]

This intensification of political competition in the context of scarce resources had one crucial consequence in terms of our analysis: even the smallest increment of power took on a higher value. Where numerous more or less equally-matched rivals are in contention, to gain any kind of advantage may have far-reaching consequences. In such a situation, alliance with a stable and secure pressure-group—a mafia family, for instance, or a federation of mafia families—is a very profitable electoral and political investment. For, thanks to the kind of business their members are involved in, the leading mafia *cosche* of Calabria and Sicily today possess an *autonomous* clientele following, and autonomous

---

[5] M. Caciagli, *Democrazia Cristiana e potere nel Mezzogiorno. Il sistema democristiano a Catania*, Florence 1978, pp. 311–312.

[6] Gribaudi, op. cit., p. 168.

[7] P. Guzzanti, 'Viaggio nella DC calabrese tra figli, padri e padroni', in *La Republica*, 18 September 1981.

power bases, of their own. The activities of the mafia of Ionian Calabria, which has specialized in kidnappings for ransom (their victims being drawn from the local leisured class and the north Italian industrial bourgeoisie), have given birth to a murderous *criminal economy*, from which a not inconsiderable sector of the population now benefits either directly or indirectly: several thousand people are involved at various levels—as organizers and informers, owners or caretakers of safe houses, guards, telephonists, nurses and drivers, in the recycling of ransom money, and so on. They constitute a growing group of real importance in collective life, which represents a reliable tranche of votes at the disposal of mafia candidates.

Similar economic networks, capable of ready transformation into significant electoral machines and political pressure groups, exist in Tyrrhenian Calabria (where the mafia is busily reinvesting its illegal profits—in construction, commerce, and other sectors) and in western Sicily (where mafia groups control the distribution of heroin along the complex and extensive channels of the southern Italian domestic markets).

If on top of this we also take into account the growing average size and overall membership of mafia families/firms—and there has been a steady increase over the last ten or fifteen years[8]— then we can begin to appreciate the opportunities for independent political influence which mafia groups now have. In Reggio Calabria province, the chief mafia *cosche* each have between thirty and eighty adult male members. Given the economic activity which the head of each mafia family controls on his own account, and the client networks over which he presides, the leading mafia group in a particular commune may exert its electoral influence over as many as 30 per cent of those entitled to vote, in the smallest districts; in larger districts, the figure will be 10–15 per cent.

The Political Autonomy of Mafia Power

The growth of the mafia's power in the political arena during the 'seventies and 'eighties is connected, as we have seen, with changes in the institutional context (in the *Mezzogiorno* and in

[8] Cf. chapter 5, above.

Italy as a whole), and especially with the increased importance, within that context, of small power-groups locked in mutual rivalry. However, the mafia's increased political power cannot be seen as a passive by-product of institutional disintegration, for the disintegration itself has been a consequence as much as a cause of the rise of the entrepreneurial mafia. The *political autonomy* of mafia power, a salient feature of the present situation, also represents a departure from the traditional model of relations between the mafia and the political world.

Mafia entrepreneurs know full well that they hold a good share of regional economic power, and constitute a largely autonomous economic force. For all their conflicts with part of the State apparatus and with non-mafia elements in the entrepreneurial elite, they feel themselves to be members of the ruling class, and have come to realise that their needs require appropriate political expression. The rise of the entrepreneurial mafia has done away with the old subordination of the local *mafioso* to the government's political representatives. In his dealings with the world beyond his own zone of influence, the mafia chief no longer seeks the mediation of the local member of parliament or government under-secretary; he acts for himself, directly and immediately. As the *mafiosi*-entrepreneurs have increased in power and widened their spheres of influence, they have entered into direct relations with a whole extensive illegal or semi-legal sector of the State apparatus, as well as with the political and administrative personnel responsible for southern Italy and its regions.

Giorgio De Stefano, Saverio Mammoliti and Gerolamo Piromalli were all found to possess the number of the Presidential telephone exchange, and a string of other numbers—those of various Ministerial offices and of the Appeal Court. Dozens of officials employed by the *Cassa per il Mezzogiorno* have been found guilty—along with many members of its Board of Governors—of administrative irregularities, from which mafia firms and big construction companies have benefited (examples include the Belice valley scandal and the 'golden dams' affair).

The style in which relations between *mafiosi* and politicians are conducted has altered, too, as the power of the former has grown. As the document reproduced overleaf shows, *mafiosi* no longer always go to call on their protectors: the protectors may make tiring journeys by sea in order to visit the *mafiosi*. The autonomy of the mafia's political power is expressed in two principal ways:

a) the development of a *mafia political lobby*, which has cemented relations of mutual economic interest between mafia leaders, political leaders, and sectors of the local and national economic and financial establishment; b) the development by mafia groups of their own, *internal* political representation: through this *internalization*, those within—or closely linked to—mafia groups now themselves seek political office.

Mafia political lobbies have become powerful competitors for supremacy in the world of government and the State. In order to consolidate and extend their power, they are quite ready to use threats, blackmail and even murder. In establishing a foothold in the world of State power, the mafia has been crucially aided by the alliances it has made with large companies engaged in public works contracts (described in the present study). The Gioia Tauro 'affair'—the building of the industrial port and the 'V' steelworks—brought to light many of the intermeshed relations and common interests that make up these lobbies. There was a bitter struggle between two competing groups: on the one hand, the mafia entrepreneurs, the large firms that won the contracts, the public agencies responsible for awarding these contracts (ASI and CASMEZ), and the Minister for the *Mezzogiorno*; on the other, a rival lobby comprising a publicly-owned entrepreneurial group, ITALSTAT, headed by the ministry responsible for State participation, supported by the mass-circulation press and represented by the Minister for Industry. In the course of this struggle, it became clear that the local mafia elites had extremely close ties with the most aggressive interest-groups in national political and economic life. A second crucial means by which mafia power has taken its place in the national political elite has been the alliance struck between the most powerful mafia groups and certain sections of national and international finance capital. The *chef d'oeuvre* of the lawyer Sindona* consisted precisely in the opening up of a channel of communication between the legal financial circuit and the circuit of illegally accumulated capital. Before the 1970s, no organic links existed between the two. The first step

---

* *Michele Sindona* : This Sicilian financier had close links with various local and American mafia groups, and was related politically to Giulio Andreotti, the Christian Democratic politician. After the collapse of his Franklin National Bank he was arrested in the USA. In Italy he was charged with the premeditated murder of the liquidator of the Banca Privata Italiana, which was also owned by him and also collapsed in 1974.

ALL'ILL/MO SIG.S.PROCURATORE DELLA REPUBBLICA
Dott.FRANCESCO Colicchia

REGGIO CALABRIA

_-'-'-'-_

Il giorno I.6.1973 verso le ore I2,30,ormeggiata
a questo molo "La Reale" il motoscafo "Olimpia C",matricola
P.T. 702,di proprietà dell'Ingegnere CHERCHI Guido,nato a
Sassari il I8.6.I922,ivi residente,presidente dell'Ordine
degli Ingegneri.

Oltre al proprietario ne discendevano:

-Dott. SECHI Pietro,sostituto Procuratore della Repubblica di Sassari;

-Dott.CAFARI Vincenzo,segretario del sottosegretario
del Ministero per la Cassa del Mezzogiorno,nato a Ferruzzano
(RC) il I.4.I933,residente a Roma;

-Dott.CHESSA Antonio,segretario del Sottosegretario del
Ministero dell'Agricoltura e Foreste,nato a Sassari l'8.6.I926,
ivi residente,ma di fatto domiciliato a Roma.

Da riservati accertamenti è risultato che i predetti
il giorno precedente avevano richiesto al Questore di Sassari
il motoscafo della Polmare per potersi recare all'Asinara,ma
questo non gli era stato concesso.

Poco dopo il loro arrivo sopraggiungevano i soggiornanti
calabresi Scriva Salvatore,Tripodi Giuseppe e Rugolo Francesco,
che manifestavano verso i quattro cordialità,in principalmodo
verso il CAFARI Vincenzo.

Li invitavano quindi a seguirli nella loro abitazione,
ove si trattenevano fino ad oltre le ore I5,30.-E' voce
diffusa che abbiano consumato il pranzo insieme.

Al momento di partire,date le avverse condizioni
atmosferiche,trovavano ospitalità a Cala D'Oliva presso
la foresteria della Direzione della Casa di Lavoro allo
Aperto ove consumavano la cena.

Durante la permanenza in Cala d'Oliva il Cafari
affermò tra l'altro che lo Scriva Salvatore si trovava
all'Asinara per un errore,che apparteneva a famiglia per
bene e che trattavasi di brava persona.

I quattro lasciavano l'Isola alle ore 7 circa del
giorno successivo,dopo avere sorbito un caffè nell'allog-
gio dei soggiornanti suddetti.-

IL BRIGADIERE
COMANDANTE DELLA STAZIONE
Pasquale Lubinu-

TO: Dr Francesco Colicchia, Public Prosecutor
REGGIO CALABRIA

FROM: Commanding officer, 'Pasquale Lubinu'
carabinieri station [on the island of Asinara, off north-
western Sardinia: the island is a place of detention for
criminals].
On 1 June 1973, towards 1230 hours, the motor vessel
Olimpia C moored here, at La Reale pier. The vessel
bears licence no. P.T. 702, and is the property of Guido
Cerchi, engineer, President of the Order of Engineers,
born in Sassari on 18 June 1922, and presently resident
there.
   In addition to the owner, the following persons
disembarked:
   —Dr Pietro Sechi, deputy Public Prosecutor at Sassari;
   —Dr Vincenzo Cafari, secretary to the under-
secretary of the Minister for the *Cassa per il
Mezzogiorno*, born at Ferruzano (Reggio Calabria
province) on 1 April 1933, and resident at Rome;
   —Dr Antonio Chessa, secretary to the under-
secretary of the Minister of Agriculture and Forestry,
born at Sassari on 8 June 1926, and nominally resident
there, though living in fact at Rome.
   Subsequent investigations revealed that the
above-named persons had on the previous day requested
permission from the Sassari police-chief to use the
Polmare motor-launch to travel to Asinara; but this had
not been granted.
   Shortly after their arrival, they met up with the
following detainees from Calabria: Salvatore Scriva,
Giuseppe Tripodi and Francesco Rugolo. These three
seemed on cordial terms with the four visitors, and in
particular with Vincenzo Cafari.
   They then invited the visitors to accompany them to
their dwelling, where they remained until 1530 hours.
It is said that they all ate lunch together.
   They were about to depart when, on account of the
poor weather, they sought hospitality at Cala D'Oliva [in
the more northern part of Asinara], in the guest-rooms
belonging to the Directorate of the Outdoor Labour
Agency, where they dined.

> While at Cala D'Oliva, Cafari declared—among other
> things—that Salvatore Scriva was only on Asinara
> because of a mistake, that he came from a good family,
> and that he was a fine person.
> The four left the island at about 0700 hours next day,
> after drinking a cup of coffee in the lodgings of the
> above-mentioned detainees.

towards unifying the mafia financial market, based in Sicily, with the legitimate national financial market was taken by Sidona in the early 'seventies, when he launched a speculative drive aimed at the Interfinanziaria Spa company. This speculative manoeuvre also involved many entirely 'clean' savers and businessmen, who helped increase its scope:

> Interfinanziaria Spa, whose headquarters were in Milan, . . . had succeeded in opening up more than twenty branches in Agrigento province . . . Quite suddenly, the mafia—both old and new—began to take an interest, and set about attracting deposits: there was an absolute savings boom, as money poured in from emigrants, from former property-owners, and from small- and medium-scale landed proprietors. Attracted both by the high rate of interest paid (more than double what other banks were offering) and by promises of employment in the company's branches, investors deposited more than four and a half thousand million lire with the bank in a short space of time. One leading proof that Interfinanziaria was directly connected with the mafia is that almost every employee taken on (and many of them lacked necessary qualifications and educational attainments) was the son or other close relative of some representative of the local mafia.[9]

Following the collapse of 'operation Interfinanziaria Spa', it was the Alamia-Ciancimino group that took over the task of forging links between mafia money capital and the chief centres of Italian finance capital. This group—with Sindona's continuing collaboration—set about launching a string of financial companies: these included Venchi-Unica, which had an operating capital of over 70,000 million lire in 1978.[10]

This alliance with the most adventuristic elements in the world of Italian high finance took the mafia within the space of a few

---

[9] Anti-mafia Commission, *Commissione parlamentare d'inchiesta sul fenomeno della mafia in Sicilia*, vols. I, II, III, IV, Rome. Tipografia del Senato, doc. XXIII, no. 2, p. 608.

[10] *L'Espresso*, no. 34, 1978; *La Repubblica*, 5 April 1979.

years into the heart of national political power. The Administrative Secretary of the Christian Democratic Party, Filippo Micheli, has stated that the party controlled two companies, based overseas (at Vaduz), which he himself directly managed. These companies dealt in securities and on the exchange market, and Sindona was closely involved with them; their profits were turned over to the Christian Democrats.

> If it is true, as a mass of evidence now seems to confirm, that Sindona was engaged in recycling mafia money and had links with the leading circles of the Sicilian-American mafia, then we have the word of the Christian Democrats' own Administrative Secretary that the party has been in business partnership with the mafia. And that is a far cry from simply claiming that some Sicilian politicians are in cahoots with the mafia.[11]

The nature of relations between the mafia and the world of politics has also been changed at regional and district level thanks to the joint management of common economic interests by political leaders and mafia bosses. Well-known *mafiosi* have gone into partnership with well-known politicians (behind the cover, often, of men of straw) to run a host of businesses—building societies and finance companies, life assurance agencies, industrial and agricultural firms, investments in tourism and hotels. Small and medium-sized mafia political lobbies have sprung up across Sicily and Calabria, and in other regions too; and this has caused a visible alteration in the way public power is exercised and in the functioning of elected assemblies. The number of administrators and public officials working in mafia areas who have been charged with or found guilty of offences connected with the discharge of their duties now runs into hundreds. In the 1980 communal and provincial elections in western Sicily, a good proportion of those candidates who had held executive office in the previous assemblies actually had criminal records:

> Among these doubtfully-qualified administrative officials, place of honour must go to an associate of the ex-mayor Vito Ciancimino. This worthy communal councillor, Francesco Paolo Alamia by name, had

---

[11] Sindona himself confirmed that he was indeed in relations with the Christian Democrats in a television interview subsequently published in *La Repubblica*, 8 October 1982. See E. Biagi and E. Scalfari, *Come andiamo ad incominciare*, 1981.

only been released a few months earlier from his prison cell in Turin . . . At Palermo, Alamia's friend and colleague Salvatore Castro ('Totuccio' to his friends), a loyal supporter—naturally—of the Christian Democrat, Ruffini, was sentenced to seven months imprisonment and barred from public office for eight months: as the councillor responsible for traffic, he had let his friends off paying their fines, and had also slandered the police commander. Next comes the outgoing mayor, Salvatore Mantione, indicted by the Public Prosecutor on a charge of polluting the sea on the Palermo shoreline. We must not leave out another council member, Giuseppe Cascio, also a Christian Democrat, who headed the Estates Department and became the subject of inquiries owing to his habit of paying two lots of rent at the same time on the same building . . . A place of honour must surely be kept, too, for the former Provincial President, Gaspare Giganti: he is currently out on remand, awaiting prosecution on charges relating to a fraudulent highway maintenance contract, in which he is alleged to have interfered with the bidding in pursuit of personal gain and to have deliberately given false information. Another Christian Democrat administrator, councillor Sisto Merulla of the tax department, has also fallen foul of the law: together with a former departmental head, he was sentenced last March to three years' imprisonment, and barred for five years from holding public office, for giving a local government contract to a firm on the point of going bankrupt. The ex-mayor, Giacomo Marchello (one of the 'Fanfani group'), faced a similar fate but was acquitted for lack of evidence. The list may be fittingly closed with the name of Salvo Lima, one of the bosses of Palermo Christian Democracy—former mayor, former member of the Italian parliament, and today an MEP. For ten years, the judicial authorities have been awaiting authorization to bring charges against Lima for offences ranging from the pursuit of personal gain to the dereliction of official duties.[12]

The appearance of so many convicted criminals in the ranks of the people's representatives has led to a gradual change in the conduct, atmosphere and even the language of public business. The political class in Italy today has its own incomprehensible jargon, full of metaphors and complicated circumlocutions, but this manner of speaking is not much favoured by politicians who are linked to the mafia or who are themselves *mafiosi*. They have a more direct approach to problems, and a less elaborate style. In defending the mafia interests which they represent, they often

[12] 'Quando la DC della Sicilia sfila davanti al magistrato', in L'Unità, 25 May 1980.

speak quite openly, in the ordinary course of council meetings, and what they say is regularly set down in the record.

One among the host of episodes witnessing to the changed relations between the mafia and the world of politics took place in July 1981 at Polistena, a township in the Plain of Gioia Tauro. Gerolamo Tripodi, the communist mayor, had given evidence a few days earlier at the trial of some 230 members of mafia *cosche* from the Plain of Gioia Tauro, then in progress at Palmi. During the subsequent meeting of the local council, Tripodi was violently attacked by the leader of the Christian Democrat group, who declared that 'the mayor has ruined several families and made criminals of the town's whole population, by making Polistena notorious everywhere—more notorious than Gioia Tauro—as if our town was the centre of the mafia.' He went on to say that the mayor was 'an informer . . . a despot, like a medieval governor, backed up by the council—and someone in the Italian communist party will pay the price for this . . . It pains me to refer to all this this evening, but I have nothing on my conscience, it's the communists who have a guilty conscience! . . . We're playing with fire, here!'[13]

The speaker is a typical representative of the stratum of local political leaders that has established itself during the 1970s, in parallel with the expansion of the entrepreneurial mafia. The local administration—communal, provincial and regional—is now crowded with such people. The leader of the Christian Democrats on the Polistena council

is by his own admission . . . a business associate of the Longo mafia clan, the most feared clan in the area. Four years ago, the same man, . . . then employed in the office of a Christian Democrat councillor who headed a regional department, was condemned for his part in the swindle that Calabrians remember as the 'golden notebooks' scandal. As well as being implicated in numerous property speculations, the head of the Christian Democrat group has also recently been condemned by the council itself for his involvement in a fraudulent land deal carried out through the MOVECO SUD company in which he holds a stake worth over 50 million lire. It is in another company (IAIA SUD, a road-metal firm) that he is a partner of Rocco

[13] Commune of Polistena, minutes of council meeting: see 'Verbale della riunione del Consiglio Comunale del mese di luglio', in *L'Unità*, 14 July 1981, pp. 40–41.

Longo, a member of the local mafia *cosca*, sentenced to ten years' imprisonment. . . .[14]

The second way in which the autonomy of the mafia's power finds expression is in the fostering of its own, internal political representation—in the tendency, that is, for the leading mafia groups to mobilize their electoral weight behind candidates who are themselves members of the group, or else to support close relatives of the *cosca* chief or chiefs.

The advantage of this solution is that it simplifies the problem of relations with official power, obviating the need to negotiate agreements and alliances with politicians from outside the mafia family itself. The disadvantages stem from the fact that such a high public profile and such a dense concentration of powers may prove counterproductive at crucial moments, when the mafia finds itself clashing head on with public opinion and with the institutions of the law.

However, neither national public opinion nor the central authorities showed much interest in the problem of the mafia from the early 'seventies through until late 1982, when General Dalla Chiesa was murdered in Palermo. These years accordingly saw a widespread merging of political roles with mafia roles in Calabria and Sicily, and this process—beginning at the grass roots—has gradually become an important factor at the level of the provincial and regional administrations.

Every mafia family in Reggio Calabria province has its representatives on the relevant communal administration—its group of councillors, who, when not drawn directly from within the *cosca*, are among the closest friends or relatives of one of its most prominent members. For instance, the candidate who headed the socialist list for the 1976 elections in Locri, in Calabria, was given a prison sentence *in absentia* in 1977, and arrested in 1980, for membership of a criminal organization. One of the leaders of the Nirta *cosca*, the former university student Bruno Nirta, was elected a delegate to the 1980 regional conference of the Christian Democrat party. However, the young man was unable to attend, as the Locri Public Prosecutor had issued a warrant for his arrest for membership of a criminal organization. A socialist local councillor from Cetraro was charged with complicity in the

[14] *L'Unità*, 14 July 1981.

murder of councillor Losardo, the communist head of a communal department, killed in July 1980. Francesco Macrí (known
as *Ciccio Mazzetta*), head of the Christian Democrat group on
the Reggio Calabria provincial council, was recently found guilty
of peculation, the pursuit of personal gain, and other offences; he
was sentenced to seven years' imprisonment. And the Palermo
Provincial President, Ernesto Di Fresco, was arrested a few
months before the writing of this book and charged with peculation, together with two high officials of the Sicilian regional
administration.

Even the PCI (Italian Communist Party) has been affected by
mafia infiltration, at local level, into its elected representation—
despite the strongly anti-mafia line taken by the party nationally.
In Mammola (another town in Ionian Calabria), the entire communist group on the council, an organ of the Macrí *cosca*, was
recently charged with a variety of mafia-type offences. The murder
of Valarioti, secretary of the Rosarno branch of the PCI and
an antagonist of the mafia, took place—according to the indictment—in the course of an internecine struggle in the *Rinascita*
communist co-op, in which it seems that the Pesce *cosca* exerted a
dominant influence.

The growing political representation of the mafia in elected
assemblies has set off a process of 'circulation of elites' in this
sphere, too. The power attaching to representative office is no
longer monopolized by bourgeois members of the liberal professions: public office is more and more often held by men of the
new elite—more outspoken and more ruthless, possessed in
general of more modest educational qualifications, and at once
more aggressive and less inclined to finicking compromises in
their dealings with the old political elite. In many parts of
southern Calabria and western Sicily, it is recognized and accepted that this new power elite has entered on the scene. This quasi-
legitimation of mafia power makes it less difficult to understand
the kind of statements the local authorities have made during
recent mafia trials:

> Virtually all the 'leading figures' called on to give evidence come out
> with claims that they do not know what the mafia is, or else that it
> does not exist in their part of the world. Defendants identified as
> members of mafia groups—and even as mafia bosses—are praised for
> their exemplary morals, and described as benefactors, creators of job

opportunities who 'ought to be given a medal'. When it is put to these witnesses that the areas from which they come are the scene of numerous murders, attacks, and the like, they reply that such deeds are the work of young louts, layabouts, and so forth.[15]

Even the ecclesiastical authorities have on occasion been known to grant testimonials to the universal trust and esteem in which the most notorious mafia chiefs are held—documents that have been invoked in trials where *mafiosi* have faced prison sentences. The *mafioso* Sebastiano Mesiti, for instance, obtained a declaration from a parish priest in S. Luca, praising Mesiti's character as that of an 'honest workman' who 'spends his leisure hours with his family, taking scrupulous pains with the upbringing of his children' (see over).

The June 1980 political and administrative elections offered an opportunity to appreciate the extent to which mafia groups had 'internalized' their political representation. It became clear that the names of *mafiosi* themselves or of their relatives were appearing in the electoral lists as candidates for a wide range of political positions, and that the success of candidates related to *mafiosi* was a reflection of the way in which the old political elite was being replaced:

It is above all in Reggio Calabria province . . . that friends and relatives of *mafiosi* are actually taking up positions in political life. The process deserves a closer look. It is the Republican Party (PRI) that is under the greatest pressure. A group of lay intellectuals, who set up a campaign three years ago to renew and reinvigorate the party, have been expelled en bloc. As one of their regional councillors (who may in fact be made a departmental head), the Republicans have chosen Pietro Araniti, a tax consultant by profession, whose cousins, Santo and Domenico, are the 'bosses' of the Gallico-Sambatello-Catona area . . . Also elected on the Republican list for the provincial administration was Pietro Ligato, a local authority veterinary surgeon, . . . the son of a former mafia chief (now in retirement) and the son-in-law of the Siderno 'godfather', Antonio Macrí. Until a few weeks earlier, Pietro Ligato had been a candidate on the Christian Democrat list; he then went over to the Republicans, whose share of the vote in the area increased in a quite unusual manner. Also related

[15] V. Macrí, *Communicazione del giudice istruttor Vincenzo Macrí al convegno sulla mafia organizzato dal Consiglio Superiore della Magistratura.* Castelgandolfo, 4–6 June 1982.

to members of mafia *cosche* is Antonio Libri, the son of the De Stefano clan member Domenico Libri: the latter was another of the sixty defendants in the famous mafia trial, and, having received a five year sentence from the appeal court, was imprisoned, though he is now out on parole for 'health reasons'. Antonio Libri was elected at the head of the Republican list for the Reggio district council.

. . . Then there are the cases concerning the Socialist party. The son of Vicenzo Comisso (a mafia boss from Siderno, was with don Macrí when Macrí was killed) was elected in second place on the socialist list at Siderno. Paolo Foti, a surveyor, susbequently a fugitive from justice after being accused of dynamite attacks on the Liquichimica plant at Saline, belongs to the area's dominant family: he was among those elected on the PSI (Italian Socialist Party) list at Montebello Jonico . . .

. . . Turning now to the Christian Democrats, the most flagrant case is that of Giorgio De Stefano, a cousin of the mafia family dominant in the area. He was the second candidate elected to the communal council . . . When one goes through the election results division by division, one suspects that the *cosche* must in fact have made a proper electoral pact. It is clear that a straightforward transfer of votes took place between the Republican Pietro Araniti, who was elected to the regional council, and the Christian Democrat Giorgio De Stefano, who was elected as a communal councillor. In the very same divisions where voters plumped for Araniti, the Republicans virtually disappeared when it came to the communal elections, and the same first-preference votes went to De Stefano. Now all this seems to depend on deals having been struck in the world of politics, too. If Nucara is the 'godfather' of the 'new' Republicans of Calabria, the corresponding Christian Democrat godfathers are the members of parliament Vico Ligato and Senator Nello Vincelli (who is . . . an under-secretary in the transport department).[16]

One of the most significant results of their direct participation in the running of public affairs is that the mafia *cosche* have now gained a privileged stake in the *Mezzogiorno* State aid market. During the 'fifties and 'sixties, this was one of the most jealously guarded monopolies of the political class. Positions of patronage in client networks and positions of leadership in the mafia involved quite different spheres of interest, and the sphere controlled by clientelistic patrons was very much the larger. Many places in the *Mezzogiorno* used to resemble the Sicilian village

[16] A. Santini, 'Le strane carriere elettorali di cugini e figli di padroni', in *Paese Sera*, 2 July 1980.

PARROCCHIA S. MARIA DELLA PIETA'
SAN LUCA (R.C.)

San Luca,9.1.1972

Il sottoscritto parroco attesta-per quanto di propria
conoscenza-che il sig.MESITI SEBASTIANO figlio di
Antonio e di Marando Saveria,nato a San Luca il 7.9.1938
e residente in via Nazionale,13 di questo stesso comune,
risulta di buona condotta morale e civile.
Il suddetto signore è onesto lavoratore e nel tempo libero
trascorre la giornata in famiglia attendendo scrupolosamente
all'educazione dei propri figli.
In fede,ecc......

Sac. Trimboli Giosafatte
PARROCO S. MARIA DELLA PIETA
SAN LUCA (R.C.)

The undersigned parish priest testifies that—to the
best of his knowledge—Sig. Sebastiano Mesiti, son of
Antonio and of Saveria Marando, born in San Luca on 7
September 1938 and living in that same commune at 13,
via Nazionale, is of good moral and civil character.

The above-named Sebastiano Mesiti is an honest workman and spends his leisure hours with his family,
taking scrupulous pains with the upbringing of his
children.

Issued in good faith, etc . . .

COMUNE DI SAN LUCA

89030 - PROVINCIA DI REGGIO CALABRIA

IL SINDACO

ATTESTA

Che Nirta Francesco, nato a San Luca il 29-8-1921
e residente in questo Comune in via Indipendenza,
è in possesso dei diritti politici ed è di ottima
moralità.===
Si rilascia a richiesta dell'interessato per gli
usi consentiti dalla legge.========================
Addì 7 giugno 1977

IL SINDACO

THE MAYOR

TESTIFIES THAT

Francesco Nirta, born in San Luca on 29 September
1921 and living in the via Independenza in this
commune, enjoys full civil and political rights and is of
unblemished moral character.

The present testimonial is issued at the request of the
party concerned, in pursuance of the uses recognized by
the law.

Dated this day 7 June 1977.

studied by Blok, where declining competition for local resources, along with the control exercised by political 'mediators' over the new resources flowing from the centre, had helped speed the ousting of the mafia from key areas of economic and social life—and where it seemed true that 'before, it was mafia; today it is politics.'[17]

Now, however, the separation between political-client networks on the one hand and the special networks of mafia power on the other is increasingly breaking down. The management of what has been called the 'State-aided economy' of the *Mezzogiorno*—the distribution of subsidies, pensions, and public-sector jobs—is falling more and more into the hands of *mafiosi*-politicians, or indeed of *mafiosi* plain and simple. The traditional political elite, unable to 'master' the new competitive situation, is being elbowed aside. The *inflationary-clientelistic* process is in fact swelling the number of broken promises made by the traditional political authorities, while it spurs the subordinate population to press ever more insistently for protection. There is presently a competition as to who can best 'deliver what they have promised' and offer 'real guarantees' about someone's pension or job, some subsidy, or the payment of some contribution. Here, *mafiosi*-politicians obviously have the advantage over the traditional mediators. Nowadays, hardly a single representative of the traditional political class is possessed of sufficient power and determination to impose his own will (through favours, threats and sanctions) on the increasingly fragmented apparatus of public government. This is just what a mafia leader *can* do; and he can use many of the techniques adopted in his rise to economic power in order to gain a monopoly of public expenditure funds. The example of EEC subsidies to olive-oil producers is instructive here:

> Making use of the funds set aside to fix an integrated price for oil, producers in Reggio Calabria province have received between twelve and fifteen thousand million lire over the last three years. 70 per cent of this sum goes to just 2,000 of the 45,000 companies to whom funds are allocated—a result achieved by various means, such as the *gabella* system of farming out leases, and the forging of rental agreements. Almost all the *gabellotti* are *mafiosi*.[18]

[17] A. Blok, *The Mafia of a Sicilian Village, 1860–1960: A Study of Violent Peasant Entrepreneurs*, New York and Oxford 1974, p. 216.
[18] Italian Communist Party, *Rapporto della delegazione parlamentare del PCI sul fenomeno mafioso in Calabria*, 13–15 November 1976, p. 4.

The Ideology and Political Culture of the Entrepreneurial Mafia

Does this new constellation of political and economic interests, formed in the wake of the entrepreneurial mafia's rise to prominence, have any characteristic ideology and culture? Are there any forms of legitimation typical of modern mafia power?

There are certain important features that distinguish today's mafia power from the power wielded by the traditional *mafioso*. Originating as it did in the arena of competition for honour, the authority of the traditional mafia appealed to ideological justifications hinging on universalist arguments, supposedly endorsed by the great majority. One recalls Vittorio Emanuele Orlando's famous declaration that

> if by the word 'mafia' we understand a sense of honour pitched in the highest key; a refusal to tolerate anyone's predominance or overbearing behaviour; . . . a generosity of spirit which, while it meets strength head on, is indulgent to the weak; loyalty to friends . . . If such feelings and such behaviour are what people mean by 'the mafia', . . . then we are actually speaking of the special characteristics of the Sicilian soul: and I declare that I am a *mafioso*, and proud to be one.[19]

This is the most comprehensive summary of traditional mafia ideology, based on the identification of mafia behaviour with the cult of honour that held sway in Sicily and Calabria until the end of the second world war.

Today, ideological defences of the mafia no longer centre on general anthropological-cultural arguments. Rather, they invoke modern claims of an ethnic and territorial kind, with a definite political content. The keynote now is an aggressive regionalism, backed up by an insistence on the worth and merits of 'Calabrianism' and 'Sicilianism' as against 'northern colonialism'. The *mafioso* figures, in this ideological construction, as one of a category of indigenous producers, whom the State—as the representative of big industry and of older and more established capitalist interests—unjustly persecutes.

'*Mafiosi*? After all, they're people who make good use of our

---

[19] V. E. Orlando, 'Discussione tenuta al teatro Massimo di Palermo nel giugno 1925', in G. Pallotta, *Dizionario storico della mafia*, Rome 1977, pp. 81–83.

local resources—Calabrians like you and me.'[20]

In this perspective, the trials of prominent mafia bosses are seen as stages in the 'criminalization of Calabria' in the eyes of national and international public opinion, and talk of the mafia is considered a ploy to discourage investment from outside the region: 'But why do the papers make such a song and dance about the Reggio Calabria trials? The real mafia isn't what the bosses on trial belong to—the real mafia's in the North, in Rome and Milan. If you want to see the real mafia, look at Agnelli. . . .'[21]

Anyone who stands up against the mafia's prepotency in the villages of the Ionian coast of Calabria is seen as an informer and a spy—as happened to the communist miller, Rocco Gatto, murdered when he went to the judicial authorities and denounced the acts of violence perpetrated by the Ursini *cosca* in Gioiosa Jonica. Few moments remain more vividly in mind, from the researches that led to the results presented in this book, than a conversation I had in 1979 with a highly-placed representative of the regional political authorities, who told me that 'in a certain sense, they were right to kill Rocco Gatto. You understand what I mean. He was a spy for the *carabinieri*.'

But the most coherent and articulate attack on the judiciary's anti-mafia activities was launched in Calabria between 1978 and 1981 by a group of socialist intellectuals headed by a member of parliament, Giacomo Mancini. In a series of articles published in the weekly *Calabria Oggi*, they put forward serious criticisms of the heavy sentences passed in the Reggio Calabria court on twenty-eight top Calabrian mafia bosses found guilty of belonging to a criminal organization. In their critique, the authors argued that the accused *mafiosi* had not enjoyed their guaranteed constitutional rights, in that inquiries had not been pressed far enough and the evidence supporting the prosecution case had proved inadequate.[22] Luigi Gullo (the lawyer who defended Gerolamo Piromalli in the trial) insisted in his plea for the defence—published later in *Calabria Oggi*—that the charges showed class bias and bias against the South: those against whom they had been levelled were 'workers' and small businessmen, unable to enjoy the same freedom of action as their richer and more

[20] Interview no. 14.
[21] Ibid.
[22] In *Calabria Oggi*, no. 3–4, 1979.

fortunate colleagues living in other regions of Italy:

> Offences and crimes, speculations and business dealings—these are
> by no means one and the same thing: that is the nub of it. Offences,
> crimes, speculations and business deals cannot all be instances of
> fraudulent practice, pursued by such means as we are here concerned
> with. To combine together to speculate, or even to carry out some
> illegal business manoeuvre together—to combine together to get
> some deal, however impressive, under way—none of this amounts to
> the kind of fraudulent practice which is the distinguishing character-
> istic of a criminal organization . . .
>   If anything has in fact been proved against any of those whom I am
> defending, it has been in connection with his activity at work . . . But
> busines matters of that kind, I repeat once more, neither constitute an
> offence in themselves, nor can they constitute proof of the offences
> that my clients are charged with. And in this connection . . . I must
> say that it is hardly very just . . . that we bow down in homage before
> big business magnates, because they operate beneath the watchful
> gaze of laws that they dictated and of justice practised in the appli-
> cation of those laws—which are class laws; and that we then pass
> heavy moral judgements on those whose class background is different,
> sometimes imposing hateful preventive measures or heavy penal
> sentences on them. . . .[23]

In parallel with this campaign promoted by *Calabria Oggi*, the
daily paper *Il Giornale di Calabria* abruptly changed its attitude
to the mafia. Having traditionally expressed solidarity with the
struggles of the left and the strivings of the few judges and
magistrates conducting anti-mafia investigations, it switched to an
attitude of opposition, objecting to the proceedings of the left and
of the judges alike. The editor of the paper (it, too, backs
Mancini) wrote in the following terms of Judge Cordova's inquiry
into the sixty mafia bosses of Tyrrhenian Calabria, which is in
fact outstanding among judicial documents relating to the mafia,
and whose validity as evidence was later confirmed when—
unprecedentedly—a Calabrian court passed heavy sentences on a
group of high-ranking mafia leaders:

> For the first time in Calabria, a judge has attempted to put flesh on the
> bones of 'the mafia', that phenomenon of organized crime. Names and
> surnames, deeds and misdeeds—they are all there in writing.

[23] Ibid.

Happy event yesterday

Male Heir Born

*Elusive Castellace fugitive
Francesco, after his father,*

PALMI, 16 January. Saro Mammoliti, the 'playboy of Castellace', a wanted man for over seven years but seemingly beyond the reach of the law, today became a father for the second time, showing that he is a model husband even if he is in hiding. His wife, Maria Caterina Nava, eighteen years old and married to the well-known boss in the little church at Castellace just three years ago on 23 August last, this morning gave birth to a lively little boy in Taurianova district hospital. This was a moment long awaited by Saro, who has called the child after the founder of the family, Francesco.

The little boy—brother to a sister born in February last year—will be baptised in the same little church where the wedding of the 'chief' of the new Calabrian mafia and his young bride Maria Caterina was celebrated. The church is a stone's throw from the *carabinieri* station, and the wedding caused a storm, being seen as an outright challenge to the forces of law and order. Saro arrived at the church wearing a dark suit and accompanied by the witnesses and a few trusted friends.

When news of the wedding got out a few days later, there was a tremendous uproar. Not long before, Saro Mammoliti had denied—in an interview given to this paper—that he was in any way connected with the kidnappings that have been carried out in the North, or

Pagina 8 - mercoledì 17 gennaio 1979

at   Taurianova   hospital

to Mammoliti

names *his   second   child*

killed by the Barbaro clan

with the other criminal acts to which has name has been
linked. He is wanted by the authorities because he is
believed to be one of the brains behind the mafia's
international organization. Charged with complicity in
the Paul Getty III kidnapping, he was acquitted by the
Lagonegro magistrature.

Saro Mammoliti has been in hiding since 13 December
1972, when he escaped from custody in Nicotera prison.
He is suspected of various crimes to do with the long-
running feud between his family and the Barbaro family
of Castellace.

The members of the Barbaro clan have been forced out
of the area by the superior strength of the Mammoliti.
The latest victim of the feud was killed last year in
Perugia: Domenico Barbaro, who had served a 26-year
prison term for the murder of Francesco, founder of the
Mammoliti family, was murdered in his turn, paying
with his blood for Francesco's death.

Francesco's birth—he has been called after his powerful paternal grandfather—has caused great rejoicing in
the Mammoliti household. Mother and baby are both
doing well in the maternity unit at Taurianova hospital,
where friends and relatives have been celebrating the
happy occasion with them.

. . . The judge, from Reggio, has worked at his task for months. He has conducted hundreds of interviews, and he has had to knit together a whole fabric of facts, petty wrong-doings as well as serious crimes . . . The resulting 'Inquiry' is a journalistic masterpiece, which would have been—still would be—the delight of any newspaper editor. We are rather put out, however, by the reflection that the document in question is not meant to be a newspaper inquiry, but an *indictment*, or in other words a part of the judicial process, which entails a trial and therefore requires some evidence . . . Judge Cordova, on the other hand, has worked very much like a newspaper reporter, quite literally *interviewing* mayors and parliamentarians, and seeking confirmation, in other people's experiences and beliefs, for his own intuitions . . . Often enough, however, he has found himself just as incapable as any journalist of producing evidence of other people's guilt of the kind that satisfies judges.[24]

Over the next few months, the same paper's articles on the mafia became more and more glamourizing in tone. The *mafioso-entrepreneur* was held up as an anti-hero. One aspect of this was a sympathetic exploration of the 'human side' of the *mafiosi*, which even reached the point where the birth of 'male heirs' to a notorious outlaw could be given prominent and congratulatory coverage (see pp. 184–185).

[24] In *Il Giornale di Calabria*, 30 August 1978.

8.

The Entrepreneurial Mafia and the Heroin Economy

The Movement of Heroin

The heroin consumed in the United States and western Europe is derived for the most part from opium produced in a few small areas on the borders between Iran, Pakistan and Afghanistan. During the course of the 1970s, Turkey gradually lost its formerly central role in opium production: American pressure, and American loans, persuaded successive Turkish governments to carry out programmes designed to encourage crop substitution and control poppy growing. The result was a sharp fall in the illicit growing and marketing of Turkish opium.[1]

The world's largest source of illegal opium at present is southwest Asia: in 1979, the combined opium production of Afghanistan, Pakistan and Iran was about 1600 tonnes, as against 160 tonnes from the Golden Triangle and 10 tonnes from Mexico (see map, over).

Of these 1600 tonnes, about 100 are consumed locally. The remainder is transformed into some 50–60 tonnes of base morphine, intended for export to the West and the rest of the world. The chemical transformation of opium into morphine takes place in crude laboratories located in Pakistan's north-western frontier region and in a series of Middle Eastern countries—Lebanon,

[1] N. A. Stavrou, 'The Politics of Opium in Turkey', in *Drugs, Politics and Diplomacy. The International Connection*, ed. L. R. S. Simmons and A. A. Said, London 1974.

Estimated World Production of Illegal Opium, 1979

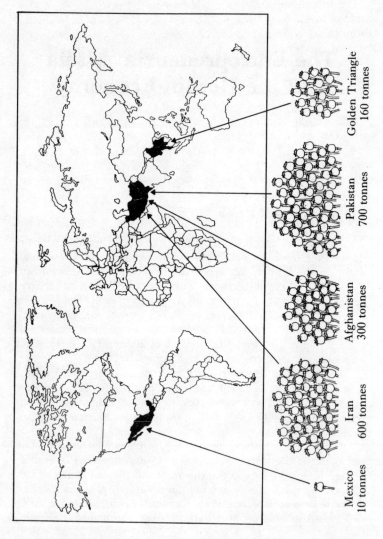

Source: Drug Enforcement Agency, *Southwest Asian Heroin: a Historical and Current Assessment*, Washington DC, Government Printing Office, 1980.

Syria, Iran and Turkey.[2]

The morphine is next transported—by car or train, or on the backs of mules—to Ankara and Istanbul, and across the Balkans. From there, still sometimes by train or car, but above all in TIR international road haulage trucks,[3] it enters western Europe. The next stage, the transformation of morphine into heroin, is the crucial moment in the whole operation, both technically and economically. Once processed into heroin, the drug is exported to north America and the rest of the world market.

Within each country, the heroin (mixed with various chemically inert substances) then finds its way via the distribution network onto the domestic market, whose consumers seem to grow in number and become geographically more widespread with every passing year. Estimates of the number of drug addicts in the USA have risen from a figure of 50–100,000 in the late 'sixties[4] to a figure of around 500,000 in 1980.[5]

The 1971 Murphy Report concluded that heroin addiction was an essentially American problem, and was seen as such by most other countries, who accordingly did little to implement their promises of cooperation with the USA.[6] Nine years later, the Biden Report noted that there were now more deaths (in absolute terms) from heroin abuse in West Germany than in the USA, and that in proportion to its population Italy had a higher drug dependency rate than the USA.[7]

Many agencies exist—at national, regional, and local level—whose brief it is to clamp down on heroin dealing. However, clandestine drug imports are particularly hard to detect because

---

[2] DEA (Drug Enforcement Agency), *Southwest Asian Heroin: A Historical and Current Assessment*, Washington DC 1980.

[3] The TIR customs convention has thirty-five member states in Europe and Asia. Its provisions allow vehicles to submit to customs control at the point of departure only, after which their doors are sealed and they are able to cross the frontiers of all member-states without any check being made until they arrive at their destination.

[4] S. Rottenberg, 'The Clandestine Distribution of Heroin, its Discovery and Suppression', in *Journal of Political Economy*, Jan. 1978, p. 78.

[5] *Southwest Asian Heroin* (cit.).

[6] Murphy and Steele, *The World Heroin Problem*, Report of special study mission, House of Representatives, Committee on Foreign Affairs, Washington DC, 1971, p. 36.

[7] J. R. Biden, *The Sicilian Connection: Southwest Asian Heroin en Route to the United States*, Report by Senator J. R. Biden to the Committee on Foreign Affairs, 1980, p. 1.

drugs are very easy to transport and conceal, and have a very high money value with respect to their weight and volume. The authorities are thus unable to intercept and impound more than a small fraction each year: the proportion of imported heroin normally seized in the USA and in Italy is estimated at somewhere between 5 per cent and 10 per cent.

The Heroin Cycle

The production, transport, distribution and consumption of hard drugs involves different groups of people at every stage. Each group has its own quite distinctive character in terms of the numbers involved, their level of organisation, and their socio-economic profile.

Poppies are grown, and raw opium is extracted from their seed-capsules, by small peasant farmers for whom the sale of opium-cakes is an essential item in the family budget, being indeed in very many cases their only source of cash income and thus their only means of paying taxes and acquiring whatever goods they do not produce themselves.[8]

Part of each year's crop is sold to the State agencies responsible for controlling opium production; part is sold, more or less clandestinely, to local dealers who pay anything from twice to five or six times the official price.[9] In those places where no recognized State authority exists (as in the Pathan tribal lands, on the Afghanistan-Iran-Pakistan border, where some seven million people live),[10] and where it is thus possible for several hundred

---

[8] Bureau of Narcotics and Dangerous Drugs, *The World Opium Situation*, Washington DC, 1970, pp. 4ff.

[9] J. F. Holahan and Herningens, 'The Economics of Heroin', in P. M. Wald and P. B. Hutt, *Dealing with Drug Abuses: A Report to the Ford Foundation*, NY 1972, p. 261.

[10] The situation in Pathanistan is the result of English colonial rule. At the end of the last century, the British administration, faced by the armed resistance of the Pathans, was obliged to accord them a special status, which led to the system of 'tribal representation'. This formula allowed the Pathan tribes to enjoy virtually complete autonomy (see A. Fletcher, *Afghanistan: Highway of Conquest*, New York 1966). When governmental authority passed to the various nation-states of the region, the latter were obliged to retain the previous system in many important respects. 'Independent as they are of any constituted authority, the areas of tribal representation are states within the State of Pakistan—but inside them, there is no administration, no police, and no law': C. Lamour and M. Lamberti, *Il sistema mondiale della droga*, Turin 1974, p. 208.

tonnes of raw opium to be produced each year, the bulk of the crop is bought up by specialist wholesale merchants who (after transforming part of it into base morphine) then arrange for its sale in the Middle East. In *Il sistema mondiale della droga*, Lamour and Lamberti record a conversation they had with one of these wholesale dealers:

'At the moment, my selling price for opium is 600 rupees (about 34,000 lire or £20) a kilo,' the dealer explained. 'It never drops below 400 rupees. *Charras*[11] costs about 200 rupees. In Karachi, quality as good as this will cost you at least 600 or 800 rupees.' And to back up his sales talk, he slipped a quarter of a tablet into our pockets, so we could 'try some before deciding' . . .

When we asked him how much opium he could supply us with, the dealer pointed to his shelves. There, alongside a whole variety of armaments, were piled a number of large square bales wrapped in jute sacking. 'I've got a tonne in the shop here, and if you like I can give it to you now. If that's not enough, it'll take me a few days to collect the stuff together—but I could get you between five and eight tonnes without much delay . . .'

The Pathan explained that we could 'trust him': 'Some of my foreign customers buy anything up to three or four million rupees' worth over a few months' (that is, over £100,000 worth—the equivalent of six tonnes).[12]

The drug cycle's second geographical and economic stage takes place in the Middle East, where its agents are members of the political and military elite in a position to control sectors of the State administration and of the local community. From the early 'seventies on, there were numerous arrests of Middle Eastern diplomats, and Turkish Army colonels and captains, implicated in heroin- and morphine-smuggling—indicating a pattern (very similar to that found in Latin American cocaine-producing countries like Bolivia and Colombia) in which there is a blurring between political and criminal roles in economic activity. In a trial held in New York in the autumn of 1981, an international smuggler 'employed' by the top Sicilian mafia groups gave a detailed description of how he had purchased some 200 kilogrammes of base morphine in Beirut. The drug was supplied by

---

[11] *Charras* is a kind of hashish.
[12] Lamour and Lamberti, op. cit., p. 212.

Mohammed Dallal, a member of the Lebanese parliament.[13]

The cycle's third stage takes place in Europe, and it is at this point that French and Italian organized crime comes into the picture. The groups involved are comparatively independent of the political authorities, and dispose of considerable financial resources. The protection of political leaders is sought in more *mediated* ways, either through client-electoral relationships (as in the dinners and election meetings held jointly by the Italian minister, Ruffini, and a leading western Sicilian heroin-producer,[14] or as in Marseilles, where the socialist mayor, Gaston Deferre, has been a protector of the Venturi brothers),[15] or else through bribery and mutual back-scratching with miscellaneous political figures.

The final stage of the drug cycle comprises all the various transfers of the merchandise between its entry into each national market, European or American, and its eventual sale on the street to the individual addict. These transfers parallel the transactions of the legal market, but there are more of them. In his study of the structure of heroin distribution in New York City, M. H. Moore identifies no less than six distinct marketing stages separating the producers from the eventual consumers.[16] The distribution chain is longer for drugs than would be necessary for legal merchandise, because of the need to restrict what dealers at any given level know about the identity of those higher up in the operation, and because each seller has to keep the number of his or her transactions to a minimum in order to reduce the chances of being arrested.[17]

The purchase of heroin for distribution on the domestic market is the point at which figures from the legitimate, respectable world are most likely to get involved. This involvement is often transitory, being limited to a single large operation or to one of its phases. But the prospect of multiplying their capital several times

[13] U. S. Courthouse, Brooklyn, record of questioning of Albert Gillet and Eric Charlier in the trial of Richard Cefalú and six other *mafiosi*, NY, 1981.

[14] G. Falcone, *Sentenza Istruttoria del processo contro Rosario Spatola più 119*, Palermo court, 1982, pp. 693–695.

[15] See the account in A. W. McCoy, *The Politics of Heroin in S. E. Asia*, NY 1973.

[16] M. H. Moore, *Buy and Bust. The Effective Regulation of an Illicit Market in Heroin*, Lexington 1973, pp. 67–108.

[17] Rottenberg, op. cit.

over within a few months or even weeks, by investing it in the
purchase of a quantity of heroin, attracts members of the liberal
professions, businessmen, and people from the world of trade and
commerce:

> Any financier who wanted to acquire a bigger stake in the deal, and
> was prepared not to ask questions, was offered a profit of at least 2
> million dollars, within six months, in return for an outlay of 100,000
> dollars. To be sure, he ran a risk—the risk of losing his money; but
> the 'shares' were negotiable. Had he found himself short of cash, he
> would have been able to sell them back. This financial transaction,
> seemingly a matter of banal routine, actually concerned the shipment
> of heroin from the Middle East to the USA . . .
> This example shows how drug-traffickers have changed over the
> last ten years. Although they are criminals in the fullest sense of the
> term, they operate like businessmen and use business methods. Their
> reputation for knowing how to earn huge sums of money (for them-
> selves and other people) gives them ready access to financiers bent on
> making big tax-free profits in a hurry.[18]

The Market

The heroin market is characterized by a permanent imbalance
between supply and demand, favouring the suppliers and allowing them to enjoy large and assured profits. There is always a
shortage of heroin. The drugs market is a classic 'seller's market',
in which the seller can vary his prices and the quantities he sells
within very wide margins.

A more 'ideal' structure of demand could not be imagined. The
consumers are an amorphous mass, unable to influence the market in any way, and likely to buy goods come what may, being
forced to disregard their quality and price.[19] The market is
supplied by way of a more complex structure, within which two
basic sectors can be distinguished—a *competitive* sector, where a
series of independent small and medium-sized units are active,
supplying heroin to a non-criminal public; and an *oligopolistic*

---

[18] R. H. Steel, in *Vista*, Mar-Apr 1972: quoted in Lamour and Lamberti, op.
cit., p. 80.
[19] Programmes of methadone-substitution, which governments have been introducing in recent years, represent an attempt to make the demand for heroin
more elastic.

sector, comprising a limited number of criminal family businesses of various nationalities, who sell drugs to members of the first sector. It follows that the *visible* presence in the heroin economy of the mafia, and of organized crime, is inversely proportional to the actual importance of their involvement.

Each family/firm has a market share determined by its ability to lay hold of and combine together three leading goods and services: capital, physical violence, and the inaction of the police and the judiciary. There is a strict—even mathematical—proportionality between the criminal firm's capacity to supply these factors, and the quantity and value of heroin it gets to deal in.

Capital must be available to purchase large amounts of base morphine for chemical transformation into heroin, a process carried out in clandestine laboratories run by the mafia groups themselves. Every transaction in an illegal market shows a marked discrepancy between purchase price and resale price. There are numerous intermediate stages, and every milestone in the drug's long journey sees another rise in the price it will command. Eric Charlier, one of the international smugglers implicated in heroin-trafficking between Sicily and the USA in the course of the major investigation carried out by the Palermo court, told judge Falcone he had found out that in Afghanistan, a kilo of base morphine cost 2,000 dollars, and you could export it with no problems. The same amount cost 3,500 dollars in Turkey, 8,000 dollars in Greece, and 12,000 dollars in Milan.[20]

The progressive increase in the cost of morphine as it draws nearer Europe and the USA entails a corresponding increase in the minimum capital required for entry into the market. While virtually any Pathan tribal chief can set about buying up opium and producing morphine, only a relatively small number of State officials, political functionaries or military officers are in a position to deal in drugs in Turkey, the Lebanon or Syria. And very few European criminal organizations are likely to dispose of the millions of pounds needed to supply a string of morphine-refining laboratories.

On the other hand, every criminal group wants to deal in base morphine, because the transformation of morphine into heroin offers profits of between 1,000 and 2,000 per cent—a rate un-

---

[20] G. Sciacchitano, *Requisitoria del PM Sciacchitano nel processo contro Rosario Spatola piú 119*, Palermo Public Prosecutor's Office, 1982, pp. 173–174.

matched at any other stage of the cycle. We have seen that a kilo of morphine (from which a kilo of heroin can be obtained) costs 12,000 dollars on the European market. The same amount of heroin costs 250,000 dollars on the US wholesale market, and between 120,000 and 150,000 dollars on the European market (1982).

Recourse to physical violence makes it possible, first of all, for the criminal firm to set up a protected enclave within the market where it operates, by erecting a barrier to discourage the entry of possible rivals. In the final stages of the distribution chain, such barriers are weak or non-existent, and virtually anyone who wants can enter the market and set themselves up as a drug-peddler.

Criminal firms also employ physical violence through their use of special personnel ('hit-men' and so on) to get rid of unforeseen obstacles—inconvenient witnesses, members of the criminal group who turn police informers, magistrates and police officers who show greater investigative zeal than is customary in the locality or who infringe any of the unwritten laws governing relations between the judicial authorities and the world of organized crime. In southern Italy, mafia and *camorra* groups can rely on a 'reserve army' of individuals prepared to endanger their own—and other people's—lives in the execution of especially risky and violent tasks, because the problems of the inner-city environment and youth unemployment are growing continually worse in the *Mezzogiorno*, so that the supply of criminal labour is continually increasing.

To ensure the inaction of the police, it is necessary to establish a very tight cordon of secrecy around the group's activities in buying and selling drugs, processing them, and transporting them. If a particularly large quantity of drugs or capital is impounded, if one or more key members of the family itself are arrested, or above all if one or more clandestine laboratories are discovered, then the smooth running of the business is disrupted. As a result, one criminal firm may be forced out of the market and replaced by another. The inaction of police officers and members of the judiciary may be obtained by way of corruption and political pressure, or attempts may be made (as has happened in Palermo in recent years) to achieve the same end by establishing a climate of terror through the murder of high-ranking political, investigative and judicial authorities active against the mafia.

At its highest levels, the drug business requires *all three* of these factors simultaneously. The conditions can then be created for initiating economies of scale beyond the reach of criminal firms operating in the competitive sector of the heroin market, which have to turn to the more powerful groups, not only for the drugs in which they deal, but also for special services—in particular, for the opportunity to corrupt or pressurize elements in the judicial and investigative system. These economies of scale enjoyed by criminal families/firms in the sphere of corruption and manipulation amount[21] to a 'negative by-product' of the complexity of the modern criminal justice system.

Small criminal entrepreneurs cannot command resources of this kind; and even if they could, they require them only occasionally, so that it would not be worthwhile investing in them. Those operating in the competitive sphere must thus turn to the monopolistic groups whenever they need to manipulate the judicial system, or to employ personnel specializing in the effective execution of violent and illegal acts.

The availability of capital, the use of violence and the capacity to ensure police inaction: these are the factors underlying the economies of scale that tend progressively to reduce the optimal number of criminal families/firms active in the oligopolistic sector of the drug market. Eventually, only a small number of groups continues to operate in each of the main commercial channels. Until recently, just four Sicilian mafia groups held a market share amounting to 30 per cent of *all* heroin introduced annually into the USA.

The Problem of Trustworthiness

The top operators in the heroin market can be sure of making very high profits; but they also run very high risks. The risks inherent in this kind of criminal activity derive first of all from the likelihood of being found out, and secondly from the lack of any legal authority capable of enforcing the terms of contracts. Transactions must therefore always be completed at sight, and payment must always be in cash. A very high degree of secrecy must also be established, much higher than is found in more traditional sectors of organized crime (gambling, prostitution, racketeering

---

[21] As we have seen: cf. chapter 6 above.

and so on), where very close 'confidential' relations often exist with the police, and where—in the USA—it is common practice for deals involving the passing on of information to be struck with the judiciary and the FBI.

Operational secrecy is the crucial element in drug-trafficking. Here, the police authorities and members of the world of organized crime exchange very little or no information about their respective activities. It is very rare for the police to get information *at the time*—or even immediately afterwards—about the opening up of a new drug-trafficking channel, the individuals and groups active in it, or the means by which their activities are being camouflaged.

Narcotics trafficking involves an endless game of cops and robbers, in which the robbers have one fundamental advantage: the time factor. When a new channel of illegal dealing is opened, operations are at first undisturbed, and big profits can be made in this initial period. This is because the resources of the investigative authorities are committed, for the time being, elsewhere— concentrated on recently discovered people, markets and geographical areas which are therefore under the spotlight of official political concern and public opinion. In the mid-'seventies, at the very time when the leading Sicilian mafia groups were expanding their activities in the heroin market to an unprecedented degree, it was believed by the investigating authorities that the centre of Italian drug-trafficking was in the Campania. On the basis of inquiries carried out on its behalf, the Anti-mafia Commission concluded that 'while the Italo-American mafia still recruits its international drug-couriers from Sicily, the organizational centres for operations at the Italian end are no longer confined to the island, but have been transferred—for the most part, at any rate—to the Campania, and above all to Naples.'[22]

The same lag between the actual geography of drug-smuggling and the current state of police awareness and information is found at the international level, where the whole problem is exacerbated by the existence of institutional barriers that prevent the various separate police authorities from pooling information and acting in concert.

The costs of enforcing contracts and protecting their own

[22] Anti-mafia Commission, *Commissione parlamentare d'inchiesta sul fenomeno della mafia in Sicilia,* vols. I, II, III, IV, doc. XXIII, no. 2, p. 252.

property do not for the most part fall within the company budgets of the majority of businessmen. Society provides police forces and courtrooms designed to maintain the security of public and private property and enforce some essential ground rules of economic life. The illegal entrepreneur is in a different position. When he draws up contracts or makes investments in the illegal sector, the security of his transactions is guaranteed by no laws or formal institutions. For this reason, mutual trust is far more necessary among criminals than among businessmen. If they are to avoid the costs of continual recourse to violence or the threat of violence, criminals must establish, within their own world, their own conventions, codes of behaviour, traditions and relations of mutual confidence. In the criminal world, the social contract is never given a priori. In a sense, it must be created anew each day.

The social and anthropological make-up of the criminal world is heavily influenced by the need for secrecy and the impossibility of turning to State laws for the regulation of market relations. For what can better guarantee the preservation of secrecy and mutual trust than common membership of the same culture, the same ethnic and regional community, or indeed the same family?

The world drug system is controlled by a series of criminal elites made up of members of ethnic minorities or family- and kinship-groups. The south-western Asian drug routes are monopolized (at the point of departure) by the ethnic minorities of Kurdistan, Baluchistan and Pathanistan: 'opium production in Pakistan is in the hands of the Pathans; it is smuggled into Iran by the Baluchis; and drug-trafficking and smuggling between Iran and Turkey is carried on by the Kurds.'[23]

In the distribution of heroin throughout southeast Asia, a very important role is played by the 'mafia' of *expatriate Chinese*, belonging to the Chu Ch'ao community whose native region is in Swatow. The members of this community, emigrants at various times from mainland China, retain a very clearcut ethnic identity: their language, cuisine and lifestyle are all Chinese. They form networks of kinship and relationship extending across geographical frontiers into a dozen major Asian cities and a similar number in Europe:

[23] DEA (Drug Enforcement Agency), op. cit.

Their financial operations are extremely hard to follow: they have their own idiosyncratic methods of exchange, . . . whether or not they are involved in drug-trafficking. It is rare for a consignment of goods to be paid for by cash or cheque. In Bangkok, perhaps, the courier who brings the drugs will be given a piece of paper no bigger than a postage stamp. This will bear Mr Wang's written authorisation for the courier to request the sum of X thousand dollars from Mr Chiang—a native of the same region, but a man quite unconnected with opium or heroin smuggling, who leads a quiet life running a restaurant or grocer's shop in Singapore, New Delhi, London or Paris. However, when he sees the piece of paper signed by Mr Wang, Mr Chiang will hand over the sum requested, borrowing it if need be. Months later, he will perhaps pay one of his Asian pickled-fish suppliers with a little piece of paper, drawn against the name of Mr Wang of Bangkok. In this way, a clandestine financial network is set up, based on mutual trust among the members of a single community —and on ruthless reprisals should that trust be broken.[24]

The 'Marseilles clan' (as it was known) was made up of members of four Corsican families: the Venturi brothers, Marcel Francisci, Joseph Orsini and the Guerini brothers. As we shall see below, the Marseilles group later lost control of heroin shipments between the Orient and the USA, being supplanted by their Sicilian rivals—the Spatola-Inzerillo, Gambino, Bontade and Badalamenti families.

The internal cohesion of each of these groups tends to be further strengthened by the apparently irrational practice of inter-marriage, adoption, and numerous other forms of natural and artifical kinship. In the case of the Sicilian mafia families, an extremely fine web has been spun, as can be seen from the indictment drawn up (on the basis of a May 1980 police report) by P. M. Sciacchitano:

The starting-point [of the report] is the observation that the four above-named families made up a compact and homogeneous group, operating in Palermo and in the USA, a group . . . headed by the now dead Carlo Gambino. The latter, according to the report, was related to the brothers Giuseppe, Pietro and Antonio Inzerillo (and, of course, to all their rather numerous children), as well as to Tommaso Gambino and his sons Giovanni, Giuseppe and Rosario.

The report goes on to describe the dense web of links (of kinship,

[24] Lamour and Lamberti, op. cit., pp. 56–57.

affinity, and sponsorship) that unite the members of the different families, and which have transformed the four original nuclei into what is really a single group—as can be seen from the facts that the Gambino brothers are cousins of the Spatola brothers Rosario, Vincenzo and Antonio, their father, Salvatore, being brother to the Gambinos' mother; that Giuseppe Inzerillo married Giuseppa Di Maggio—sister of Calogero, Giuseppe and Salvatore Di Maggio—while Calogero Di Maggio married Domenica Spatola, thus strengthening the kinship links between these families; and that intermarriage between cousins has been very frequent, whereas it is a matter of remark for women from the family to marry outsiders—who are thenceforth regarded as forming part of the group. . . .[25]

The criminal groups active in the world drugs trade display a strange blend of tradition and modernity. On the one hand, the nature of the trade and its geographical scope entail a developed division of labour within the group, whose members must take on specific tasks and possess specific skills, familiarizing themselves with a variety of languages and cultures and with fairly difficult technical notions in chemistry and economics. On the other hand, the need for secrecy and the requirements of managing and controlling the trade itself make those involved heavily dependent on the maintenance of traditional relations of trust, friendship, kinship and family relationship.

It follows that firms operating in the heroin economy need personnel with special characteristics, not easily come by even in the criminal market itself. There is a call for people able to move from country to country, capable of making rapid decisions, and aware of the machinery and procedures of control deployed by their opponents. And these people must at the same time be trustworthy: they must not turn traitor, play a double game, or go back on what they have agreed.

The *mafiosi* of the Spatola-Inzerillo group, to take one example, were partners in a legitimate firm, the Inzerillo sanitation company. Within this, there was an organized technical and professional division of labour. Some people were occupied in the running of the laboratories, in cooperation with French chemists who came to Palermo in secret. Others took care of the dispatch and concealment of the product, which obliged them to turn for outside help to a clerk in the Alitalia forwarding office. Then

[25] Sciacchitano, op. cit., p. 36.

there were the 'couriers', one of the most sensitive links in the chain, whose task it was to transport heroin from Sicily to the USA, and to bring money back from the USA to Sicily. Two different groups of people were often involved in a single exchange of heroin for dollars, one on the outward journey and one on the way back. The dollars were very often changed into lire outside Italian territory, in Swiss banks, either by the couriers themselves or by some other individual active in some other sector (armaments, gold, diamonds and so on) of the illegal world market.[26]

There was also yet another group of people—its members drawn, sometimes, from other groups or sub-groups of the same firm—who took charge of reinvesting the profits and depositing them in banks. Even the supply of morphine to the laboratories depended on the coordinated work of specialists, able to make contact with the political-military-criminal groups, from Turkey, the Lebanon and Syria, who handled drug exports. The entire business was supervised by an elite of top leaders, who intervened in person in certain operations and at particularly crucial moments.[27]

The whole process we are describing has two essential prerequisites: it must remain impermeable to police investigation, and those involved must abide by undertakings and verbal agreements concerning transactions each of which run into thousands of millions of lire.

To find people who respect agreements, who will not make off with enormously valuable goods and capital in situations where it would be very easy to do so, and who will reveal nothing to the authorities if captured, the mafia has had to turn to those under obligations of natural or artificial kinship. This severely limits the dimensions to which any of the criminal firms has been able to expand its dealings. There is in fact a direct relationship between the number and strength of the primary bonds that unite those employed in the firm, and the extent to which its operations (both internal and external) run smoothly and in secrecy:

> If it is necessary to intervene in some particularly important affair, then it is logical that the task should invariably be allotted to a

[26] U. S. Courthouse, Brooklyn: document cit. in note 13 above.
[27] Falcone, op. cit., pp. 514 ff.

relative—both because the job is then certain to be done, and because the remainder of the group can rest assured that in any case nothing will be revealed to the outside world.[28]

If the level of secrecy surrounding its activities drops through unforeseen circumstances, or because of betrayals or leaks of whatever kind, then the firm's network of operations will contract, leaving only the core members still active: 'It seems clear that after the Gallina consignment was lost, a decision was reached that it was best for people to carry the stuff themselves: it was so valuable that it could not be entrusted to a stranger . . . but must rather be transported by two family members who had the necessary skills.'[29]

Once operations exceed a certain scale, the need to turn regularly to people and facilities from outside the original family- and kinship-networks ends up by creating leaks in the secrecy surrounding the operation and gives rise to growing 'irregularities' in the group's internal accounting (goods disappear; there are 'misunderstandings' about prices, about how the stuff is to be forwarded, and about its quality; anomalies arise concerning how, and at what rate, dollars are to be exchanged for lire; and so on). From this angle, one can appreciate the significance of the fact that the most important leaks about heroin-trafficking between Sicily and the USA took place at the very moment when the scale of operations grew large enough to entail the recruitment of individuals from outside the Sicilian mafia families. It was two international smugglers, one Swiss and one Belgian, together with a number of airline employees involved in trafficking at various levels, who collaborated with the police, following their apprehension, to reveal a number of details about the workings of the biggest drugs business ever set up by the Sicilian mafia.[30]

The Place of Mafia Firms

The great power of the modern western Sicilian mafia in the heroin-smuggling market is something new, and is bound up with

[28] Ibid., p. 61.
[29] Ibid., pp. 85–86.
[30] G. Falcone, *Sentenza istruttoria del processo contro Mafara Francesco più 23*, Palermo court, 1982, pp. 1–95.

broader developments affecting the power of the mafia over the last ten or fifteen years. Until the early 'seventies, Sicilian *mafiosi* were prevented from acquiring any oligopoly within the drugs market because they were insufficiently competitive with other European criminal groups, in particular with the French groups based in Marseilles.

The mafia had indeed been involved to some extent in the hard drugs business all through the 'fifties and 'sixties. At that time, a series of police operations implicated leaders such as Genco Russo, Angelo La Barbera, Tommaso Buscetta and Gaetano Badalamenti. However, they never had anything more than a secondary role in the world drugs system: according to the investigations of the McClennan Committee, Sicily and southern Italy were no more than staging-posts in the shipment of French-produced heroin to the USA.[31]

Throughout these two decades, the Sicilian families/firms were at a marked disadvantage compared to their competitors—above all when it came to the availability of capital. Before the development of the modern entrepreneurial mafia, the *mafiosi* were hampered by the *cult of honour*, which obliged them to squander their time and resources in gaining supremacy over their rivals, and by the fact that their income was drawn from extortion and from parasitic activities: in consequence, they were unable to amass the large cash sums needed to get involved at the highest levels of the world drugs import-export circuit.

This disadvantageous position was transformed by the emergence (during the early 'seventies, in Sicily) of a stratum of mafia entrepreneurs, and also of small and medium-scale *non*-mafia entrepreneurs and speculators, who had an excess of liquid funds and were looking for new investment outlets. At this same period, Sindona was working with masterly skill on the creation of communication channels between the Italian legal financial circuit and the circuit of illegally-earned capital. As mafia capital began to avail itself of this new freedom of movement, and as the simultaneous crisis of the State's monopoly of violence led to a growth in police inaction, the Sicilian *mafiosi* rapidly gained in market power, until by the mid-'seventies they were able to alter the international division of criminal labour that had prevailed for

---

[31] U. S. Senate, *Organized Crime and Illicit Traffic in Narcotics*, Report of the Committee on Government Operations, Washington DC 1965.

over thirty years, shifting the crossroads of the heroin route from France to Italy.

It is worth considering in rather more detail how these reserves of ready cash, used by the mafia to break into the world heroin trade, were built up. Today, a decade after the event, it is far easier to discern the overall shape of incidents and processes which seemed at the time to be isolated and unconnected, so that even those actively involved perhaps failed to appreciate their full implications.

Everybody knows—from the documents published by the Anti-mafia Commission, and from accusations made in the press —that the mafia made profits and accumulated capital from its activities in the construction sector. Two other less well-known sources also contributed to the build-up of excess liquid funds that characterized the western Sicilian economy in the early 'seventies, allowing the mafia—via intermediate stages and transfers of varying complexity—to buy up drugs in the quantity needed for industrial processing. These two sources were a) the accumulation, in bank deposits, of unspent public funds, forming part of the 'support funds' allocated to the Sicilian Region by the central State; and b) the vast sums of liquid cash available to the Sicilian families who ran the island's Revenue Offices.

Article 38 of the statutes of the Sicilian Region provides for the Region to receive each year from the State an enormous sum of money by way of national support funds. This is intended to finance public works. Between 1947 and 1971, no less than 830 thousand million lire were transferred to the Region, and 630 thousand million were allocated for the period 1972–1976. If we bear in mind the big delays in payment of these sums, and the incapacity of the regional administration to spend them, we shall understand how it came about that in 1973 'out of a total sum available of over 45 thousand million lire,[32] almost 290 thousand million—more than 65 per cent of the total, in effect—had still not been put to use.'[33] The Anti-mafia Commission expressed its concern about the situation; in its final majority report, it devoted several paragraphs to an analysis of the problems arising from the use made of these funds by the mafia and in client systems:

[32] 450 thousand million lire in 1973 had the same value as at least four times that number today.

[33] Anti-mafia Commission, op. cit., vols. I, II, III, IV, doc. XXIII, no. 2, p. 299.

As a result of the facts and circumstances that we have been outlining, an exceptional quantity of unused liquid funds built up over the years, in the sense that the money paid to the Region remained on deposit in banks for long periods and in large amounts. This helped to introduce artificial features into the banking system, and gave an opening for mafia involvement and for parasitism. In fact, this exaggerated liquidity . . . led to the capital involved being put to use in schemes which quite often had a speculative intent . . . Situations of this kind eventually offer fertile ground for the mafia, giving them excellent opportunities to intervene and opening up large areas in which they can get involved in bank credit and the use of financial resources.[34]

. . . There have in fact been several cases in which credit has been given, on vague security, to well-known mafia characters, such as Mariano Licari. More generally, there have been other occasions when banks appear to have been managed against the interest of the credit institutions, and in disregard of the provisions laid down. This gives good grounds for suspecting that well known mafia personalities have benefited from illicit favourable treatment.[35]

The four families holding the contract for the operation of the island's 344 Revenue Offices have represented a major concentration of wealth and power, because the State has allowed them to retain a high percentage of sums collected (until a few years ago, this was set at 10 per cent, as against a national average of 3.3 per cent), as well as to exceptional arrangements of all kinds—such as so-called 'allowances' concerning the time before sums collected must be paid over, granted sometimes in respect of as much as 20 per cent of the total tax receipts; 'reimbursements against expenditure' in excess of the normal percentages; and so on.[36] Thanks to their access to money capital running into hundreds of thousands of millions of lire, and to their very close links with mafia groups and with the dominant political groups in Sicily, the revenue-collectors, who constitute an organised lobby, have opened up speculative and financial opportunities for Sicilian criminal firms to break into the world heroin trade. Pio La Torre

[34] Ibid., p. 300.
[35] Ibid., p. 200.
[36] On the power of the Revenue Office lobby, and its role in Sicilian political life, see the evidence given to the Anti-mafia Commission by the former Regional President Giuseppe D'Angelo (Anti-mafia Commission, op. cit., doc. XXIII, no. 2–VII, p. 1067).

wrote—in the minority report of the Anti-mafia Commission—
about the Salvo group, from Salemi:

> The Christian Democratic party in Trapani province . . . is today in
> the hands of a power-grouping dominated by the Salvo family of
> Salemi—who control, as is well known, the communal Revenue
> Offices to which this Commission has devoted so much attention . . .
> In recent years, the Salvo group has gained a clear ascendancy over
> the other groups, and it has become clear that it is aiming to control
> the province. All this is quite apart from the numerous analyses of
> drug-trafficking which (while they of course lack corroborative evi-
> dence) suggest that the Salvo group has provided the financial backing
> for a distribution network in which Zizzo [the Salemi mafia chief]
> would seem to have played a very important role, along with certain
> groups from Alcamo.[37]

The growing imbalance between financial reserves and investments that affected Sicily from the late 'sixties to the early
'seventies would not have led to such a major increase in the
mafia's economic power but for the fact that the credit market on
the island was closely controlled by an alliance between political
power and mafia power. To get an idea of how the main Sicilian
banks functioned during the period of the Anti-mafia Commission's investigations (1962–1976), we need only consult what the
Commission's own majority report concluded about the issuing of
credit in Sicily:

> We were able to establish, among other things, that the supervisory
> bodies did not always carry our their responsibilities with due rigour
> or with the necessary firmness; . . . that agricultural credits were
> sometimes issued in a manner inconsistent with the provisions of the
> law; that special funds were often employed in sectors other than
> those for which they had been created; that on more than one
> occasion, credits were issued to groups or financial companies which
> then made use of them to lend money at interest . . . But above and
> beyond such particular incidents, the entire credit system was con-
> ducted on typical mafia lines.[38]

Public funds, then, were to a large extent the source of the
massive capital sums invested, from the early 'seventies on, in one

---

[37] Anti-mafia Commission, op. cit., doc. XXIII, no. 2–VII, p. 603.
[38] Ibid., p. 200.

of the most lucrative illegal markets in the world. This was how the four most financially powerful criminal families managed to set up four heroin-producing laboratories around Palermo in the mid-'seventies, each capable of producing about fifty kilos of heroin per week. Allowing for interruptions in the supply of morphine and for the problems of keeping the industry secret, we can estimate—on the basis of· records of proceedings in Italian and American courts—that between four and five tonnes of pure heroin were produced each year from 1975–1976 until the discovery of the laboratories in August 1980. This quantity represented, as we have said, some 30 per cent of total us demand. More than 80 per cent of it was distributed in New York city, via a system of couriers, importers and wholesalers involving several hundred people.[39] Subtracting the costs of production and transport, this gives a net annual profit somewhere around 700 or 800 thousand million lire (not 20,000 thousand million lire—a figure often quoted, which corresponds, however, to the overall annual volume of the *retail* heroin sales in the usa).

However, the sum of money was in any case large enough; and it was concentrated in a few hands. These *narcolire* have certain special characteristics, namely: a) they come from outside the local economic system, thus constituting a credit entry in the Sicilian balance of payments; b) they do not originate from the State, and are saved or redistributed along channels independent of classical political clientelism. The old clientelistic system certainly never allowed a butcher to become the owner of a palatial mansion worth a thousand million lire in the space of a few short months—the kind of thing that happens more and more often in Palermo.

Thanks to the *narcolire*, the *mafioso* now enjoys increased autonomy and greater political clout in his relations with official Sicilian political power. The *narcolire* have also had a disruptive and disintegrative effect on society and its institutions, on one hand, while on the other hand they have helped create a new consensus around the *mafiosi* and around mafia-linked groupings and parties.

This new consensus is pragmatic, and devoid of the charisma associated with the traditional mafia. Ever larger sections of the population now depend on the running of illegal and criminal

[39] Biden, op. cit., pp. 1–3.

business—not only directly, but also in indirect and entirely above-board ways, as for instance in construction, where new employment has been created through the impetus given by the investment of illegal profits.

Such a high rate of profit is now assured from investments in the illegal sector of the western Sicilian economy that people from the legitimate, respectable world are making brief forays into illegal business. Those named by judicial reports as intimates or accomplices of major heroin-traffickers include clerks, officials and managers of small, medium-sized and large banks; members of the professional middle classes; and directors of public agencies—especially those connected with the Regional adminis-tration. Transitory or part-time involvement in a single recycling operation can bring in as much as a whole year of tedious routine work.

Now that they have access to several million million lire, the chief Sicilian mafia groups have, what is more, a different relation than did the old-style rich *mafiosi* with the financiers and business-men who operate at higher levels of the economy. They are now approaching the threshhold of big business properly so called— and this is something quite new in the history of the mafia phenomenon, in Italy and the USA. The fact is that (outside the realms of rhetoric and mythology) no American mafia chief or organized criminal group has ever crossed the frontiers of *big* power or *big* money. As G. Lundbergh writes in his study of the wealthiest strata of US society, *The Rich and the Super-Rich* :

> While it is no doubt true that people like Costello have accumulated a nest egg of dimensions that might be envied by the common man, I doubt that it is very great in the terms under discussion. If Costello or any other underworld character of 1965 had a net worth of more than five million dollars it would be surprising. No available evidence shows great underworld wealth unless Wall Street is located in the underworld.[40]

When the anthropologist F. Ianni studied one of the five famous New York mafia families in the early 'seventies, he found that its financial assets did not exceed fifteen million dollars.[41]

The limits of their financial fortunes have curbed the real

[40] G. Lundbergh, *The Rich and the Super-Rich*, NY 1968, p. 119.
[41] F. Ianni, *A Family Business*, London 1972, p. 90.

independence of American *mafiosi*, circumscribing their effective sphere of action and helping to keep them subordinate to the wishes of the top US financial and military groupings.[42]

Today's Sicilian mafia entrepreneurs find themselves in a very different position. They have amassed wealth on a scale that allows them an autonomy of action far beyond what their political protectors themselves can enjoy. Without such substantial autonomy, they could never even have conceived their murderous plans—plans whose victims have been top-ranking political and judicial authorities, killed in Sicily during the last few years.

Let us note, finally, how the *narcolire* have been employed. They would appear to flow along four main channels. One portion—the smallest—returns into illegal circulation, being used to purchase more drugs. A second and more sizeable portion is illegally exported: either it is deposited in Swiss banks or, more and morre often, it makes its way to the various Latin American countries where there are already substantial investments made by venture capitalists and by Italian financiers such as the late Licio Gelli, Ortolani and others.

A third portion enters the legitimate economy, following the familiar pattern of mafia investment (in construction, agriculture, tourism, and so on)—something that helps explain why the suburbs of Palermo have enjoyed a building mini-boom, in stark contrast to the national economic situation. Perhaps the largest portion of the *narcolire*, however, remains in Sicily in the form of liquid funds, recreating in exacerbated form the same imbalance in the financial market as was present (as we have seen) ten years earlier. But *narcolire* are far less amenable to control than were the capital and cash sums, derived from public funds, that flooded Sicily in the early 'seventies. Heroin profits a) are now held *in private hands*: they can be employed, and moved around, without the mediation of the political powers that be; and b) are deposited in a string of small and medium-sized banks that have grown up during the 1970s. These banks have enjoyed the protection of the Sicilian Regional authority's special powers over the opening up of new bank branches, and have also had *de facto* immunity from the strict periodic checks carried out by the central supervisory authorities.

[42] F. Pearce, *Crimes of the Powerful: Marxism, Crime and Deviance*, NY 1976, pp. 115, 124.

The presence of *narcolire* has been a contributory factor in the rapid development of cooperative and popular banks, and of other small private institutions, which taken together have doubled their share of the investment market at the expense of the larger credit institutions (see Table 11). The performance of the popular and cooperative banks has been especially notable: from 345 thousand million lire in 1970, their deposits have grown to 1,007 million lire in 1980 (both figures converted to 1981 values). During the same period, publicly-established institutions saw their investments shrink from 2,280 to 2,028 thousand million lire (1981 values).

Table 11

Market Share of Credit Institutions Operating in Sicily
(1970–1980)

Legal category of institution	Investments		Deposits	
	1970	1980	1970	1980
Publicly and nationally established institutions	51%	44%	52%	52%
'Vittorio Emanuele' Savings Bank	35%	27%	30%	21%
Popular and cooperative banks, private banks, other institutions	14%	29%	18%	27%
Total for Sicily	100%	100%	100%	100%

Source: Bulletin of the Banca d'Italia

IV

Afterword
to the
English Edition

Current World Trends
in Organized Crime

Alongside an overall growth in 'classical' criminal activity in most developed and developing countries,[1] *large-scale crime* has recently emerged as a real and pressing problem on a global scale. The term 'large-scale crime' is used to designate those powerful groups able to engage in political and economic activity both through legitimate official structures and by illegal means, and which can adversely affect whole areas of productive, social and institutional life. The presence of large-scale crime reveals itself in a variety of forms, which can be classified provisionally under four basic heads: organized crime, financial and economic crime, political and administrative corruption, and illegal lobbying.

There is no doubt that the world-wide growth of large-scale crime presents a challenge to the national and international agencies charged with its prevention. It also tests the capacity of the social sciences to offer interpretative guidelines adequate to the complexity of the problems that we face. The world of big crime is in many respects novel and unfamiliar, and its features cannot easily be understood in traditional terms: alongside concepts drawn from the sociology of deviance, from the law and from criminology, we must employ the techniques of economics, anthropology and political studies.

Since there is no space for an examination of large-scale crime in all its aspects, I limit myself here to a survey of the new

[1] UN General Assembly, *Crime Prevention and Control: Report of the Secretary General* (A/32/199), 22 September 1977.

trends of international organized crime in the context of the
development of illegal world markets.

Illegal Markets

In recent decades, a range of large-scale illegal activities has
sprung up, carried on by groups disposing of huge economic
resources, able to impose their power by means of private violence, and to manipulate large sectors of the political system and
the state apparatus. These groups take the form of firms or
enterprises with a particular specialized structure and personnel,
whose organizational features vary widely.

Criminal enterprises have developed as part of a wider process
of change. In parallel with the post-war development of international commercial and economic exchange, a very sizeable
illegal and criminal world market has developed in labour, in
goods, and in capital. Arms, drugs, industrial and military
secrets, illegally acquired currency, professional gunmen and
agents provocateurs, and human beings reduced to economic or
sexual slavery—all now circulate throughout the world more
readily and on a larger scale than ever before.

The exchange of such commodities has given birth to a distinct
and identifiable sphere of economic activity, whose presence
is arousing general fear and anxiety in a growing number of
countries.

An undeclared and sometimes subterranean war has broken out
for control of these illegal world markets. The combatants include
businessmen of irreproachable public character, soldiers and
military chiefs, political leaders, criminal bosses, secret service
agents, diplomats, straightforward criminals, and mercenaries
from virtually every country under the sun. Within certain particularly lucrative sectors of the illegal economy, however, the
struggle was resolved some time ago, in favour of a small number
of the contending parties—the most battle-hardened outfits in
the world of international organized crime.

In the most important branch of the criminal market, the trade
in drugs cultivated in Asia and Latin America and destined for
western consumption, the predominance of these illegal groups
has led to the internal division of labour we discussed in Chapter
Eight: on one hand, there is a *competitive* sector, where a number

of small and medium-sized outfits operate, supplying drugs to a non-criminal public; on the other, there is an *oligopolistic* sector, made up of a limited number of criminal firms of various nationalities, who sell drugs to those active in the first sector.

It is only recently that a world market in hard drugs has developed. Its growth has been linked to the rising demand for heroin (in the USA, from the end of the Second World War through to the 1960s; in Western Europe, the Third World and the socialist countries, during the 1970s and 1980s), and also for cocaine (among the European and American middle classes from the mid-'seventies up to the present). The UN Narcotics Division's published figures for worldwide drugs seizures show how the market has expanded:

World Heroin and Cocaine Seizures
1947–1982

	Heroin (kg)	Cocaine (kg)
1947–66 (annual ave.)	187	41
1967–74 (annual ave.)	953	625
1975	1708	2406
1976	2586	2419
1977	2377	3977
1978	2441	5391
1979	2070	8365
1980	2510	11820
1981	5613	9541
1982	6153	12092

Source: UN Division of Narcotic Drugs, *Review of Trends in Drug Abuse and Illicit Traffic*, MNAR/1/1984.

During the boom of the 1970s and 1980s, heroin seizures rose from just over one tonne to over six tonnes. At the same time, worldwide cocaine seizures were rising from two to twelve tonnes. If we assume that the amounts intercepted represent a relatively constant proportion of the overall quantity of drugs available on the market (taking the world as a whole, and confining ourselves to recent times), then we can say that the demand for and supply of narcotics has increased more than fivefold since the beginning of the 1970s.

This estimate is borne out by the data available for some countries concerning the number of users, the price of drugs, and the illegal market turnover. In the USA, the proceeds of retail heroin sales rose from little over a thousand million dollars in 1970[2] to 8.7 thousand million dollars in 1980,[3] while the wholesale price of heroin on the New York market rose during the same period from fifteen thousand to two hundred and thirty thousand dollars per kilo.[4] Turnover in the US cocaine market more than doubled in the space of just three years, rising from 13.4 thousand million dollars in 1977 to 29.4 thousand million dollars in 1980,[5] while the number of users doubled between 1977 and 1979.[6] During the five years from 1975 to 1980, there was an approximately threefold increase in the number of drug addicts in western Europe: two rather conservative estimates put the figures respectively at somewhere between eighty six thousand and one hundred and three thousand, for 1975,[7] and two hundred and seventy thousand for 1980.[8]

This quantitative growth in the drugs market was accompanied by an important transformation of the relationship between demand and supply. This grew tighter as drug use spread to large areas of the Third World, free of addiction problems until the 1970s, and as both the price of drugs and the demand for them increased in western Europe. Each increase in demand began to have immediate repercussions on decisions about what to produce, and on the structure of distribution. Conversely, the rising quantity of drugs on the market actually began to create demand,

[2] J. F. Holahan, 'The Economics of Heroin', in P. M. Wald and P. B. Hutt, *Dealing with Drug Abuse: A Report to the Ford Foundation*, New York 1972, p. 291.

[3] *The Supply of Drugs to the US Illicit Market from Foreign and Domestic Sources*: report of NNICC (National Narcotics Intelligence Consumers Committee), 1982, p. 77 (Govt. Printing Office, Washington DC).

[4] Ibid., p. 30; and M. Moore, *Policy Concerning Drug Abuse in New York State*, Vol. III, July 20 1970, Hudson Institute, New York, 1970.

[5] See NNICC reports (note 3, above), 1977 and 1982.

[6] Drug Enforcement Agency (DEA), *Southwest Asian Heroin: a Historical and Current Assessment*, Govt. Printing Office, Washington DC, 1980, p. 20.

[7] J. S. Russell and A. McNicoll, *The British Experience with Narcotics Dependency*, British Columbia Ministry of Health: Alcohol and Drug Commission, Vancouver, 1978, p. 9.

[8] NNICC, 1982, p. 37.

becoming an active factor in the establishment of market conditions in the most varied geographical and cultural contexts.

Before the emergence of a world drugs system properly so called, which took place between the 1960s and the present, there was not such a close relation between the supply of and the demand for opiates, coacaine and other drugs. There did exist, as there had done for a couple of centuries, a certain amount of long-distance trade and a series of local drug markets in Asian countries and in some western capitals. But there was no system of competitive, interdependent national markets, extending into every continent and involving large transactions, such as we have known during the recent past.

For much of the human race, drugs were not a commodity to be bought, sold and exchanged like other goods. Cocaine and opium, as well as cannabis and other drugs, took their place within long-established and stable cultural patterns.[9] For hundreds of thousands of small farmers and fieldworkers, they were a part of everyday life or of religious experience. The drugs themselves very often provided some comfort, some relief—whether regular or occasional—from the drudgery of life; and their use had its meaning within a particular cultural context.

Outside that context, the consumption of the drug lost its sense. One had only to travel a couple of hundred miles, within traditional Mediterranean or Oriental societies, and this relationship between a given drug and a given culture ceased to hold good.[10] Here, the mere fact that the drug was available, that it could be obtained, could not create any demand for it.

Thus the production and circulation of drugs was very limited so long as they remained bound up with a particular cultural context, and had not become mere objects of consumption and profit—so long, that is, as they had not become commodities.

Other big illegal markets have grown up in parallel with the world drug market. For instance, western manufacturers have illegally supplied weapons of war to governments and insurrectionary

---

[9] National Institute on Drug Abuse (NIDA), *Perspective on the History of Psychoactive Substance Use*, Govt. Printing Office, Washington DC, 1979.

[10] NIDA, *International Drug Use*, Govt. Printing Office, Washington DC, 1978.

movements in the Third World,[11] their intermediaries being traffickers, businessmen and secret service agents who make enormous profits from this trade.[12] This sector of the illegal world market, too, has been thriving since the 1960s. The end of the Cold War, and the outbreak of a range of conflicts in Asia and Latin America, have given rise to a tightening of the supply and demand relation analogous to that found on the drugs market: the interests of pressure groups linked to the clandestine arms trade are now so extensive that they play a part in determining the outbreak and duration of wars, while the kinds and quantities of weapons sold on the illegal market are giving rise to a widespread feeling that the process is beyond control.

For the purposes of the present analysis, there is no need to give a detailed description of professional crime's involvement in the clandestine arms trade. There are, however, two points of cardinal importance: a) transactions on the arms market tend to rely on the same network of logistic, informational and financial infrastructures used for drug trafficking and other illegal marketing:[13] b) those involved in political conflict or war within areas where opium or cocaine have traditionally been cultivated, or which lie near the chief drug-trafficking routes, are increasingly impelled to use drugs as a source of money with which to buy arms.[14]

Organized Crime

The expansion of illegal markets has had a profound influence on the structure of organized criminal groupings, and on their relations both with ordinary and juvenile crime and with other elements of the large-scale criminal world.

---

[11] According to A. Monti ('Economia e politica dell'aiuto pubblico allo sviluppo', *Ispe Quaderni (serie studi e ricerche)*, December 1983), developing countries spent some 129 thousand million dollars on arms purchases and defence in 1979—which is almost six times as much as the sum of 22.8 thousand million dollars which the OECD countries spent on aid in that year.

[12] See Judge Carlo Palermo's *sentenza istruttoria*, Trento court, 1984.

[13] Ibid; and see also the article by N. M. Adams, 'Armi e droga: il mercato bulgaro', in the November 1983 Italian edition of the *Readers' Digest*.

[14] Commission on Narcotic Drugs, *Report and Recommendations of the Meeting on Drug Trafficking and Other Crime*, Vienna (E/CN/657), 1980.

There has been, first of all, an acceleration of the process by which the criminal elite identifies with the forces of accumulation and of the market. In some cases, this process was already at work several decades ago (as among the Chinese secret societies associated with the Triad, or certain groupings in the Colombian mafia).[15] In the case of the Italian mafia, on the other hand, we have seen that it is only in quite recent times that an entrepreneurial and capitalist outlook has come to play the leading role in determining the *cosca*'s activities—with the result that the mafia ceased, during the 1970s, to carry out its ninety-year-old role of political, economic and cultural mediation between the central state and the periphery.

Both the Chinese secret societies and the *cosche* of the Sicilian mafia were already involved in economic activity, legal and illegal, during the last century: the former had a hand in urban racketeering and smuggling, and controlled opium-dens and prostitution,[16] while the mafia were engaged in cattle-rustling, extortion, and the control of commerce between the countryside and the cities.[17] In both cases, however, these activities were just one piece in a broader mosaic of roles and functions.

These two 'mafias' were admittedly quite different both in their organizational basis—the Sicilian mafia being built around a nucleus of friends and relatives, while the Chinese secret societies depended on mutual solidarity between the members of a sect whose structure and values were rigidly anti-familial—and in their political and cultural perspective, the Sicilians being individualistic and conservative while the Chinese had a nationalist-revolutionary outlook. At bottom, however, both were excellent instances of *polyvalency*; they were 'total social facts', able to express values and forms of behaviour deeply rooted in the cultural heritage and collective consciousness of the peoples in question.

The economic dimension did not acquire its predominance in

[15] See W. P. Morgan, *Triad Societies in Hong Kong*, Govt. Press, Hong Kong, 10; pp. xvi-xix, Fei-Ling Davis, *Le società segrete in Cina (1840–1911)*, Turin, Einaudi, 1971, pp. 231 and 256ff; P. A. Lupsha, 'Drug Trafficking: Mexico and Colombia in Comparative Perspective', *Journal of International Affairs*, no. 1, 1981, p. 104.

[16] Davis, op. cit., p. 238.

[17] See J. Schneider and P. Schneider, *Culture and Political Economy in Western Sicily*, New York 1976, pp. 70–71.

the activities of the most powerful international criminal groups in the course of some abstract process of modernization. Traditional values were not jettisoned; in the majority of cases, 'selective' use was made of them, with the aim of facilitating economic exchanges.[18]

The most influential criminal entrepreneurs in Colombia, Sicily and South-East Asia have a double cultural identity. For all their integration into multinational networks of personal contact and business dealing, and for all their adoption of universal patterns of behaviour and consumption, they remain traditionalists, firmly tied to their native cultural world—the world of the family, the kinship group, the village, the quarter, or the sect.

When they intervene in local social and cultural life, these criminal bosses tend to act in suprisingly similar ways, whether in Europe, the USA, Asia or Latin America. Handsome 'disinterested' contributions are often made in support of public activities that symbolize strong local traditions or arouse widespread popular interest. In southern Italy and the United States, the *camorra* and the mafia fund and organise sporting associations and public festivals;[19] in Colombia, the mafia has set up radio and TV stations, film companies, and even zoological gardens;[20] and ethnically-based interest groups have been organized in immigrant areas, both by members of the Chinese sects in Southeast Asia and the USA,[21] and by Sicilian *mafiosi* in New York's Little Italy during the 1970s.[22]

Their cultural traditionalism, and the roots they have in their own local territory, are not just part of the anthropological identity of criminal entrepreneurs, and a ready means of access to political influence; they are also (as we saw in Chapter Eight) a fundamental condition of illegal economic activity itself. Shrewd management of kinship and family relations and of bonds of race and sect allows a substantial network of 'contacts' to be built up. Formed as they are in the context of large waves of spontaneous emigration, these contacts cover wide geographical areas.

[18] See J. Boissevain, *Friends of Friends: Networks, Manipulations and Coalitions*, Oxford 1974.

[19] L. Rossi, *Camorra*, Milan 1983, p. 159.

[20] 'Los "capos" colombianos caen en Madrid', *Interviu*, 10 December 1984.

[21] See 'A Chinatown Merchant Portrayed as Crime Boss', *New York Times*, October 25, 1984.

[22] See *Time* magazine, 12 July 1971.

There is, furthermore, the major problem of *trustworthiness*. Trust is essential to every kind of illegal transaction: indeed, as we have argued, the absence of legal and officially enforced guarantees forces entrepreneurs on the illegal market to trust one another to a far greater extent than is necessary among ordinary businessmen. Together with the need to maintain secrecy, this factor leads criminal entrepreneurs to seek partners among the members of their own family and kinship networks, their own sects, and their own cultural communities. We discussed several examples of such cooperation in Chapter Eight: a further instance is given in a recent report by the New York police, which emphasizes that the top levels of the illegal cocaine trade between Latin America and the USA are controlled by the innermost members of a dozen criminal family firms from Colombia, who organize the distribution of raw cocaine harvested in Peru and Bolivia.[23]

The growth of illegal world markets has not only hastened the full conversion of the mafia ethic into the 'spirit of capitalism'; it has also led to mobility and internal competition, both within particular criminal groups and between each large criminal association and its rivals. At the same time, it has encouraged a process of *vertical integration*, linking the organized crime of the international mafias on the one hand with common and juvenile crime on the other. The interaction between these two spheres has been intensified by the expanding *demand for criminal labour* generated by the increased scale of activities of the major criminal groups. The setting up of drug distribution chains in each different national market has involved a whole range of operators, some of them recruited from the legitimate world and some drawn from what used to be called the 'underworld'—the domain of thieves, prostitutes, gamblers, robbers, extortion racketeeers and smugglers. Those caught up in these chains now number several thousand, each with their own specialist 'profession' and distinctive subculture, but all now taking on the more anonymous roles of wholesalers, distributors, couriers, peddlers—and users—of heroin and cocaine.

In some cases, where the urban environment degenerates as disastrously as it had done in Naples by the late 1970s, the

[23] New York City Police Dept., *Report on Organized Crime in New York City*, delivered to US Senate Committee on the Judiciary, 1983, p. 251.

demand for criminal labour has expanded so rapidly as to engender criminal associations of unprecedented size. The so-called *Nuova Camorra Organizzata* ('new organized *camorra*'), run by Raffaele Cutolo, succeeded in bringing together over two thousand young gangsters in the years 1978–83. These were split up into around fifty bands, whose operations were directed by a small elite of older professional criminals.

In the USA, too, juvenile crime, studied since the 1920s by the pioneers of American social research, is showing signs of transformation as the illegal market expands. In the metropolis of Los Angeles, multi-racial bands of young criminals (there are over four thousand such gangs) are being incorporated into the hard drug distribution system. Their members are subject to a discreet but effective hierarchical power, exercised by the criminal operators who supply them with drugs, employ them in particularly hazardous undertakings, and sometimes protect them from the police.[24]

In Colombia, the long period of political conflict and social disorganization known as *la violencia*, which the country endured from 1946 until 1959, left some two hundred thousand people dead. The aftermath of *la violencia*, and the traditional contraband trade in coffee, electrical appliances and consumer goods, created a reservoir in Colombia's cities and countryside of men 'above the law', who ignored the State's decrees—smugglers, *bandidos, bandoleros*, who roamed about the country, sometimes taking refuge in neighbouring states. At the beginning of the 1970s, many members of this outlaw army became involved in international cocaine- and marijuana-smuggling, often meeting the manpower and military needs of the Colombian mafia families.[25]

Organized Crime and International Finance

As organized crime has come to take its place in the development of illegal world markets, some very large fortunes have been

[24] See 'Increase in Gang Killings on Coast is Traced To Narcotics Trafficking', *New York Times*, 29 October 1984.

[25] Lupsha, op. cit. (see note 15 above), p. 104.

amassed. They have been accumulated thanks to the extraordin-
arily large profits obtainable in the illegal economy. Although
current estimates of illegal profits differ widely both in reliability
and in the figures they put forward, it is possible to make
reasonably dependable assessments in certain areas.

For instance, the us Embassy in Colombia has estimated that
profits from cocaine- and marijuana-smuggling totalling some 3
thousand million dollars were 'repatriated' into the Colombian
economy in 1979. Of these profits, a proportion—between six
and seven hundred million dollars—entered directly as us currency, while the remainder had been converted into Colombian
currency, as shown in the following Table:

Estimated Returns on Drug-Trafficking in Colombia,
and their Percentage of the Colombian Money Supply,
1975–1979

	Dollars (millions)	Colombian Pesos (000 millions)	% of Colombian Money Supply
1975	150	4.6	7.9
1976	400	13.6	17.5
1977	450	16.6	17.0
1978	500	19.6	14.5
1979	600–700	25.6–29.8	16.4–19.7

Source: Ambassador Diego Asencio, us Ambassador to Colombia: in
us Congress, Senate Committee on Governmental Affairs, Permanent
Sub-Committee on Investigations, *Illegal Narcotic Profits* Hearings,
96th Congress, First Session, 12 December 1979.

In the summer of 1980, the Superintendent of the Central Bank
of Colombia stated that about half of that country's foreign
exchange holdings derived from activities connected with smuggling and drug trafficking.[26]

We saw above (p. 207) that the Sicilian mafia 'cartel' which
owned the heroin-refining laboratories operating around Palermo
between 1977 and 1982 was able to make net annual profits of
around six hundred million dollars from wholesale sales in the

[26] Foreign Broadcast Information Service, Latin American, June 3, 1980:
'Banking Superintendent's Speech on *La Ventanilla Siniestra*'.

North American market. American scholars have given a similar figure as an estimate of the sum that entered Mexico during the mid-1970s through the drug-trafficking operations controlled by the ten or twelve leading families in the world of Mexican organized crime.[27]

As wealth accumulated in the illegal sector became concentrated in a few hands, the economic, political and military power of organized crime kept growing, all through the 1970s, to unprecedented levels. Without this massive economic base, the chiefs of the Sicilian and Colombian mafia could never have planned the assassinations of leading anti-mafia campaigners from the world of politics and the judiciary that were carried out in Palermo and Bogota between the mid-70s and 1983.

The fact that criminal groups now dispose of hundreds of millions of dollars has also altered the traditionally subordinate relation of the criminal bosses to the financiers and businessmen active at the highest levels of the economy. In approaching the frontiers of 'big business' properly so called, the mafia—in Italy and the USA—has opened a new chapter in its history. In the USA, for all the abundant myths to the contrary, not one mafia chief and not one organized criminal group had succeeded, before the 1970s, in entering the world of *big* power and *big* wealth (see above, p. 208). Nowadays, after a decade and a half of illegal accumulation on a vast scale, things are very different. For some years now, the names of well-known mafia chiefs have been appearing in the roll-call of the USA's wealthiest citizens.[28] One Sicilian finance group linked to the mafia possesses a fortune estimated to exceed a thousand million dollars. Investigations carried out under the new Italian anti-mafia legislation are bringing to light almost unheard-of concentrations of wealth: an obscure mafia entrepreneur from a little town near Palmero turns out to have accumulated a personal fortune of some two hundred and fifty million dollars, and still larger amounts are being discovered in the course of investigations in northern Italy.

What use is made of the profits acquired by international

---

[27] P. A. Lupsha and K. Schlegel, 'The Political Economy of Drug Trafficking: the Herrera Organization (Mexico and the United States)', *Working Paper No. 2* of the Latin American Institute of the University of New Mexico, Albuquerque, New Mexico, November 1980.

[28] See Forbes (13 September 1982), quoted in E. Mandel, *Delightful Murder*, London 1984.

organized crime? Until a few years ago, this question was particularly difficult to answer. There was a dearth of available information; what there was simply pointed in the general direction of Switzerland as a favoured repository of 'dirty money'. It is now possible to sketch a provisional overall picture, based on results obtained from various very recent investigations into public and private sources covering a number of different fields.

We remarked earlier on the imbalance between the speed with which illicit fortunes are accumulated, and the actual opportunities for investing them. Because enormous sums have been amassed so quickly, by people who have neither the skills nor the economic and financial infrastructure needed for the rapid investment of large capital sums, illegal profits have not been entirely transformed into investment goods.

As we saw above (p. 209), these profits would seem to have flowed along three main channels hitherto. One portion, of modest overall size, returns into the illegal sector, being used to maintain and extend ongoing operations. A more sizeable portion enters the legitimate economy—either in the criminal group's country of origin, or in the country to which the illegal merchandise is exported. As a rule, this money is invested in sectors where there are few technological barriers to investment, where good profits can be made, or where there is a high level of internal competition (such as construction, agriculture, wholesale trade, the modern tertiary sector, and so on).

However, the largest portion of criminal wealth is retained in the form of liquid currency and exported beyond the frontiers of the country in which it was produced. According to US Senate hearings, the 3 thousand million 'narco-dollars' that returned to Colombia in 1979 represented no more than half of the profits made that year by the drug-traffickers: the other half was put into overseas holdings.[29]

For reasons of efficiency and security, the criminal bosses cannot personally administer these capital sums. Specialized skills are required, and these are to be found only in certain sections of the financial community, among those in a position to direct the international operations of banks and finance companies.

The alliance between capital of criminal provenance and an entire section of international finance capital, which came into

[29] US Senate Hearings, 1979, p. 205.

operation during the 1970s, would not have been cemented so easily had the development of illegal international markets not been parallelled by a quite extraordinary growth in world financial markets, and had the latter not given rise, internally, to the Eurodollar market and to the phenomenon of so-called 'tax havens'.

Today, the Eurodollar market is the most important source of private international liquidity. It has developed at a headlong pace, its overall size rising from around 14 thousand million dollars in 1964 to around 800 thousand million dollars in 1982.[30] This market's notable features include the very large scale of transactions made in it and the speed with which these are effected, as well as the growing tendency for them to be carried out in the least regulated zones of financial exchange—namely, the 'offshore' financial centres.

Because of its sheer size, the Eurodollar market guarantees conditions of unprecedented anonymity to illicit capital. Once deposited with a bank licensed to operate abroad, criminal profits flow into an ocean of money that knows no homeland and leaves ever fainter traces of its origins as it is moved, by telephone or telex, all over the world.[31]

If we add that some thirty 'offshore' jurisdictions, offering legal guarantees of the secrecy of all financial operations in their territory, have come into existence in various parts of the globe,[32] then we can appreciate the context within which the alliance between organized crime and venture finance capital has grown up. This alliance now takes care of much of the illicit capital that flows annually—20 thousand million dollars from the us criminal economy alone, in an average year[33]—into the tax havens of Europe, Asia and the Caribbean.

[30] See *World Financial Markets* (Morgan Guaranty Trust), 1984.

[31] See A. R. Abboud, 'Eurodollars in Today's World Markets', in L. C. Nehrt, ed., *International Finance for Multinational Business*, Intext Educational Publishers, Scranton, 1972; and us Senate, Committee on Governmental Affairs, Permanent Sub-Committee on Investigations, *Crime and Secrecy: The Use of Offshore Banks and Companies*, Staff Study publ. at Govt. Printing Office, Washington DC, 1983, p. 25.

[32] R. Gordon, *Tax Havens and Their Use by United States Taxpayers: An Overview* (study commissioned by us Dept. of Justice, Treasury Dept. and Internal Revenue Service), 1981.

[33] See us Senate, 1983 (cited in note 31 above), III.

Roots and Consequences of Organized Crime

The development of large-scale crime has altered the relationship between the illegal world and its socio-economic context in certain important respects. For several decades, scholars and social reformers have stressed the cause-and-effect relation between poverty and social disintegration on one hand, and criminal and deviant behaviour on the other.

The framework within which industrialization and urbanization have taken place over the last two centuries in the countries of the West, and the forms that so-called 'modernization' is presently taking in certain large Asian and Latin American nations—a 'modernization' that entails growing social injustice, poverty and violence—indeed leave little doubt that socio-cultural disorganization plays an important role as a seedbed for the growth of crime.

A certain level of social disintegration is an essential precondition of organized crime, whose power is based to a considerable extent on the ability to use terror and physical violence unsparingly against competitors and enemies.

The use of violence depends, however, on the availability of personnel with particular attributes—people ready to endanger their own lives, and those of others, in the carrying out of especially risky tasks. The presence of this type of human material is linked to the extent of the *supply of criminal labour*, which is linked in turn to the general pathology of socio-economic change. Criminal groups acquire their power by exploiting the delinquency and aggression produced by immense processes of deculturation.

The current decline of old-style American organized crime based on Italian emigrant stock (the famous 'five families' of New York, the twenty-four families in the USA as a whole) results, precisely, from the difficulty of recruiting young Italo-American gangsters who look to crime as a means of bettering their social position. Successive generations of Italo-Americans have risen rapidly up the economic ladder since the early years of the century, and this has made it hard for criminal groups to replenish their membership. These groups were formed, for the most part, in the 1920s and 1930s, and the average age of their members is now surprisingly old—over sixty.[34]

---

[34] New York City Police Dept., *Report on Organized Crime*.

The largest share of the drug traffic between Sicily and North America is today controlled by families of recent immigrants, who arrived during the 1960s and 1970s, and who have been obliged, because of the shortage of locally available Italo-American criminal labour, to organise clandestine 'imports' of criminal manpower from the underdeveloped areas of Italy.[35]

Nor, in considering the relations between socio-economic disorganization and the birth of organized crime, must we underestimate the role that the prevailing local economic backwardness and social and institutional disintegration played, last century, in the development of the Chinese 'secret societies' and the southern Italian mafia,[36] or the analogous role played more recently in Colombia by *la violencia*.

Nevertheless, all these considerations must not obscure the fact that one of the most important new features of the last few years has been the tendency for this classical relationship, in which crime depends upon socio-economic disintegration, to be *turned on its head*.

The most powerful criminal groups have shown (and are showing) that they can influence society and economic processes to a greater extent than they are determined by them. They are more and more capable of *creating* marginalized and ruinous enclaves, even in environments previously free of them.

This is very well illustrated by the expansion of mafia power in northern Italy during the 1970s. Here, organized crime has shown it can reproduce the social soil in which it originally grew, setting off the usual violent reactions in the economy, in society and in the political system, and subjecting even rich and stable areas to disorganization and fear.

Verona, for instance, used to have little enough in common with the southern cities that are the usual home of mafia crime. It was a flourishing, well-integrated city, with no large slums and no particularly alarming marginal enclaves. There was a healthy tradition of public participation in civic and religious life. However, a clandestine network for the distribution and sale of heroin made its appearance in Verona in the mid-1970s, and this has

---

[35] Author's conversation with J. Dintino, Deputy Chief of the New Jersey police, in 1983.

[36] See Davis, op. cit., pp. 84–88; P. Arlacchi, 'Mafia e tipi di societa', *La Rassegna Italiana di Sociologia*, no. 1, 1980.

rapidly produced the kind of results familiar in other places.

An area of social disintegration has come into being. Juvenile crime has grown more prevalent. In some districts, collective political and religious activity has declined. A feeling of hostility and uncooperativeness towards the forces of order has made itself apparent in certain milieux, though such attitudes have never been customary locally. The turnover of the drug market has begun to influence the local economy, giving rise to semi-legal entrepreneurial 'grey areas' where economic operators recycle and put to use money gained from the sale of heroin.

Effects on Economic Development

Organized crime, then, has made itself markedly *autonomous* of its roots: it can reproduce itself outside its original environment. How, though, does its presence as an economic force affect those underdeveloped areas in which—despite everything—it is still a far more potent factor than 'n developed regions?

Is it true that Sicily, Calabria, Turkey, and the ten or fifteen other developing countries and regions that play host to drug-based economies are benefitting, in terms of economic development, from the investment in their legitimate economic sector of large amounts of illegally-acquired capital?

As yet, there are no systematic studies of this matter to which we can refer. It is however possible to outline the situation, drawing on available data about the state of affairs in Colombia and the Italian *Mezzogiorno*.

In the case of Italy, it is noteworthy that the power of the mafia is still particularly strong in certain regions of the South as opposed to others, even though the 1970s saw mafia power spreading throughout Italy, as the activities directly controlled by criminal families/firms enlarged their geographical scope and as the families themselves forged ever closer links with northern economic and financial crime and with illegal lobbies active in Rome.

Is it possible, then, to establish any relationship between the presence of the mafia and such variations as may appear in rates of regional economic development in Italy over the last decade? It is indeed possible: and the correlation is negative.

Those parts of the South where the mafia is most in evidence are not those with the highest rates of growth in production and investment. The two southern regions with the highest growth-rates during the last fifteen years—Apulia and the Abruzzo region —also have rates of crime (both organized and conventional) among the lowest in the whole of the *Mezzogiorno*. The typical 'mafia areas'—Calabria, Sicily and the Campania—have experienced economic stagnation or decline at a time when every other Italian region has been growing economically.[37]

As we argued above (in Chapter Four), mafia firms and mafia investment within the legitimate economy do not take their place alongside previously existing, non-mafia firms, but to a large extent drive them out: they are forced to finance mafia capitalism —by paying 'quotas', by being excluded from the most profitable sales markets and public works contracts, and by abandoning their programmes of expansion within the geographical and economic areas beneath the umbrella of mafia 'protection'.

In Colombia, criminal wealth has had deeper and more complex effects on the economy. For around a decade, from the early 1970s until 1982, the influx of 'narco-dollars' was a credit item in the national balance of payments, helping to keep down inflation and to moderate the country's foreign indebtedness.[38]

However, these positive effects were balanced if not outweighed by other consequences: the Colombian economy grew still more dependent on the outside world, the political elite was corrupted and degraded by the pay-offs they took from drug-traffickers (who would seem to have spent some 100 million dollars on bribes in 1980 alone),[39] and the national banking system became more and more vulnerable.

The latter is in a particularly delicate position as regards both domestic and foreign operations. On one hand, the Colombian banking system is the bridge between the legitimate and the illegal sectors of the national economy, and is thus obliged to take its share in the very serious risks that typically attend the activities of many of its clients (and administrative officials); on the other hand, it is closely tied into the 'hottest' area of international finance, through the so-called 'Panama Connection' set up by some half-dozen Caribbean branches of its leading institutions.

[37] G. Beccatini and G. Bianchi, 'Sulla multiregionalità dello sviluppo economico italiano', *Note economiche*, 5–6, 1982, pp. 27–28.

[38] See 'Colombian Peso', *International Currency Review*, vol. 16, no. 1, 1984.

[39] See P. Lernoux, 'Corrupting Colombia', *Inquiry*, September 30, 1979, pp. 14–17; and *New York Times*, April 30, 1980.

Strategies for Combatting Organized Crime

These links between illicitly acquired wealth and the world of international finance lead one to consider what counter-strategies might prove effective, given the levels of interdependence and complexity at which illegal markets and criminal firms now operate. The experience of the last fifteen years has shown that no meaningful results can be obtained, in the struggle against large-scale crime, if one begins from any single national base. The USA is an instructive example. After successfully putting an end to Turkish opium production in the early 1970s, through the active collaboration of the Turkish government and other western administrations, the Americans found themselves faced with the problem of heroin imports from South-East Asia, and heroin and marijuana imports from Mexico. Having succeeded once again, thanks to the cooperation of the Mexican government, in reducing the influx of these drugs—whose share of the total national market fell from 90 per cent in 1975 to 30 per cent in 1980[40]—they had to deal with the flood of south-west Asian heroin (produced in the turbulent tribal regions of Pakistan and Afghanistan) and of cocaine from Latin America and the Caribbean.

The US authorities' efforts led merely to a levelling off in domestic heroin supply and demand between 1970 and the present, and to a decline in marijuana consumption among new student intakes.[41]

Meanwhile, as we have seen, the problem of drug addiction and organized crime was spreading all over the world. Organized crime was becoming integrated 'horizontally' with financial speculation, and 'vertically' with ordinary and juvenile crime. And the illegal market was becoming unified.

These developments have obviously posed the question of crime on a new scale; but at the same time, they offer fresh opportunities for combatting it. Since, moreover, a large number of countries, rather than just a few, are now directly involved, there are growing domestic pressures towards international collaboration.

In searching for effective counter-strategies, we shall obviously

---

[40] US Dept. of State, 'International Narcotics Control', in *Gist*, August 1980.
[41] National Institute on Drug Abuse, *National Survey on Drug Abuse: Main Findings*, Govt. Printing Office, Washington DC, 1982.

be guided to a considerable extent by how we analyze the type of crime we face. This *Afterword* has aimed above all to show that we are no longer confronted with pure and simple 'law-breaking' or 'criminal behaviour', to be prevented and punished with the classic weapons of criminal justice.

We face, rather, a phenomenon that is primarily *economic*, rather than criminal. We must strike at its real structures and seats of power—at markets, banks, and accumulated capital, and at the institutional degeneration that allows the problems to continue and grow worse.

One immediate strategy might be to extend to as many national jurisdictions as possible the measures permitting *seizure of illegally acquired property* that are having such encouraging results in certain states. Much can be learned from the first two years' implementation of Italy's anti-mafia legislation, the La Torre law: to date, illegally accumulated fortunes to the tune of around 500 million dollars have been confiscated, half of that amount being seized in just two operations, one in the North and one in the South of Italy.

By confiscating their wealth, the authorities strike a blow at the criminal groups' fundamental *raison d'être*, the pursuit of profit through violations of the criminal law.

A second strategy should take the form of international action to erect stronger barriers between the legitimate financial market and the market in 'dirty' capital. In recent years, these two markets have been linked first of all through 'offshore' finance systems, and secondly through a series of banks, active in the Eurodollar market, situated at the key junctions of the illegal exchange network.

Here, the struggle against large-scale crime coincides with the ever more urgent need for a new international financial order. For the presence of illegal currency, albeit in modest amounts in terms of today's gigantic financial markets, may prove the catalyst for a chain reaction whose gravity nobody can foresee—and whose elements are to be found in the existing contradictions of the world financial system.

Illicit capital—by bringing entrepreneurs linked to the world of large-scale crime into the system, and so introducing fresh strains of adventurism and anarchy—threatens to trigger off the explosive worldwide financial breakdown that so many people now fear.

We should not forget that the three biggest banking collapses of recent times (those of the Franklin National Bank in 1974, the Nugan Hand Bank in 1980, and the Banco Ambrosiano in 1982) were all attributable to illegal financial deals and the use of 'tax havens', rather than to other and more widely acknowledged 'danger areas' of international business.

A third strategy (which could encompass the first two) might be to draw up an international convention against large-scale crime. This would lay down the scope and aims of actions undertaken by individual states, and ensure that the struggle against crime was waged by forces as mobile and agile as those deployed by the enemy.

Note: The paper on which this Afterword is based was originally presented at a preparatory meeting for the seventh United Nations Conference on The Prevention of Crime and the Treatment of Offenders, St. Vincent, 8–10, March 1985.

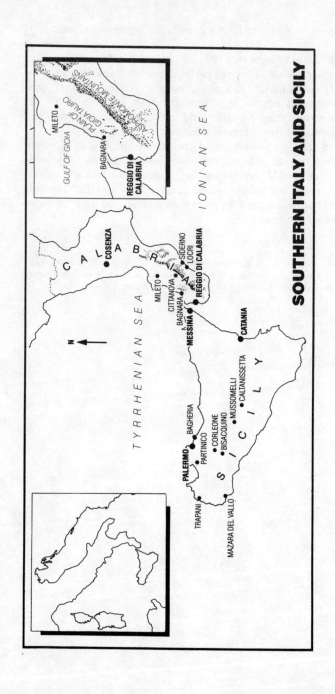

SOUTHERN ITALY AND SICILY

Index*

* Names in italics are pseudonyms